IMAGES
*of America*

# CAMP GLENN

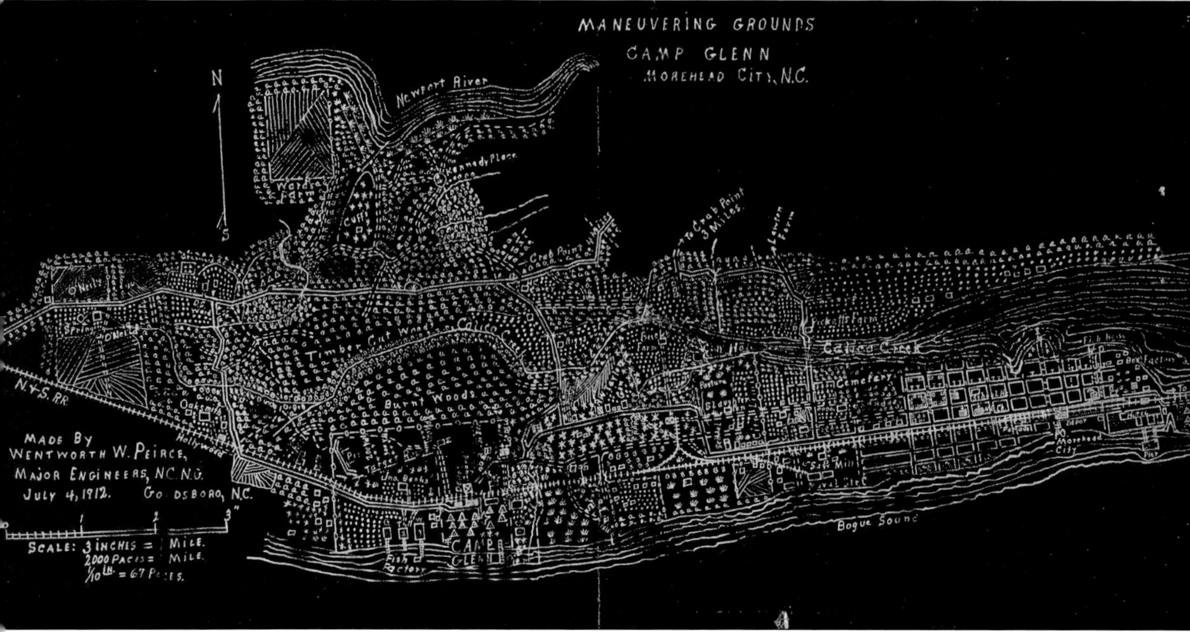

Maj. Wentworth Willis Peirce (1878–1923), assistant chief of engineers, drew this 1912 maneuvering map showing area details of Camp Glenn, located in southwestern Carteret County on a site formerly known as Carolina City. Some of the details shown are the target range, the drill hike route, and tents lining an area near Bogue Sound's shore. (Courtesy of the History Museum, Morehead City.)

**On the Cover:** Col. Wynham Eugene (W.E.) Gary (1848–1917) stands behind soldiers watching as they shoot rifles on the target practice field during summer training encampment at Camp Glenn. Soldiers sitting at tables are keeping scores while instructors keep a close watch on the practice shooting. (Courtesy of the University of North Carolina at Chapel Hill.)

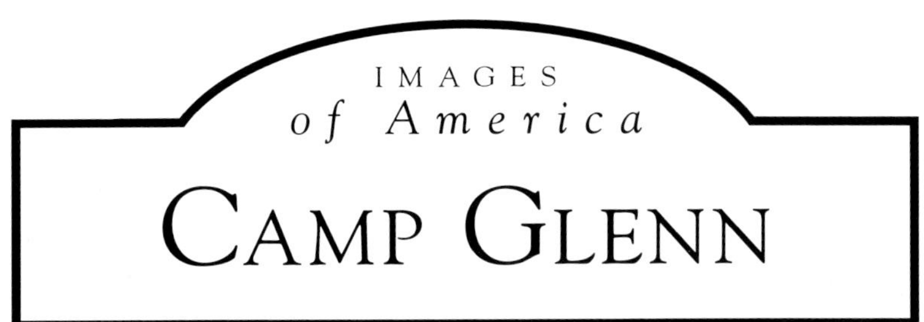


Susan Charboneau Holland

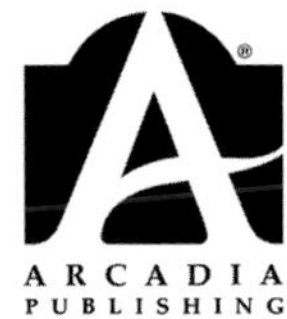

ISBN 978-1-4671-0718-1

Published by Arcadia Publishing
Charleston, South Carolina

Printed in the United States of America

Library of Congress Control Number: 2021938340

For all general information, please contact Arcadia Publishing:
Telephone 843-853-2070
Fax 843-853-0044
E-mail sales@arcadiapublishing.com
For customer service and orders:
Toll-Free 1-888-313-2665

Visit us on the Internet at www.arcadiapublishing.com

*To my husband, Gregg, for your loving support, and whose patience and understanding made this all possible. Now, let's go get that drink. For my children, friends, and family—my thanks to you as well. You are invited to come along.*

# Contents

Acknowledgments 6

Introduction 7

1. Officers and Enlisted Men 9
2. Target Practice in the Pits 43
3. Drills, Marches, and Dress Parades 63
4. Camp Life 85

# Acknowledgments

Thank you, Linda Willis Sadler, historian, for sharing your *Camp Glenn* postcards—you have an amazing Carteret County postcard collection, and I am in awe of your knowledge of this area. And thank you, John Lawrence, assistant director for Special Collections, J.Y. Joyner Library, East Carolina University, for your help and support. You are the best! Jason Tomberlin, head of Research and Instructional Services at University of North Carolina at Chapel Hill, I appreciate your answers to my many e-mails, your help in locating sources, and your willingness to work around obstacles in the time of institutional lockdowns and working from home. Thank you. Benjamin Wunderly, associate museum curator, North Carolina Maritime Museum, Beaufort, thank you for taking the time to send me that great image of the flying boat! Matthew Peek, Military Collection archivist, North Carolina State Archives, thank you for pointing me to an invaluable source of images that helped me put a few names to some unknown faces. North Carolina Army National Guard major Sean R. Daily, US Army, historian at the North Carolina National Guard Museum, your work to promote the North Carolina National Guard (NCNG), its work and mission, is impressive. Thank you for your service. Angel Prohaska, title manager, Arcadia Publishing, this book would not have happened without your help. Thank you for your patience and guidance throughout this process. I think it is very cool that you took the time to step foot on Camp Glenn soil while you were here on vacation. Thank you. And lastly—but never last in my heart—thank you to my husband, Gregg, my daughters, Renee and Megan, for being the best I could ever wish for, and to the rest of my dear, dear family and my friends. You know who you are.

All images used in this book belong to the author unless otherwise noted.

# INTRODUCTION

North Carolina has maintained a state militia since it fought in the Revolutionary War. In 1877, the state militia became the North Carolina State Guard, commanded by an adjutant general. The guard was made up of enlisted volunteers, uniformed and equipped, who were ready to be called up at any time. During the 1898 Spanish–American War the State Guard was not subject to the president's call for troops; however, the adjutant general supervised its reorganization in order to provide volunteers for the war effort. North Carolina's general assembly changed the name of the State Guard to the National Guard to conform with a 1903 act of Congress.

In 1905, when summer encampment training ended at Camp Glenn in Wrightsville Beach, commanders began looking for a new site for a permanent training camp as the land's lease had expired. The camp had used the Wrightsville site since 1899, and initially, leaders at Camp Glenn considered making it the permanent camp location. Wilmington's Board of Aldermen recognized the benefits the camp's location had for its citizens and tried to persuade the guard to remain. Wilmington had held the lease since July 31, 1899, when H.M. Bowden leased 101 acres, more or less, known as Summer's Rest at Wrightsville Beach, to Gov. D.G. Fowle and his successors in office. The town stipulated that if the State Guard failed to maintain a permanent encampment on the site, the land would revert back to the city of Wilmington for the purposes of a public park for the citizens' use and pleasure, in fee simple.

Wilmington's leaders failed in their efforts to persuade the NCNG to remain, and a special military board appointed by Gov. Robert Broadnax Glenn (1854–1920) made a unanimous decision to select a permanent training site in Carteret County. The state and guard leaders kept the name, Camp Glenn, in honor of the governor, who held office from 1905 to 1909.

In 1905, Raleigh's *Daily News and Observer* published an account of the relocation and the reasons behind military leaders' decision to move the camp to a site in an area formerly known as Carolina City that was located about three miles west of Morehead City on Bogue Sound in Carteret County. One of the most important reasons for their decision was the land for the camp was donated to the National Guard without cost by the Atlantic & North Carolina Railroad with the stipulation that the land would revert back to the company if the camp was discontinued. Also, the railroad agreed to construct platforms and other facilities as necessary to ensure safe and convenient handling of the troops and camp equipage. The railroad also agreed to provide transportation and satisfactory accommodations for the of troops and equipment.

Both officers and men thought the land, located on a sandy bluff overlooking Bogue Sound, suitable and well-adapted for encampment purposes. The sandy ground was firm, high, and well-drained. Southwesterly breezes coming off the sound would keep the men in camp comfortable and help keep mosquitoes and flies at bay. They were also pleased that there was a splendid bathing beach for the soldiers without the expense of transportation to the surf. The large parade ground adjoining the campgrounds was "level as a floor" and able to accommodate the entire North Carolina National Guard.

The Town of Morehead City agreed to repair any buildings already on the grounds and keep them in good repair as well as erect any future buildings needed. This reciprocal agreement meant that some residents would have steady employment and National Guard leaders could be assured that their property would be well looked after in their absence when summer training was not being held. Additionally, it was noted that the recent establishment of the Armour Packing Company, a storage warehouse and refrigeration plant in New Bern, and the excellent game and fish market in Beaufort and Morehead City and its location in the midst of a trucking district, meant it would be possible to supply the troops with the best food during their stay in camp.

The National Guard mobilized at Camp Glenn in June 1916 and left for service in September that year for the Mexican border to fight under Gen. John J. "Black Jack" Pershing in the Mexican Punitive Expedition war against Pancho Villa. Troops returned in February 1917 without seeing much fighting, to their great disappointment.

In 1906, New Bern native Mary Bayard Morgan Wootten had an idea for a business venture in order to make some money. The young, divorced mother of two young boys headed to Camp Glenn to set up a photography studio in order to take soldiers' pictures as they trained during encampment. She also photographed the men during leisure and camp activities. The photographs were turned into postcards, and soldiers purchased them to send to family and friends. Now folks back home received messages and pictures telling and showing what their men were doing during summer training. Wootten's photographs were also published in posters and in local newspapers for recruitment purposes. For a number of years, the business was a success, and with the help of some family members who also worked at the studio, Wootten was able to support her children and her parents.

Bayard Wootten, an intrepid soul, was one of the first women photographers to enter the field during the early 20th century. And she was the only woman who photographed soldiers at camp during training. Wootten recorded the work of the North Carolina National Guard at Camp Glenn, operating her studio, The Photo Hut, until 1926 when she closed her business. She died on April 6, 1959, at her home in New Bern, though her vision, drive, and ingenuity lived on in her inspirational camera work and the lives she influenced.

Camp Glenn was a National Guard fixture from 1906 to 1918. During World War I, the camp was converted into a naval refueling base and later the site of a US Navy base. Camp Glenn made history as the first US Coast Guard air station from 1920 to 1921. In the 1940s, Camp Glenn's site was sold for use by North Carolina's Division of Commercial Fisheries. Today, the University of North Carolina Institute of Marine Sciences occupies six and a half acres of the former National Guard site as a study and research center of estuarine and wetland habitats.

# *One*

# Officers and Enlisted Men

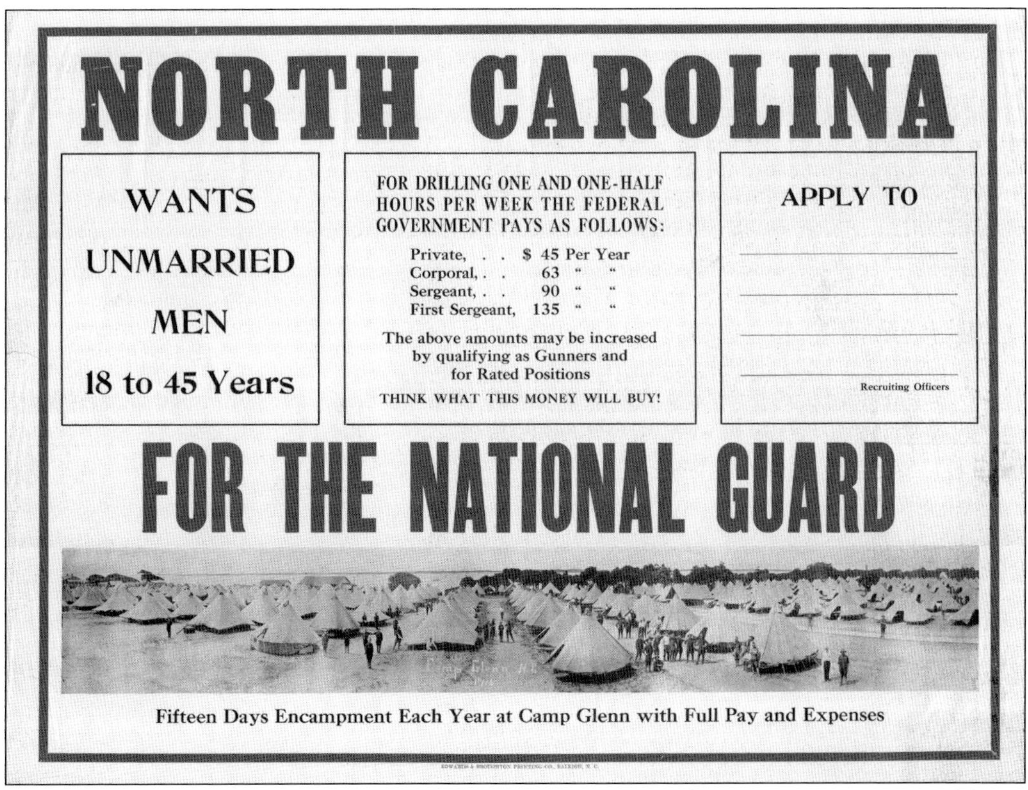


A North Carolina National Guard (NCNG) recruitment poster shows a panoramic view of Camp Glenn with tents, soldiers, and Bogue Sound in the background. Recruitment centers were set up at regimental armories, in local town armories, or at central points in the NCNG regiment localities. Each NCNG company recruited 65 enlisted men with four sergeants, six corporals, two cooks, two mechanics, and two musicians. (Courtesy of North Carolina State Archives.)

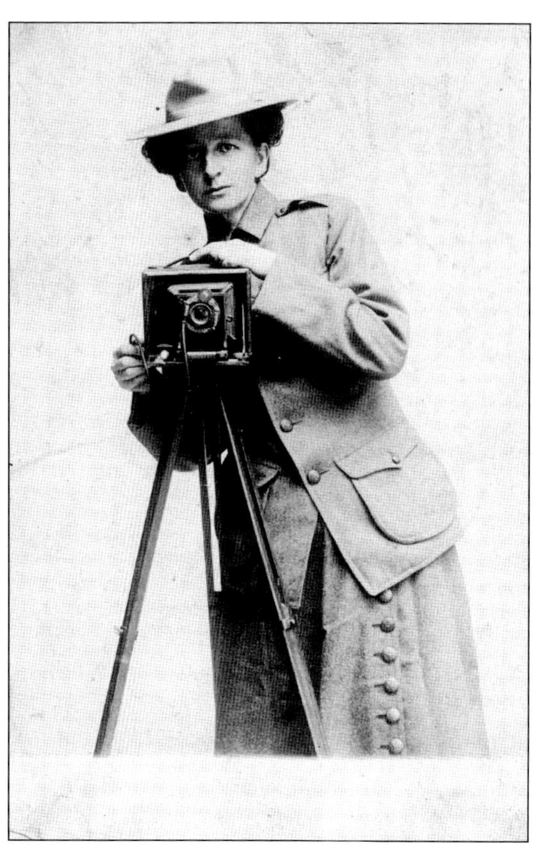

Mary Bayard Morgan Wootten (1875–1959), New Bern, learned the art of photography at an early age. Separated from her husband in 1904, later divorcing him in 1907, Wootten was one of the first female photographers in the country. She supported her two young boys and her mother and stepfather from her work at Camp Glenn from 1906 to 1926 and other photographic endeavors. (Courtesy of the University of North Carolina at Chapel Hill.)

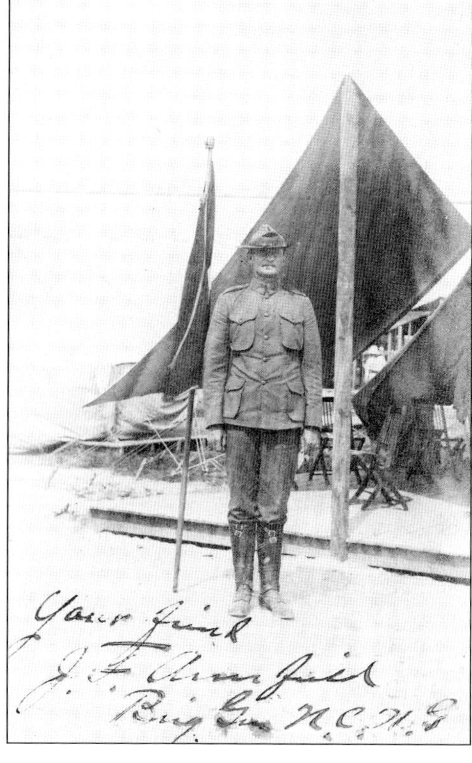


Camp Glenn's commander, Gen. Joseph Franklin Armfield (1862–1910), was a colonel in the Iredell Blues Company A, 4th Regiment, before being appointed to brigadier general of the North Carolina State Guard in 1901 by Gov. Charles B. Aycock. General Armfield was appointed adjutant general of the National Guard by Gov. William W. Kitchen in 1909. (Courtesy of North Carolina State Archives.)

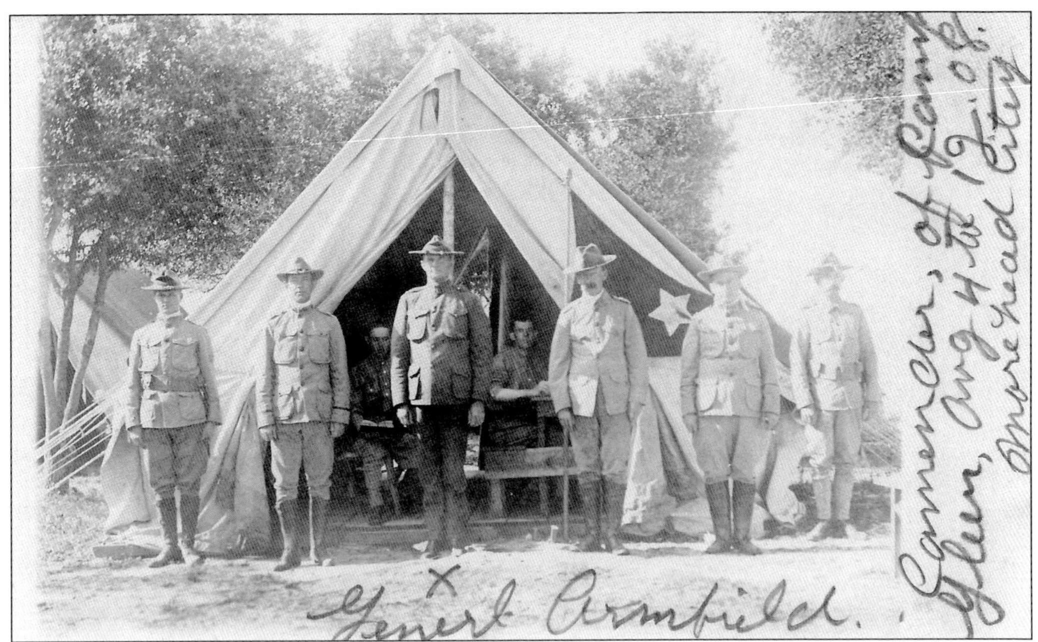


General Armfield (center) and quartermaster general, Lt. Col. W.E. Gary (right), are standing with unidentified staff in front of a tent. The card is postmarked August 7, 1908, and addressed to Alice Wyckoff, Ridgeway, North Carolina, from her brother, Will, with the following message: "This card shows where I was all day to day." Pvt. Will Orlander Wyckoff (1884–1924), Company H, 3rd Regiment, attended summer encampment August 4–11, 1908.

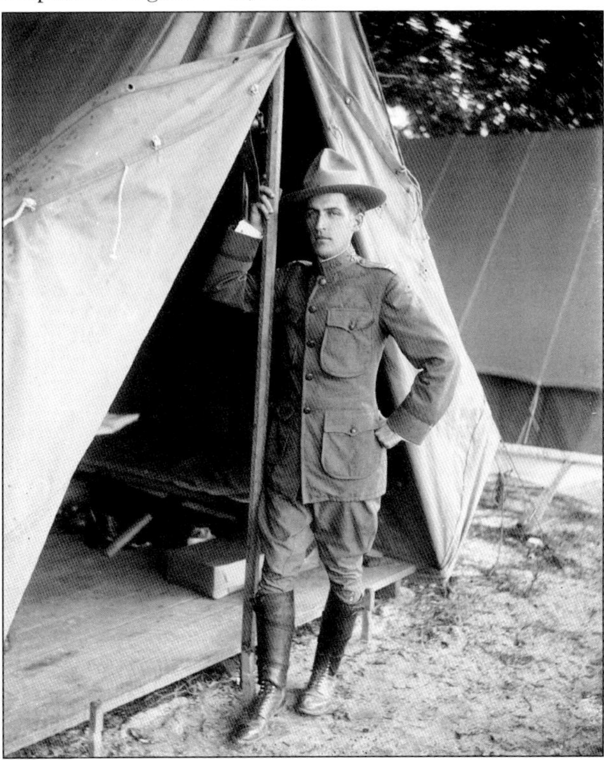

Capt. Baxter Durham (1878–1968) served as the camp's quartermaster in 1910, and his duties included providing necessary transportation and forwarding each organization commander's schedule for movement from home station to camp. Durham also oversaw the necessary quartermaster's stores and camp equipage while getting the camp ready for troop occupancy. (Courtesy of the University of North Carolina at Chapel Hill.)

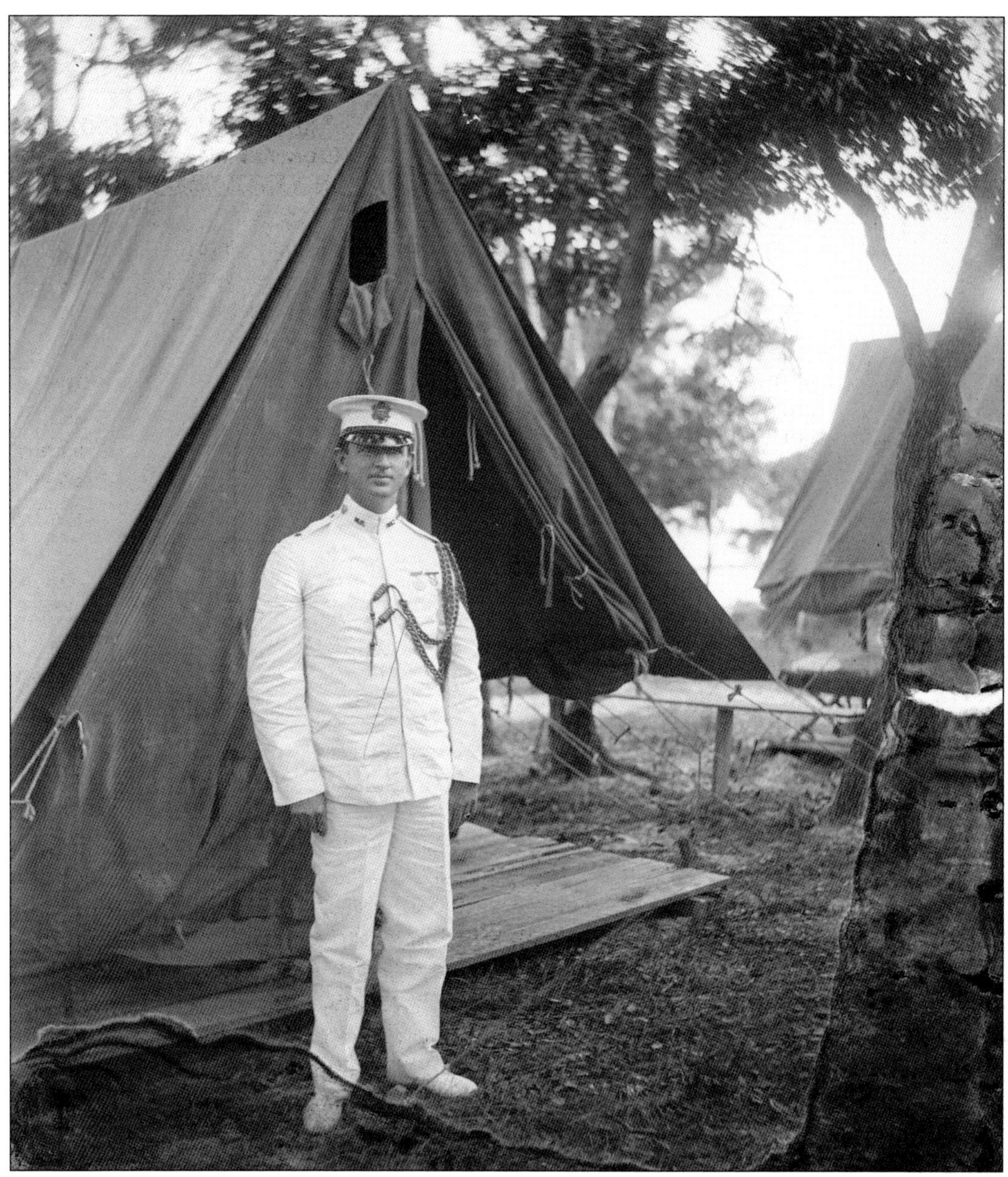

A photograph taken by Bayard Wootten shows Col. Laurence Woodville Young (1877–1966) in dress uniform. Wootten first met the adjutant general at a camp inspection when she was wearing a National Guard uniform and a hat with a lieutenant's black and gold hat cord. When Young remarked that Wootten should not be wearing a lieutenant's cord an embarrassed Wootten tried to apologize. Young smiled saying Wootten misunderstood him and then thanked her for promoting Camp Glenn's soldiers and their good work with her photographs by replacing her cord with his gold colonel's cord. Earlier in her career as the camp's photographer, Wootten had a misunderstanding with another general in charge during that time. He gave her a public dressing-down thinking that she was a "camp follower." Wootten, who came from some of the state's most distinguished families, described in an interview the general's surprise that night when he attended Atlantic Hotel's military ball and saw her dancing and mingling with some of the other finest families in the state. (Courtesy of the University of North Carolina at Chapel Hill.)

In 1911, bespectacled and smoking his ever-present pipe, Col. W.E. Gary is relaxing on a bench near Bogue Sound's shore while reading the Raleigh *News & Observer.* Tents, soldiers, a civilian, and the sound are seen in the background of the photographs. Gary served as the NCNG's assistant quartermaster general for more than 10 years, retiring in 1912. In civilian life, Gary served as postmaster, tax collector, auditor, and the first president of the Tobacco Board of Trade of North Carolina. Camp Glenn's YMCA may have provided the Raleigh *News & Observer* that published news of Henderson, Gary's hometown. (Courtesy of the University of North Carolina at Chapel Hill.)

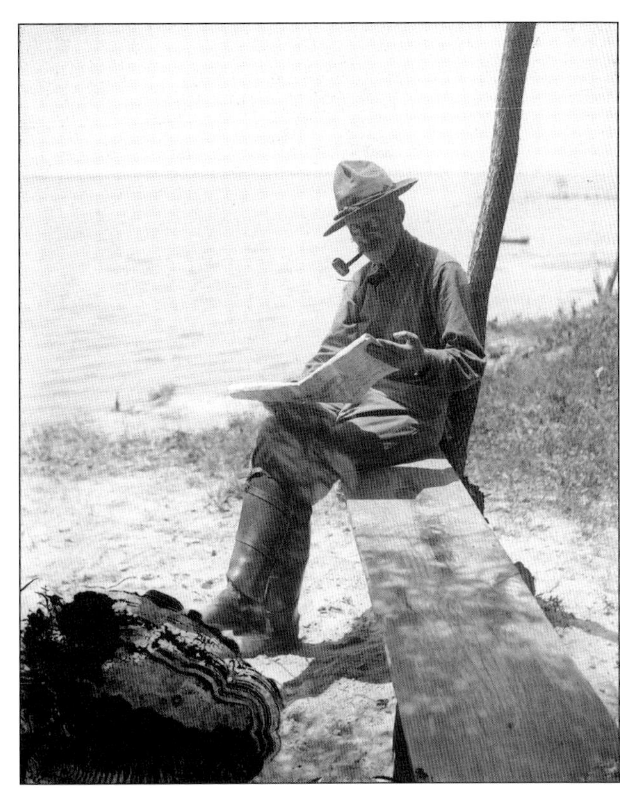

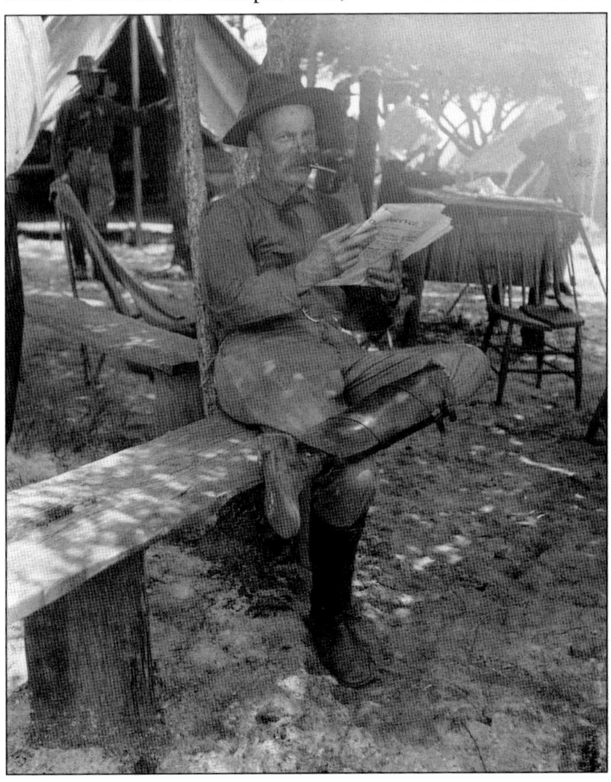

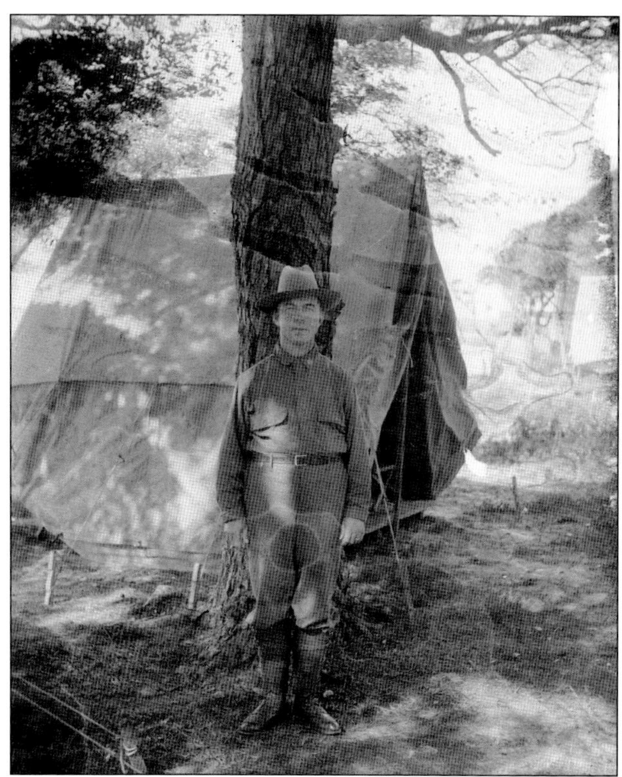

Maj. James S. Poythress (1871–1918), Company C, 3rd Regiment, served as quartermaster. In 1911, a newspaper article praised Major Poythress stating, "He is a whole-souled, companionable man, and a splendid officer. He is a favorite with all who know him, and he deserves it." When he served at Camp Glenn, Poythress was in charge of improvements that included constructing new buildings and granolithic walks. (Courtesy of the University of North Carolina at Chapel Hill.)

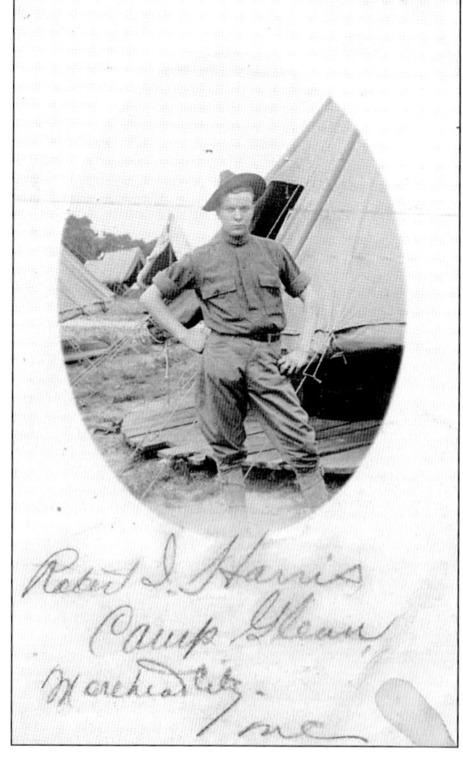


Likely from Pitt County, Robert I. Harris is in an enlisted soldier's uniform posing in front of a tent with a wooden floor. Soldiers were not allowed to bring civilian clothes to camp and had to wear their cotton uniform, with blouse and olive drab shirts, shoes, and campaign hat on the train to camp and at all times during the training period. (Courtesy of East Carolina University.)

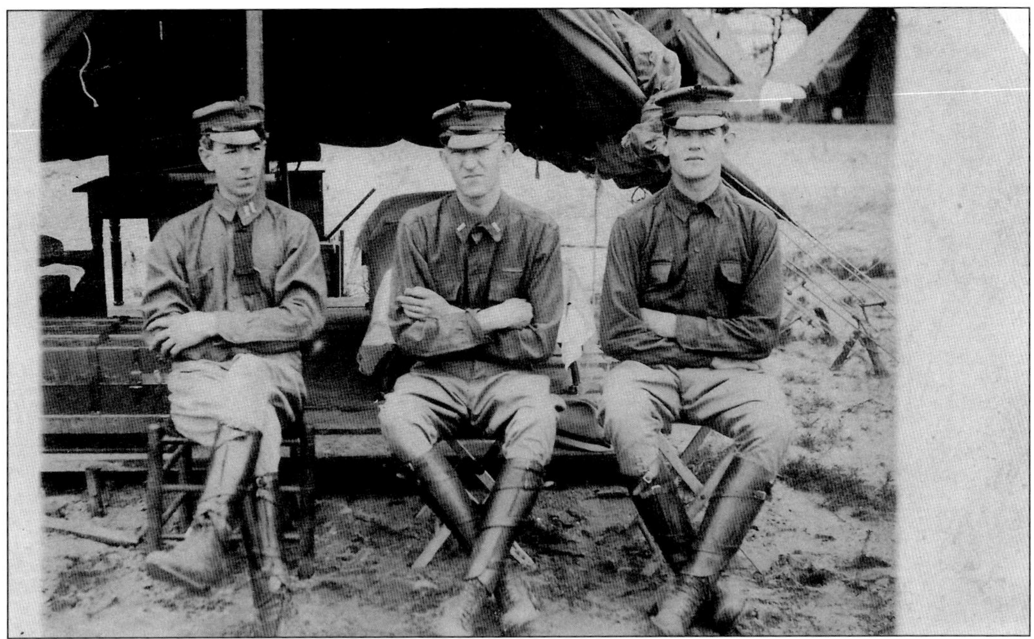

Three unidentified soldiers are shown seated in front of an administrative tent with a desk and a trunk. Camp administrators' duties were to employ the limited time during encampment to the best advantage in order to develop the soldierly esprit and the company into a unit capable of organized effort. They also strived to teach some fundamentals of military engineering.

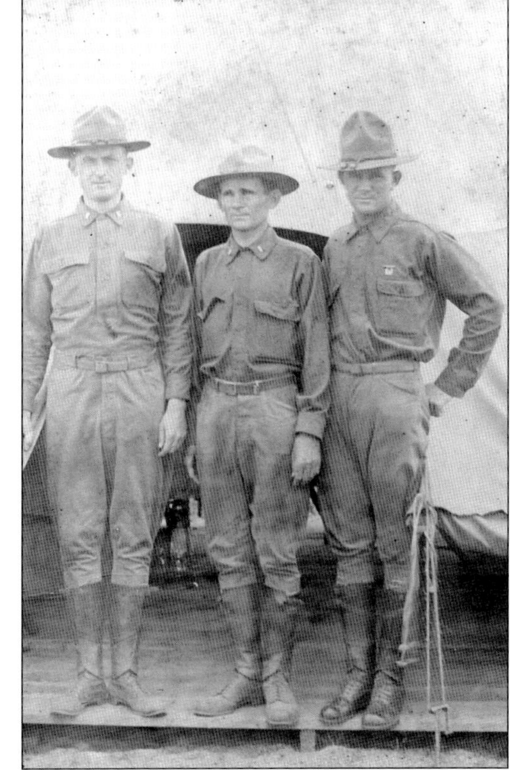

Lt. Henry Clarence Howell (1881–1958) (right) and two unidentified soldiers, Company B, 3rd Regiment, Raleigh, are standing in front of a tent. Howell served as battalion adjutant in 1915. The postcard (date illegible) is addressed to Miss Adna Howell, 11 Seawell Avenue, Raleigh North Carolina, with a message, "Hello Sweetheart—How are you this time. Father." Adna Elizabeth was Howell's young daughter.

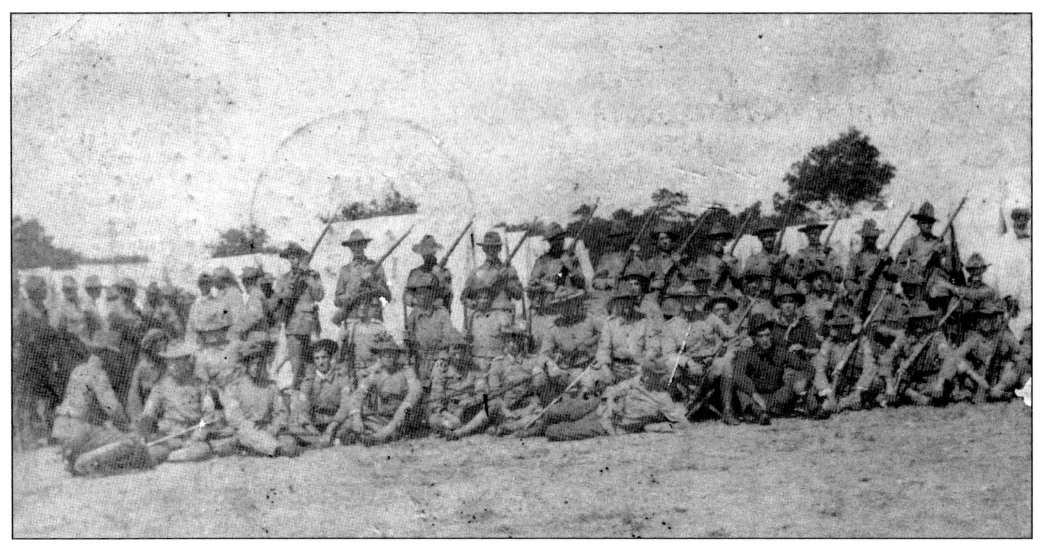

Unidentified soldiers with Company F, 1st Regiment, Asheville, are posing with weapons in front of tents, as one soldier reclines. A civilian cook in a white uniform is standing (right). Civilian cooks were hired to aid company cooks during camp training periods. Lt. James Earl Whiteside (1881–1959) mailed this postcard, dated August 16, 1906, to his wife, Nannie Whiteside (1895–1958), at 41 Searcy Street, Asheville, North Carolina.

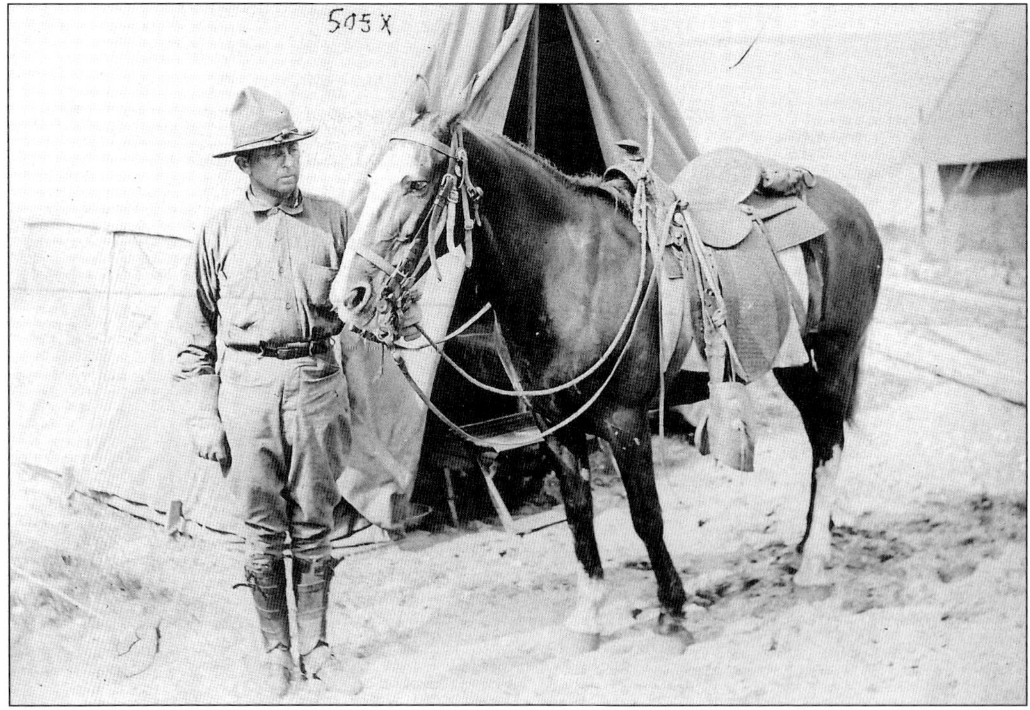


Col. Wiley Croom Rodman (1879–1942) briefly commanded the 2nd North Carolina Infantry during 1916's mobilization training period held at Camp Glenn in preparation for the Mexican Punitive Expedition against Pancho Villa. Rodman recruited and served with Battery B, 113th Field Artillery core through its demobilization. The postcard's message in part reads, "Taken at Camp Glenn, N.C. July 20, 1916." (Courtesy of Linda Willis Sadler.)

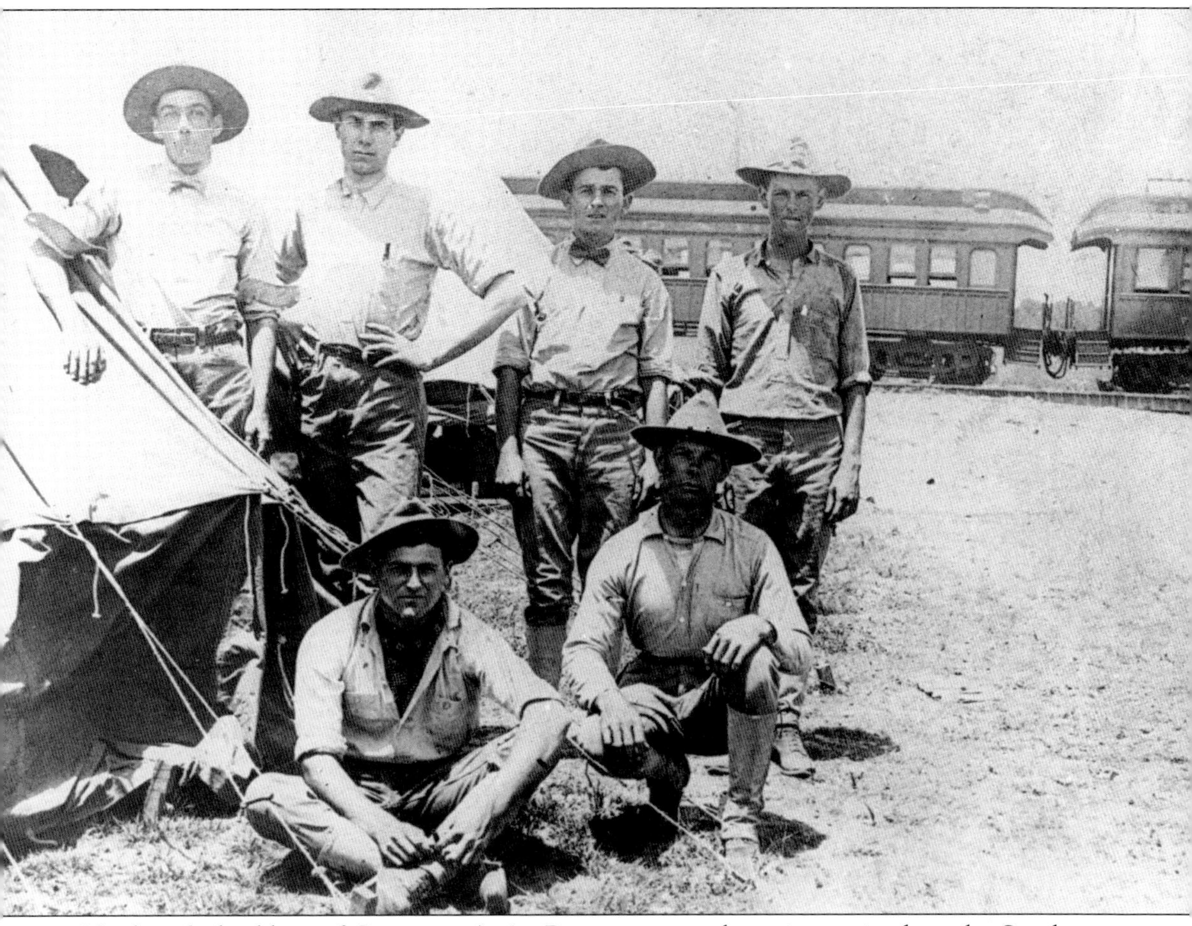

Unidentified soldiers of Company A, 1st Regiment, may have just arrived on the Southern Railways train shown in the background. Two soldiers are looking dapper wearing bow ties that are probably not part of the standard uniforms issued. In 1914, Hickory Rifles soldiers had 54 enlisted men and 3 officers and were under the command of Capt. George Lafayette Lyerly (1888–1952). They left for Morehead City on Monday evening, July 14, for the annual encampment and maneuvers of the first North Carolina regiment of the National Guard, which was made up of 12 companies and a band. Their local newspaper, *Hickory Daily Record*, kept up with their local soldiers' activities during encampment and reported, "The soldier boys fared better in making the trip this year as the State had provided sleeping cars for the long night ride." (Courtesy of North Carolina State Archives.)

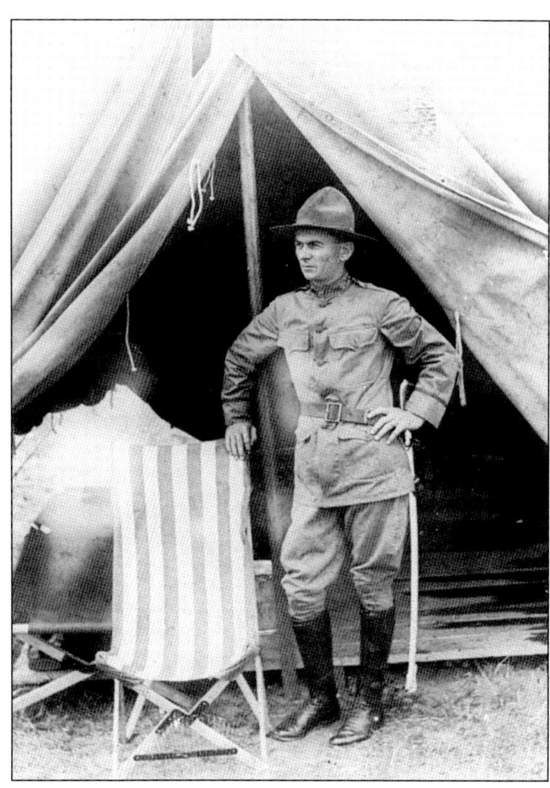

Lt. Frank Lawrence Cline (1888–?), Company A, 1st Regiment, with hand on hip, is standing in front of a tent and leaning on a striped cabana chair. The cabana chair is suitable decor for the camp's coastal environment, though it is probably not standard government issue. It does, however, show up in other Camp Glenn scenes. (Courtesy of North Carolina State Archives.)

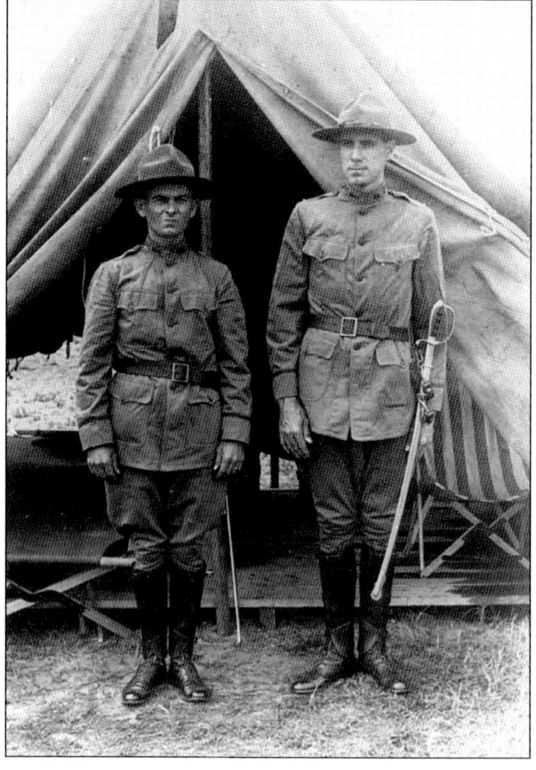

Hickory Rifles officers, from left to right, Lt. Frank Lawrence Cline and Lt. George Lee Huffman (1883–1968), Company A, 1st Regiment, are standing at attention with swords at their sides in front of a tent and the striped cabana chair. Cline and Huffman were elected 2nd and 1st lieutenants, respectively, in 1914 upon the untimely death of Lt. W.C. Keever. (Courtesy of North Carolina State Archives.)

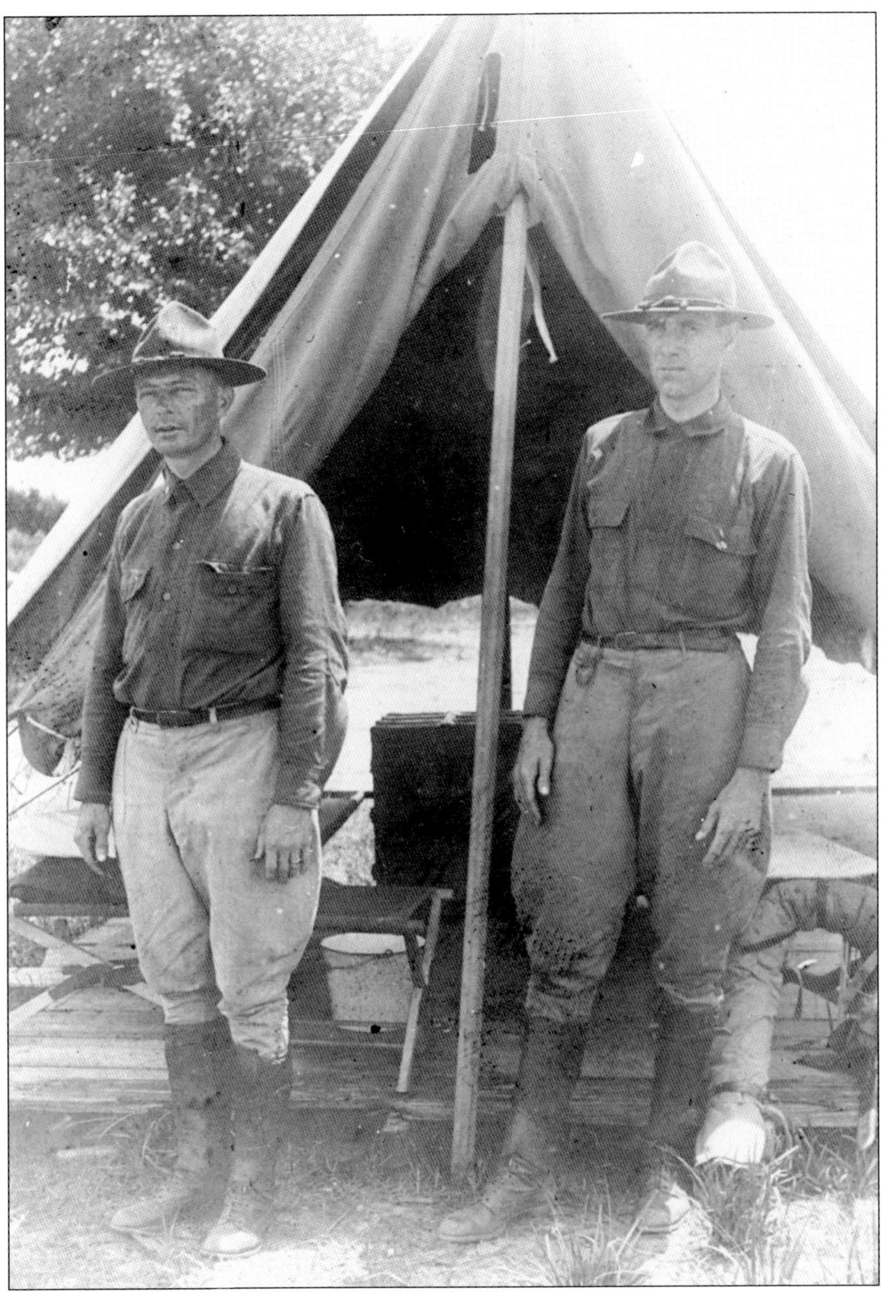

1st Lt. Walter Claude Keever (1879–1914) (left) and 1st Lt. George L. Huffman (right), Company A, 1st Regiment, Hickory, are wearing Montana peak–style Stetson campaign hats featuring hat cords with acorn tips. The acorns tips bouncing on hat brims were designed to keep riders awake while riding horses. Keever, who attended the officers school of instruction in Raleigh in 1912, was 34 and unmarried when he died after a brief illness in 1914. At his funeral, Company A fired a salute of three volleys, and taps was played by the company's musician. Claude Keever was a partner in Bost and Keever, Hickory, North Carolina. Huffman also attended the officers school of instruction in 1912 and was the recruitment officer for the Hickory Rifles. In 1917, Lieutenant Huffman was promoted to the rank of captain. (Courtesy of North Carolina State Archives.)

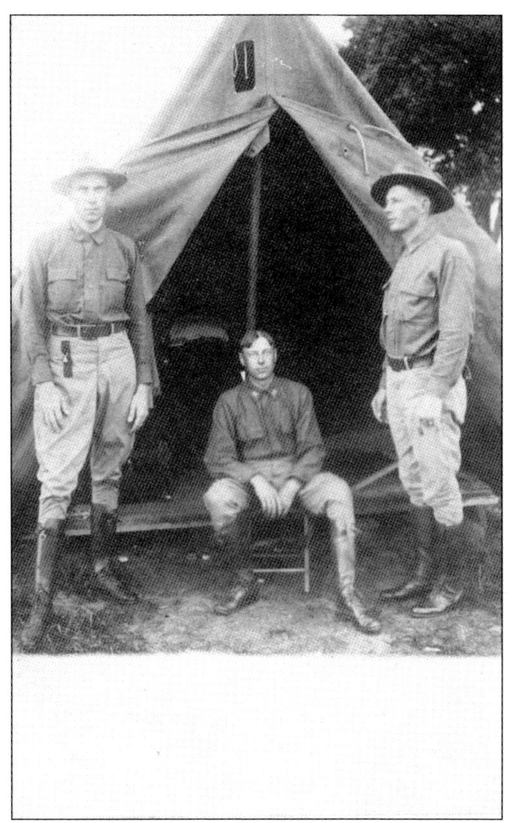

Company A officers, from left to right, Lt. George L. Huffman, Capt. Gustus William Julius Payne (1879–1920), and Lt. Claude Keever, are in front of their tent during 1910 encampment. In 1910, the *Hickory Democrat* reported, "Lieutenants Claude Keever and George Huffman deserve commendation for their unceasing efforts to make the company what it is today." Payne, promoted to major, was a Hickory businessman and died of influenza in 1920. (Courtesy of the University of North Carolina at Chapel Hill.)

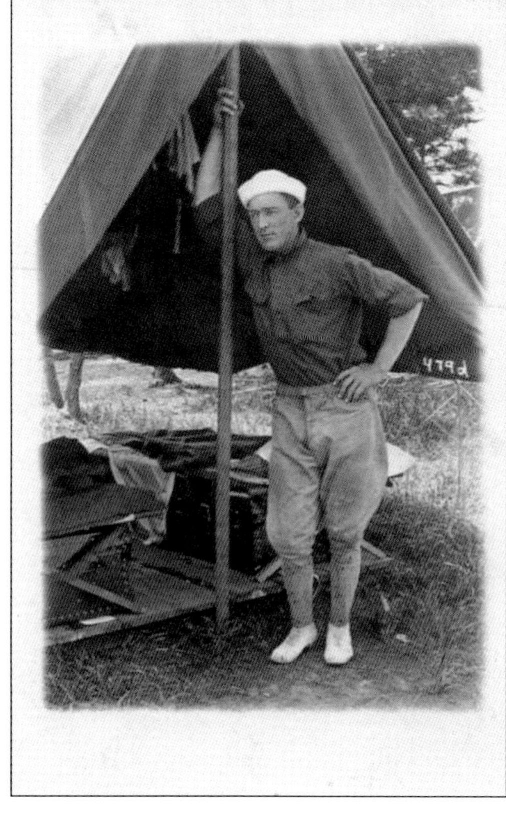

An unidentified soldier of the Coast Artillery Corps is posing at a tent's entrance and is dressed in issued blue denim trousers and jumper. In 1910, Brig. Gen. Arthur Murray, chief of the Coast Artillery Corps, strongly advocated an increased detail of artillery troops to man the coast defenses. In 1914, the Coast Artillery had 6 companies with 21 officers and 374 enlisted men. (Courtesy of North Carolina State Archives.)

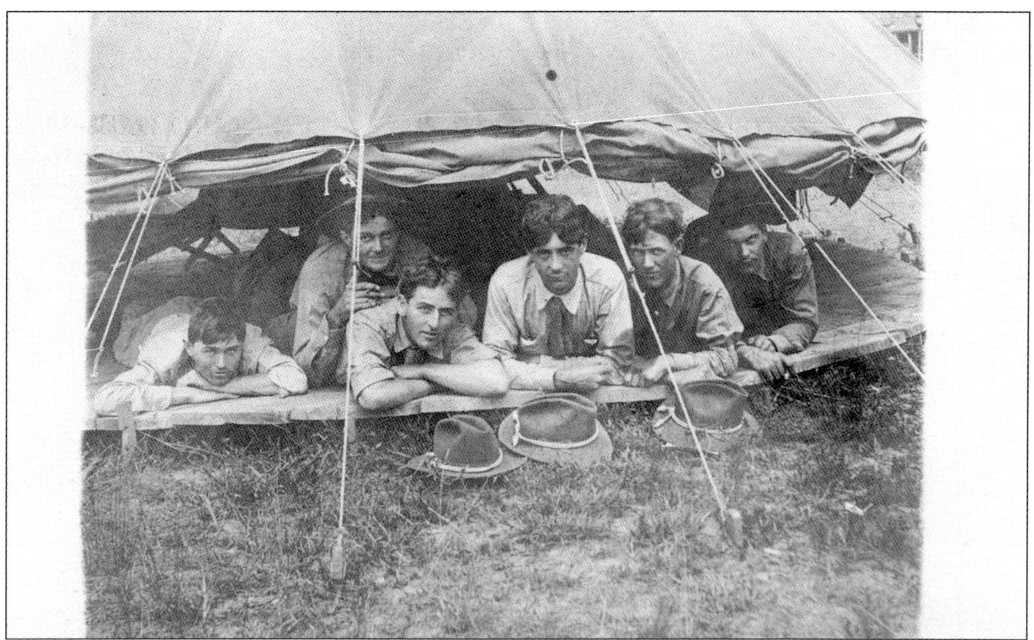

During summer training camp in 1912, unidentified soldiers are lying on a wooden tent floor peering out from underneath. Camp conditions and equipment were reportedly good; however, that year's report noted that the wooden tent floors were badly in need of repair and should be replaced. (Courtesy of the University of North Carolina at Chapel Hill.)

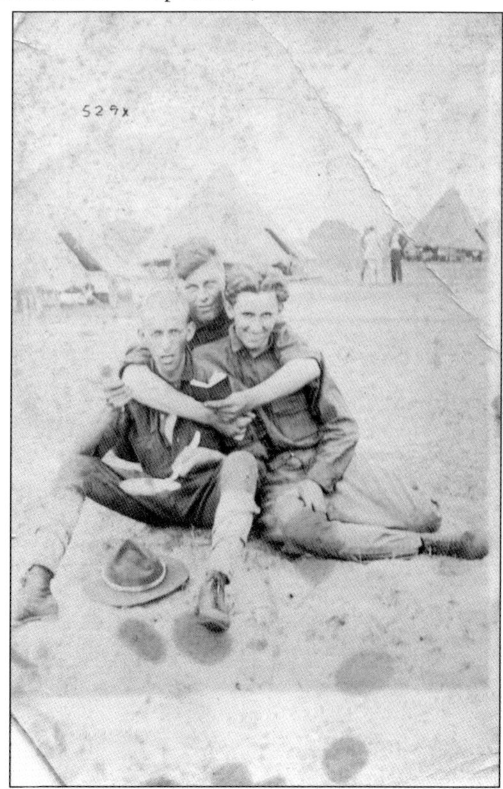



Three unidentified soldiers, possibly with the 3rd Infantry, are sitting on the ground with their arms around one another. One soldier, with a plate and utensil, appears to be having a meal. Another soldier is holding a book that may be a field manual or a bible. Two officers and a civilian are seen in the background. (Courtesy of North Carolina State Archives.)

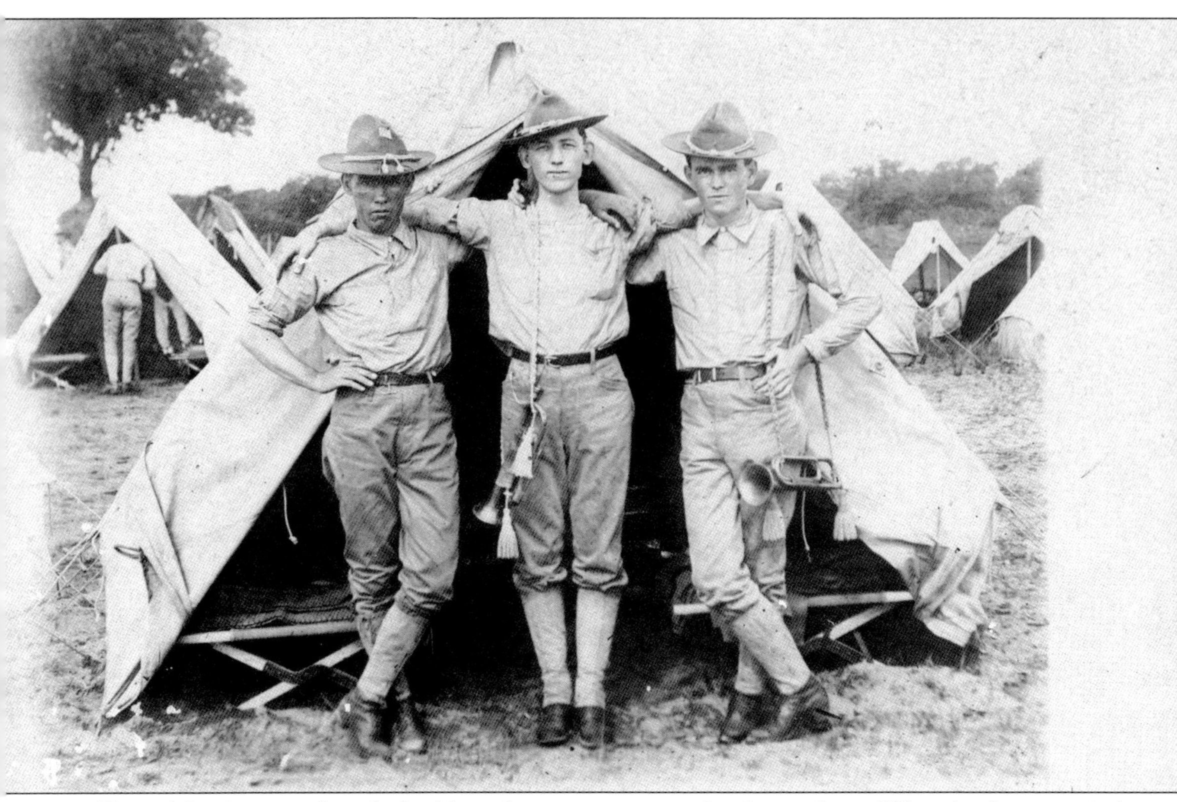

Two of the three unidentified soldiers shown are carrying bugles on slings. When buglers sounded the "call to arms," every man quickly grabbed his gun and belt, falling into line. One 2:00 a.m. call to arms woke a soldier who had trouble finding his shoes and the tent's opening in the dead of night and in a hurry. Eventually, the soldier found his shoes and the tent's opening and remarked, "It is better to be late falling in than to walk bare-footed on sand-spurs." The bugler stationed at the brigade headquarters tent had the unusual duty of sounding the wedding march as Camp Glenn held its first wedding in 1916 when Selma Young, the sister of General Laurence Woodville Young (see page 12), married Lt. Wallace Stone, Company L, Thomasville, 3rd Infantry, during summer encampment. After the wedding, the couple headed for points north on their honeymoon. (Courtesy of the University of North Carolina at Chapel Hill.)

In 1917, a Camp Glenn soldier (unidentified) is posing in front of a tent. In February and March, most National Guard units mustered out of federal service after returning from the Mexican border. On April 6, 1917, the United States declared war on Germany, and on August 5, 1917, the entire National Guard was drafted into US Army in preparation for World War I. (Courtesy of the University of North Carolina at Chapel Hill.)

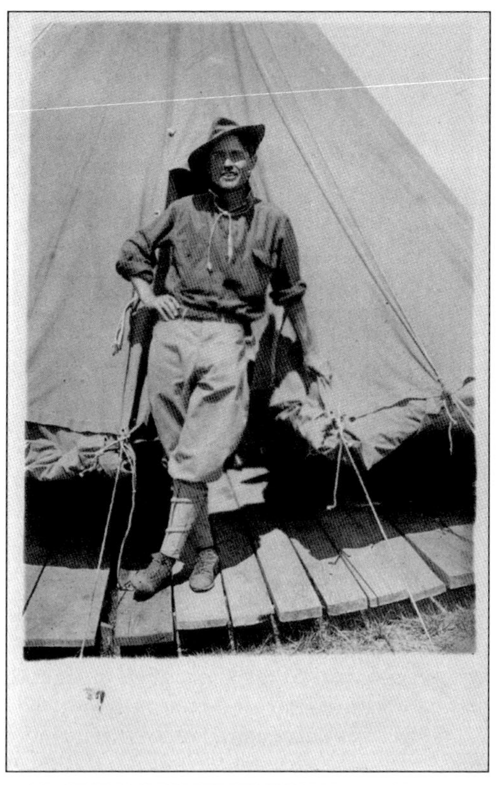

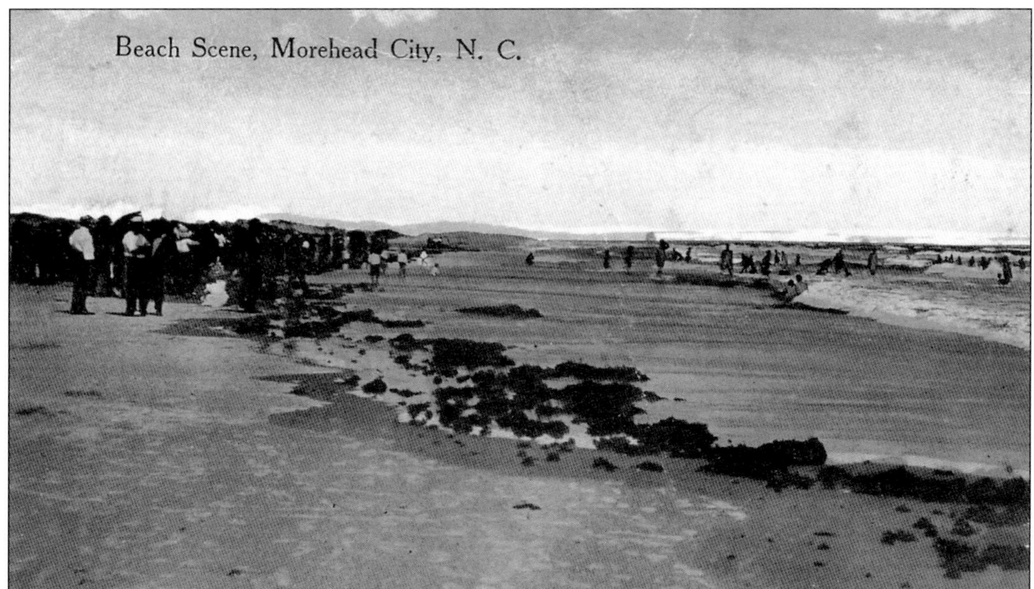


Clyde Justinary Pope (1895–1974), Company A, 1st Regiment, Hickory, was training at Camp Glenn to prepare for war with Mexico when he sent this beach scene postcard postmarked July 2, 1916, to "Miss Grace Pope, Rt. #1, Clearmont, [*sic*] N.C." The message reads, "Hello Grace how are you fine I guess. I am ok but aint [*sic*] having much of a time down here fighting mosquitoes. Guess we will go to Mexico before long. Would like to see you all. tell everybody hello. and soon from Clyde Pope."

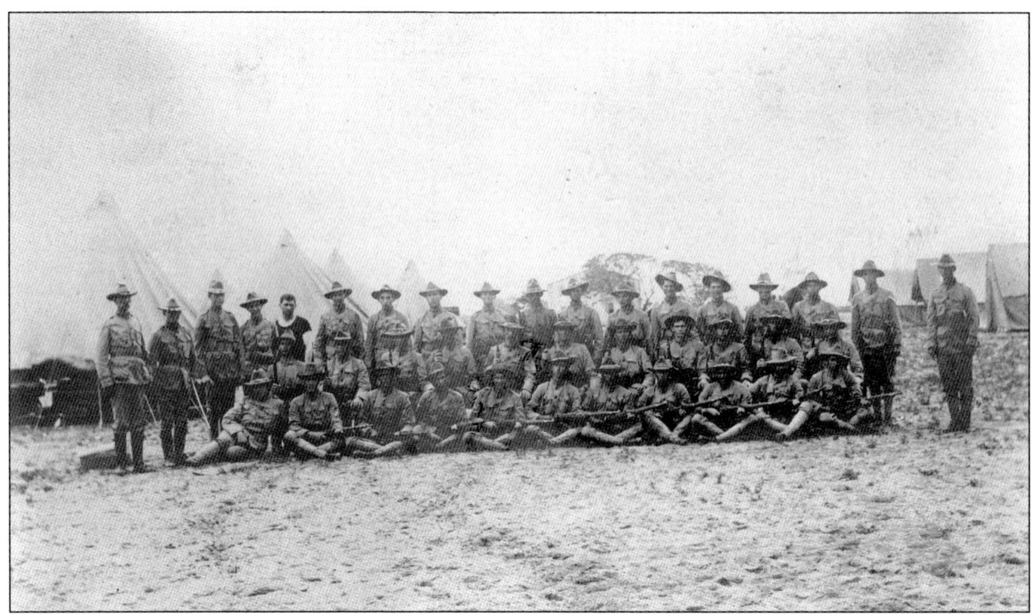

"Hollywood" is written on the back of this postcard showing unidentified soldiers, tents, and one person in a bathing costume (third row, fifth from the left). Camp Glenn was located in an area called Hollywood, named for a plantation home located nearby and owned by Capt. Appleton Oaksmith who was an accused slave trader, Civil War blockade runner, and, in 1874, an elected representative in the state's legislature. (Courtesy of the University of North Carolina at Chapel Hill.)

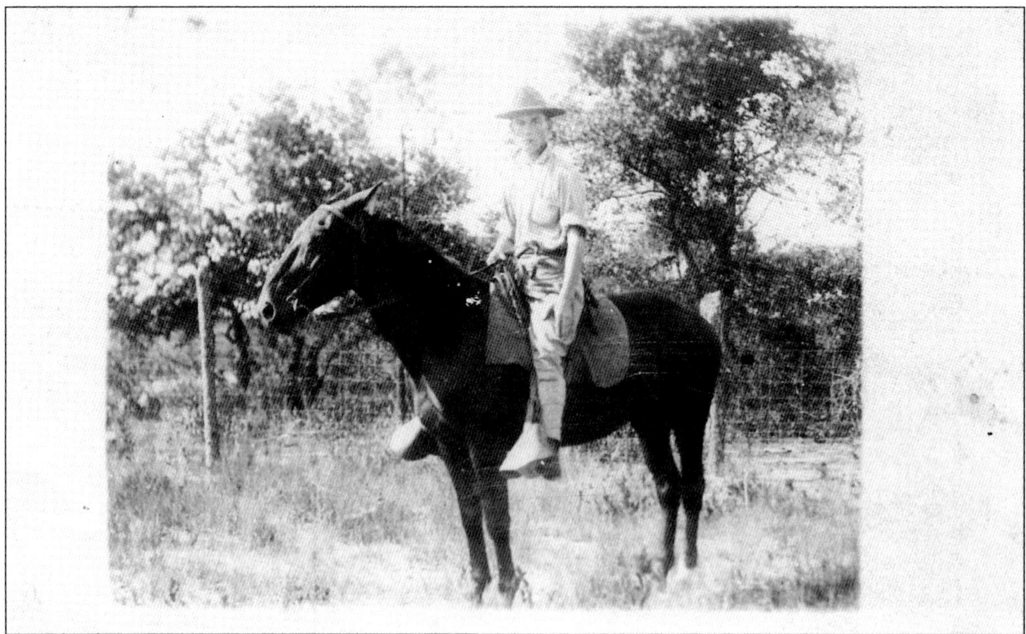

The soldier on this horse is likely a member of the NCNG's cavalry. In 1920, the cavalry had three troops, Troop A, Lincolnton; Troop B, Asheville; and Troop C, Hickory. Each troop brought 32 horses to camp by train in Pullman cars. The cavalry drill encampment was held September 7–23, 1920, making camp life better for both men and horses because there were fewer tormenting mosquitoes and flies.

Pvt. Silas K. Triplett (1887–1918), of Hunting Creek, is kneeling and pointing his rifle. Triplett enlisted on June 19, 1916, serving with Company M, 3rd Infantry, Durham. In 1917, he was drafted into the US Army during World War I. Triplett served in several units in the 26th Infantry, 1st Division, US Army. He was killed in action in France on May 26, 1918. (Courtesy of North Carolina State Archives.)

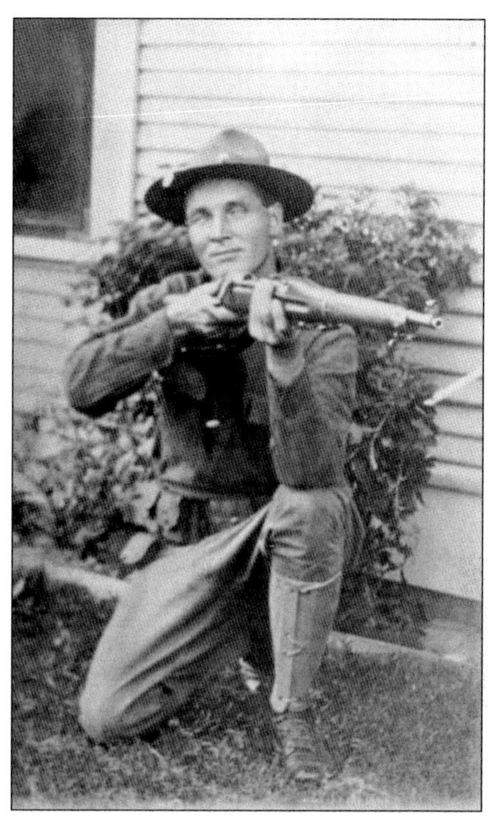

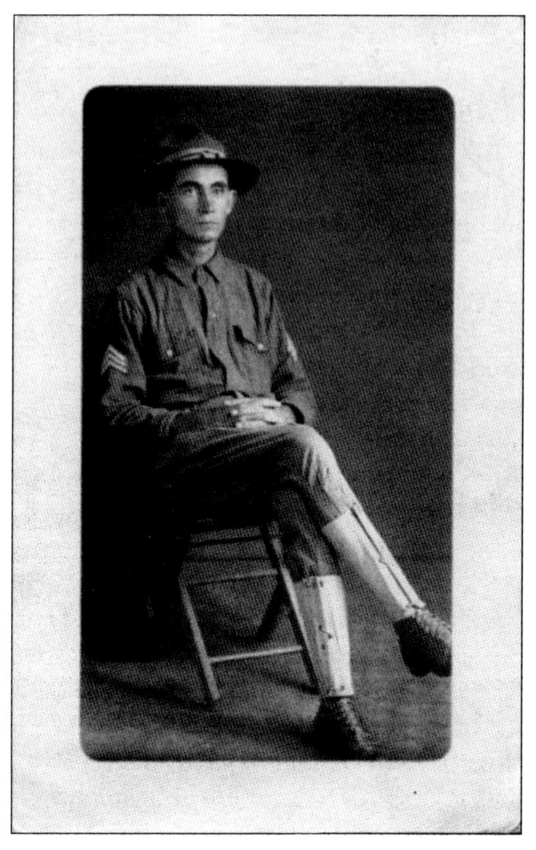

Sgt. Joseph McAlister White (1899–1985), Company L, 120th Infantry, 30th Division, wearing his Army uniform, poses for a studio portrait. White, served in Company L, 3rd Infantry, Thomasville, as a NCNG soldier and was a student at North Carolina State College when he enlisted during World War I. After the war ended, he was employed by Caldwell Furniture Company of Lenoir, North Carolina. (Courtesy of North Carolina State Archives.)

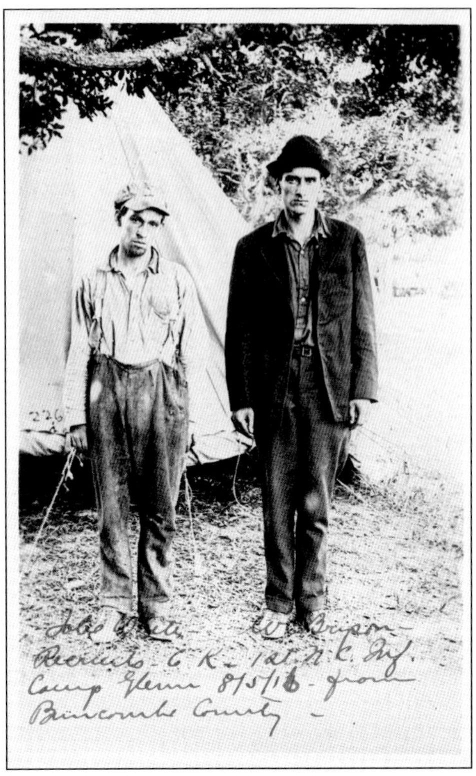

In 1917, the *New York Times* published an article, "In Uncle Sam's Service—Before and After," about the overall benefits of enlisting in the National Guard. Two photographs were taken at Camp Glenn in 1916. The first, titled "In Uncle Sam's Service—Before," was taken on August 15, showing two North Carolina men when they first enlisted in Company K, 1st Infantry, Asheville. Pvt. Jobe White (left) and Pvt. Walter E. Bryson (right) are standing in front a tent, slouching and looking a little shabby. The second photograph, taken five months later, shows both soldiers standing tall, looking healthier and confident after gaining 30 and 50 pounds, respectively. An officer in the State National Guard remarked that the improvement was proof that military training "will raise the standard of citizenship in this country from 50 to 75 percent." (Courtesy of the University of North Carolina at Chapel Hill.)

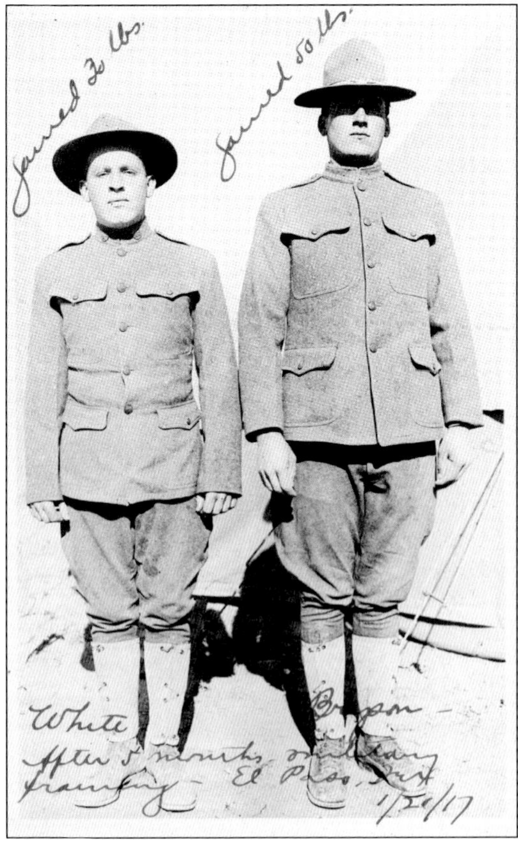

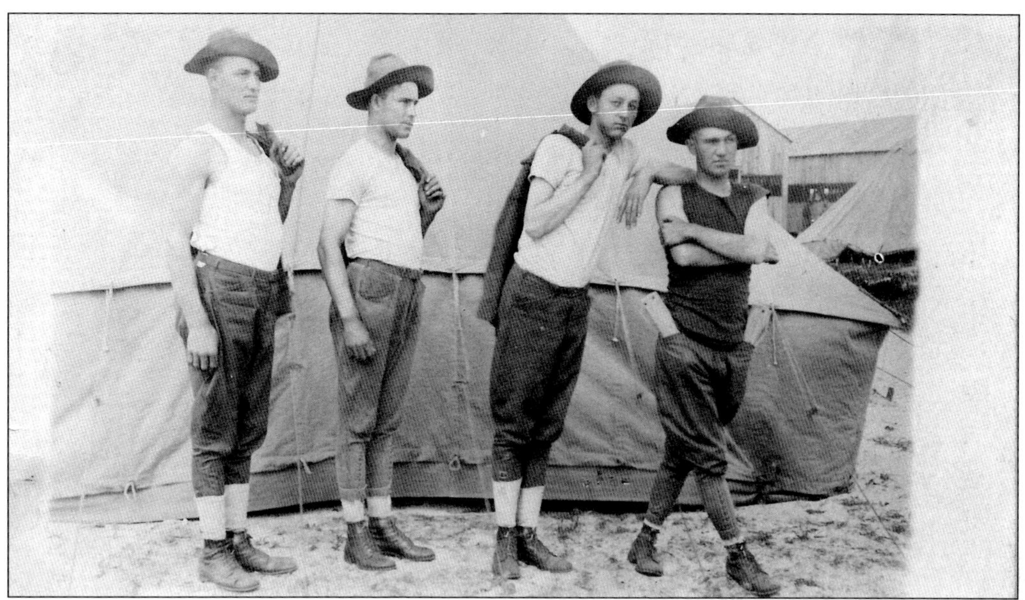

Partially dressed in uniform, four soldiers pose in front of a tent. One soldier (right) appears to have rolled-up papers in his pockets. These men might be relaxing between drills and other camp-related duties. Soldiers' off-time activities included swimming, boating, fishing, and baseball games. Drinking and card games were prohibited.

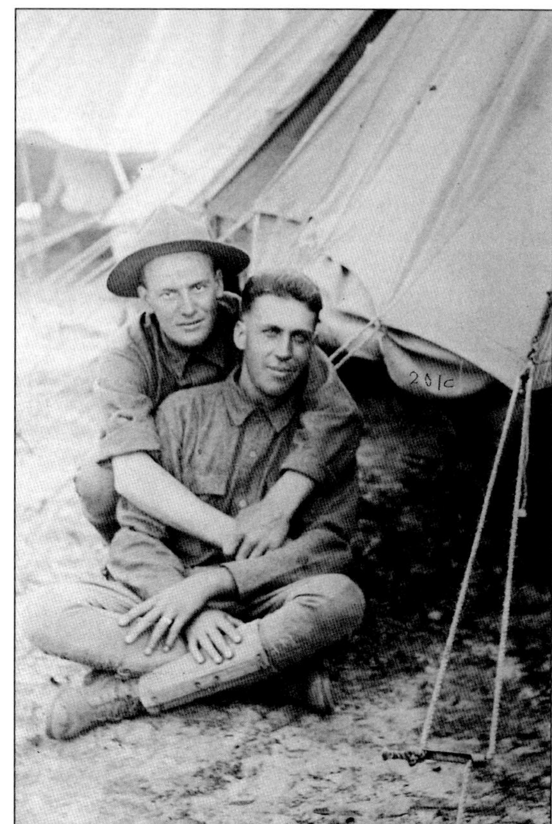

Two soldiers pose for a photograph taken by Bayard Wootten. These unidentified soldiers may be friends or relatives who belong to the same company and know one another well back home. Friends and family members, including brothers, cousins, and other close relatives, often served in companies together, providing companionship and a familiar face while away from home during summer training camp.

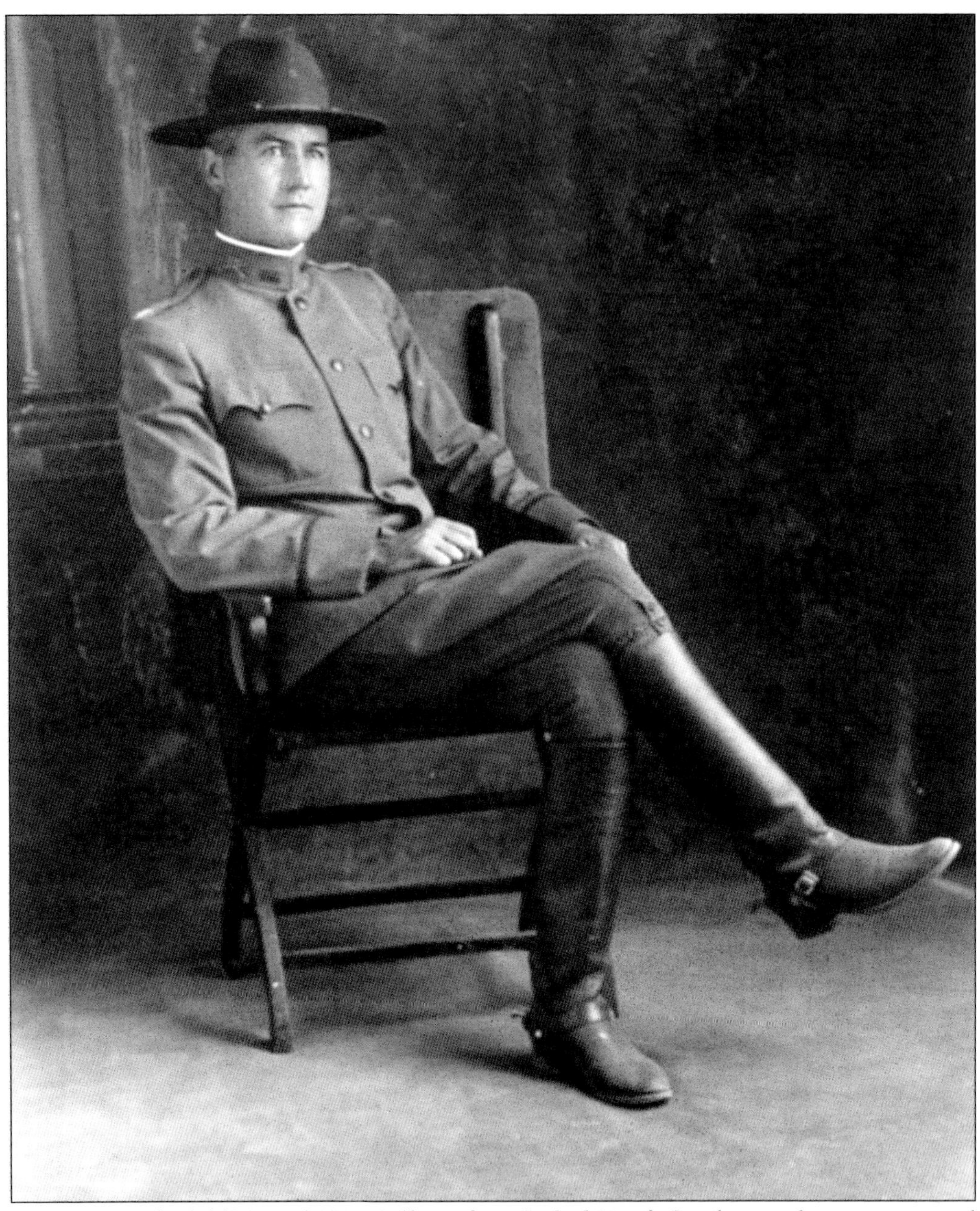

Col. Sidney Whitfield Minor (1873–1945) was from Oxford, North Carolina, and was in command of the 3rd Regiment, NCNG. The *Durham Morning Herald* reported that the colonel was popular with the soldiers, both officers and enlisted, because of his "deep manifested interest in their welfare and advancement." Minor led the 3rd Regiment in 1916 in El Paso, Texas, when North Carolina troops fought during the Mexican Border War. As commander of 120th Infantry, 30th Division, US Army, during World War I, Minor was equally popular with the soldiers under his command, and after the war was over, Minor eloquently stated in a speech printed in the same newspaper article that the "North Carolina troops didn't win the war but they came darned near to it." Minor received the American Distinguished Service Medal in recognition for exceptionally meritorious and distinguished services during the Great War. (Courtesy of North Carolina State Archives.)

Standing next to a military biplane during World War I, Capt. James Wiggins Jenkins (1893–1976) is in his US Army uniform. He enlisted on July 22, 1915, in the NCNG commanding Company C, 3rd Infantry, Henderson. Captain Jenkins was at Camp Glenn in 1917 and commanded Company 120th Infantry during World War I in the US Army Air Service. (Courtesy of North Carolina State Archives.)

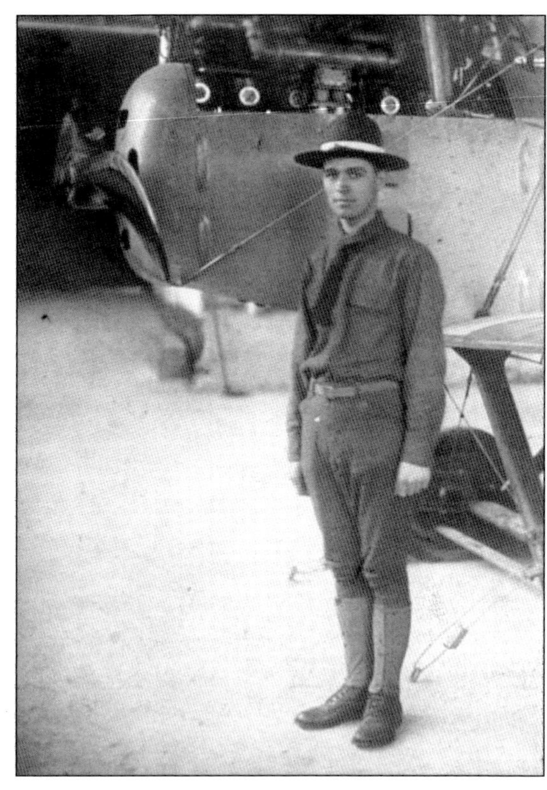

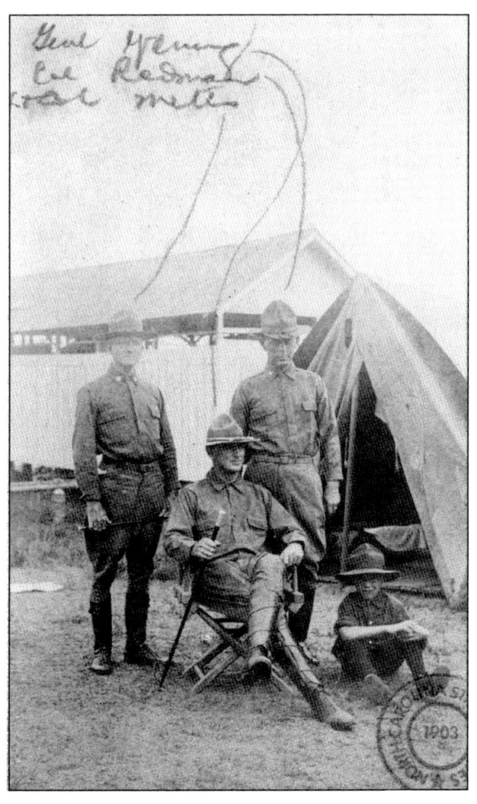

Col. Laurence Young (seated) is pictured with Lt. Col. John Van Bokkelen Metts (1876–1959) (left) and Capt. Wiley Rodman (right), during the 1916 mobilization. Metts, 60th Brigade, 119th Infantry, was promoted to colonel in 1917 while serving on the Mexican border. An unidentified young boy, perhaps a son of one of the officers, is seen sitting on the ground. (Courtesy of North Carolina State Archives.)

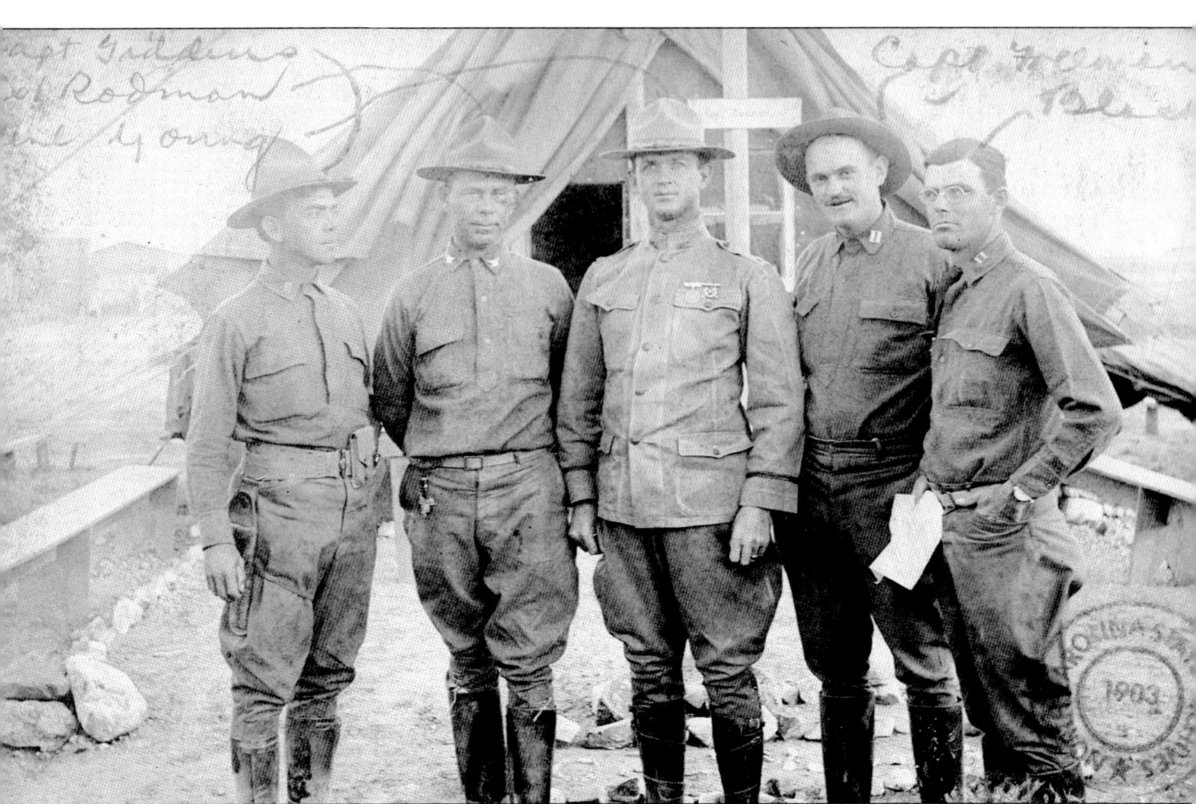

A military tent with a cross served as Camp Glenn's chapel where Capt. Arthur Wiles Freeman (1866–1952) held services for soldiers during the 1916 mobilization. Benches lined up on either side of the chapel served as additional seating for soldiers attending services. In 1923, Col. Don E. Scott required the men to attend church services in order to give the chaplain "an opportunity to talk to the men in a body." The camp's YMCA also held services. Each regiment had a chaplain in its Field and Staff Company. Pictured are, from left to right, Capt. Lewis Devereaux Giddens Jr. (1873–1923), Company K, 2nd Infantry, Wilson; Capt. Wiley C. Rodman; Adj. Gen. Laurence W. Young; Capt. Arthur W. Freeman, chaplain, Field and Staff, 1st Infantry, Raleigh; and Capt. Fred L. Black, quartermaster, 2nd Infantry. (Courtesy of North Carolina State Archives.)

This 1916 photograph shows three unidentified Louisburg soldiers from Company D. That year, the troop was one of the last to arrive at camp for summer training. The soldiers were eager to get started, and within three minutes of their arrival by train, the men and equipment were in their tents and ready for duty. (Courtesy of North Carolina State Archives.)

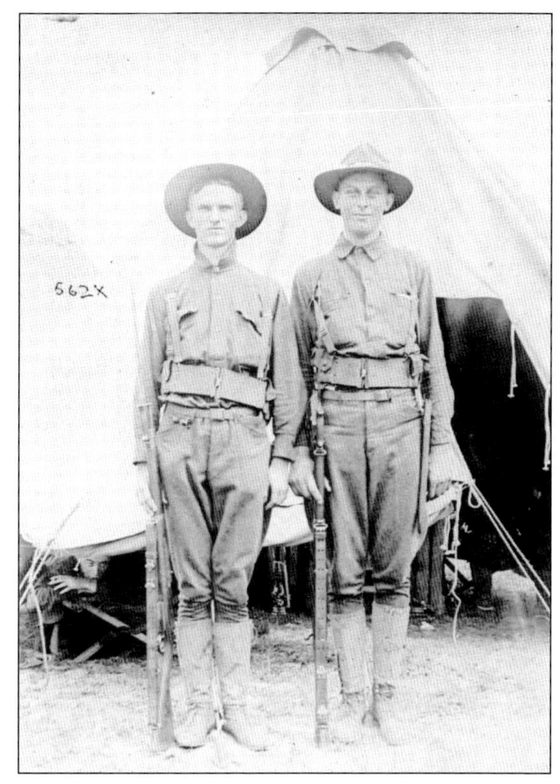


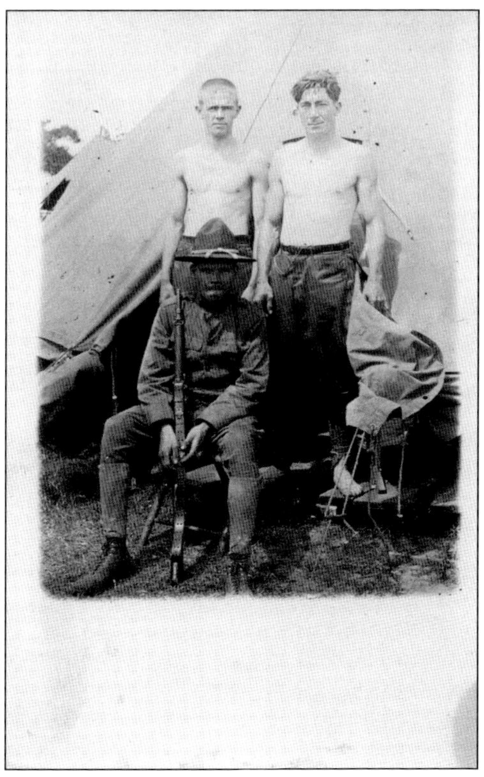

During the 1916 mobilization, Sgt. Thomas Alston (left) (1894–1938), with other Company D, 3rd Infantry, Louisburg, soldiers, is standing in front of a tent. The men left Camp Glenn on September 27, 1916, for Camp Stewart in El Paso, Texas, to take part in the Mexican Punitive Expedition. Alston enlisted as corporal on April 9, 1915, and was promoted to sergeant during his Mexican border assignment. (Courtesy of North Carolina State Archives.)

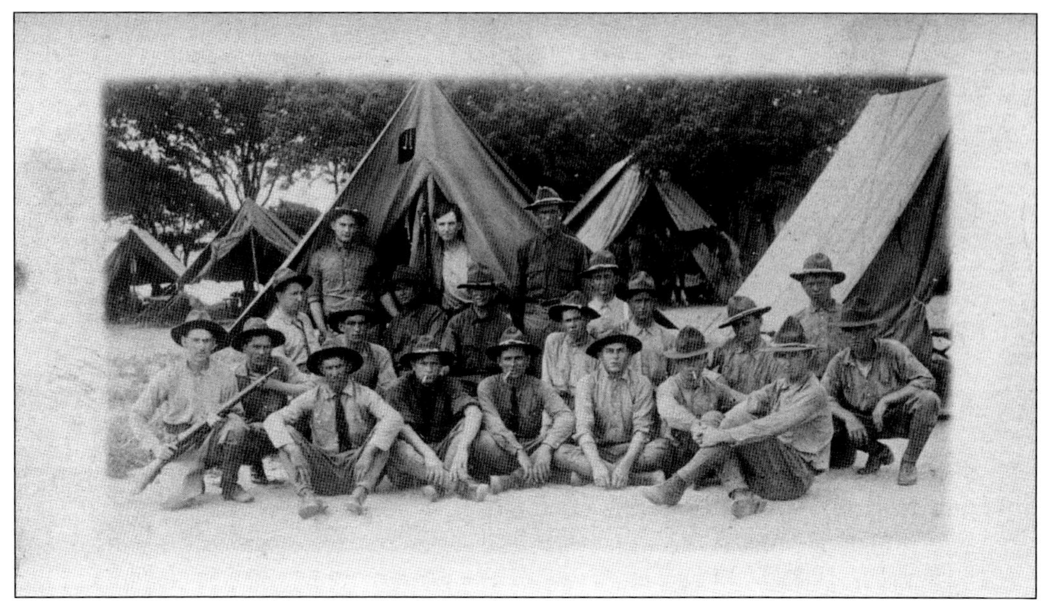

In 1916, Company D, 3rd Infantry, Louisburg, soldiers pose during training at Camp Glenn, and with rifles in hand, they appear ready for action at the Mexican border. A horse, saddled and hitched in the background, also appears to be ready for some action. All Company D soldiers enlisted or were commissioned from 1915 to 1917. (Courtesy of North Carolina State Archives.)

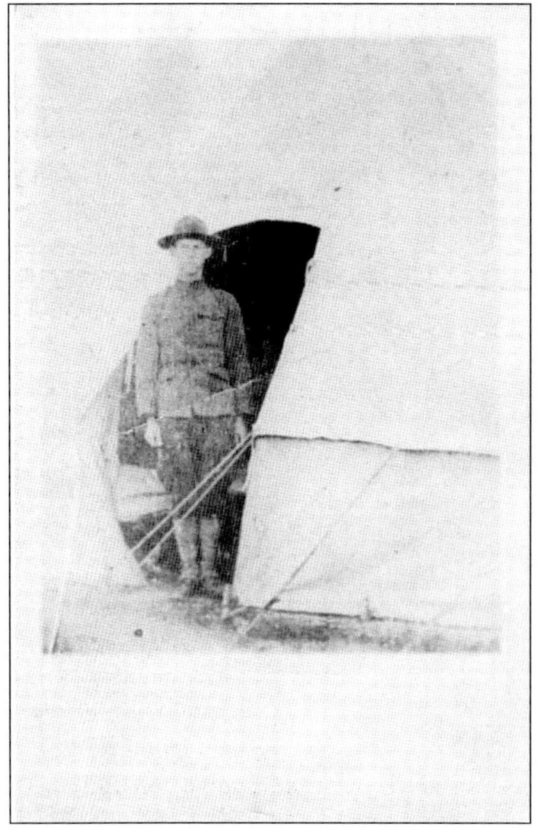

Pvt. William E. Nicholson Jr. (1897–1974) enlisted in Company H, 3rd Infantry, Warrenton, on April 6, 1917, as a corporal and was promoted to private January 1, 1918, during his service in World War I. Nicholson was from the town of Airlie and served in the 120th Infantry, 30th Division, US Army, during World War I. Nicholson was wounded severely on July 25, 1918, and honorably discharged on April 18, 1919. (Courtesy of North Carolina State Archives.)

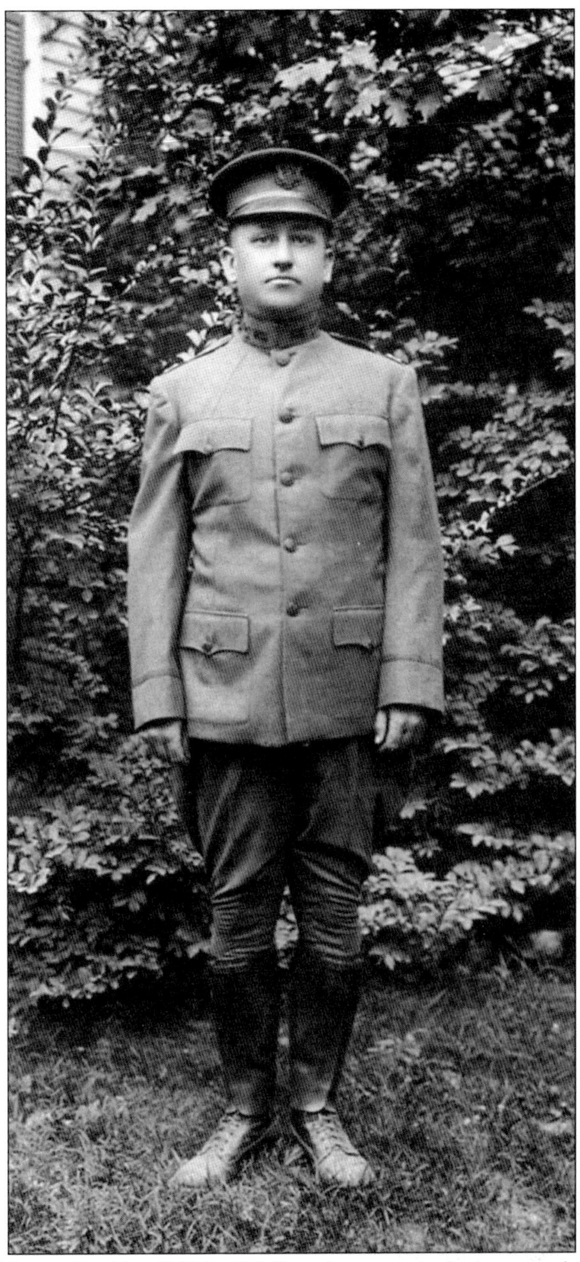

When Capt. Samuel Perry Boddie (1880–1936), a druggist and commander of Company D, 3rd Infantry, Louisburg, enlisted on April 9, 1915, it was said in the *Franklin Times* that, though every man at Louisburg's Tar River Drug company rallied to the colors, Boddie was the "chief man in the store." After serving in the Mexican Border War, it was also said that Boddie led Company D from the Mexican border through the Hindenburg Line as he commanded the 3rd Battalion, 120th Infantry, 30th Division, US Army, during World War I. In January 1918, while fighting overseas, Boddie was promoted to major and, in October of that year, was wounded by machine gun fire when taking the Hindenburg Line. Though it was first reported that he was slightly wounded, that report was later amended when it was discovered that Boddie's wounds were severe. Major Boddie recuperated at a hospital in France. (Courtesy of North Carolina State Archives.)

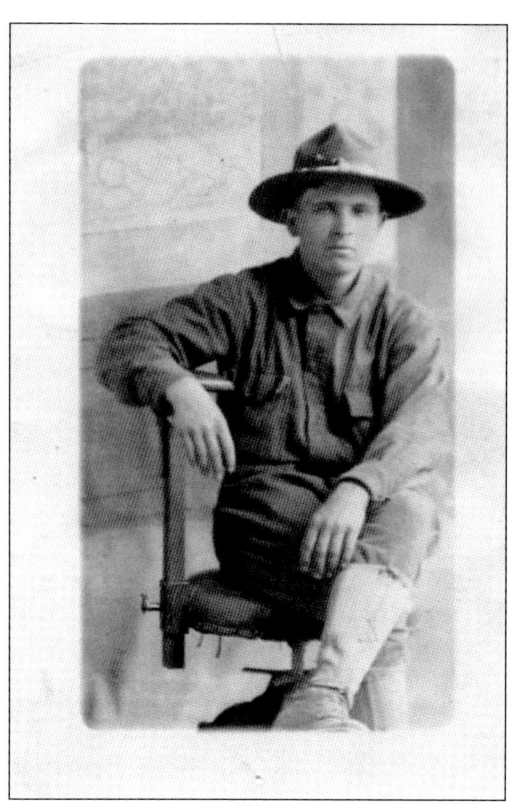

Pvt. Beverly M. Allen (1896–1918) of Airlie in Halifax County, North Carolina, enlisted on May 22, 1917, serving in Company H, 3rd Infantry, Warrenton. At the start of World War I, Allen served in Headquarters Company, 120th Infantry, 30th Division, US Army. Private Allen was killed in action on September 29, 1918. (Courtesy of the North Carolina State Archives.)

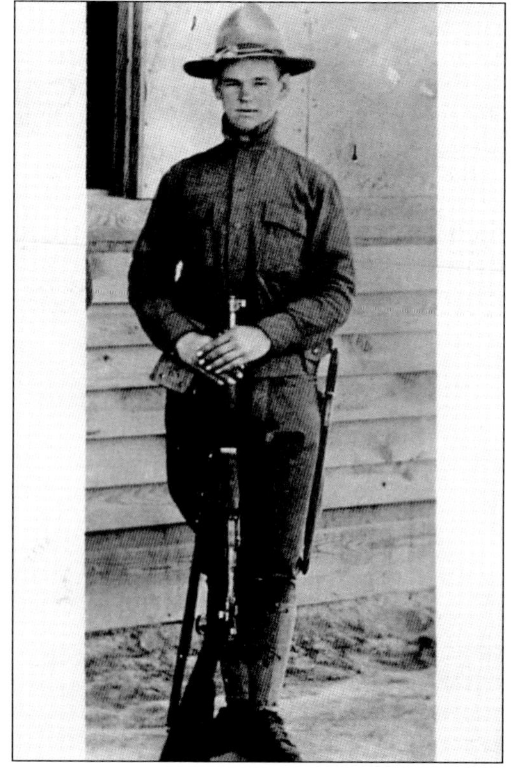

Sgt. William G. Hewitt (1890–1918) of Southern Pines, North Carolina, enlisted on May 4, 1916, and served in Company K, 2nd Infantry, Asheboro, and in Headquarters Company, 119th Infantry, 30th Division, US Army, during World War I. He was killed in action in France on August 31, 1918.

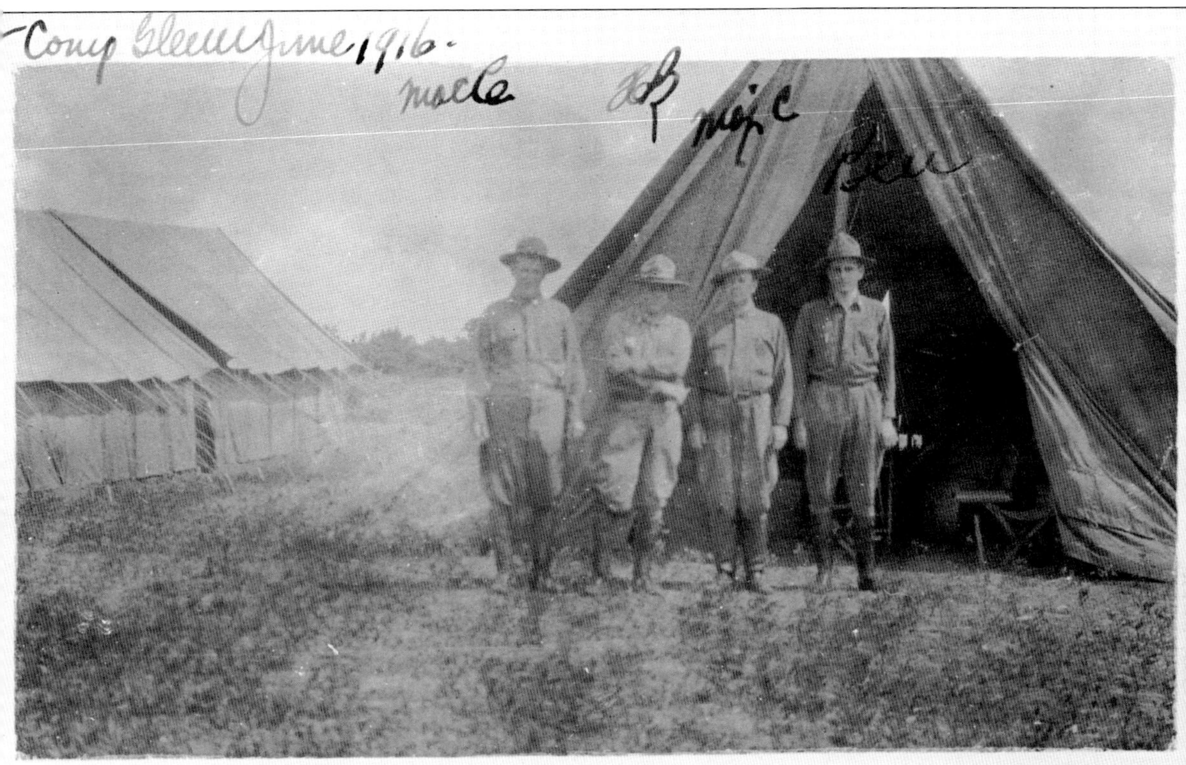


The Sanitary Detachment was ordered to Camp Glenn in June during the 1916 mobilization. Created by the War Department under the General Orders No. 80, on June 30, 1917, and called the Sanitary Corps "for want of a better name," the organization enrolled newly commissioned officers with "special skills in sanitation, sanitary engineering, in bacteriology, or other sciences related to sanitation and preventive medicine, or who possess other knowledge of special advantage to the Medical Department." The corps was the precursor to the Medical Service Corps. The medical detail pictured in this photograph includes, from left to right, Lt. John Wilson MacConnell (1878–1950); Lt. Houston Boyd (H.B.) Hiatt (1886–1941); Maj. Francis Jonathan (F.J.) Clemenger (1877–1931), commander, Field Hospital Company No. 1, Asheville; and Capt. William (Bill) Blair Hunter (1886–1967), infirmary, 1st (1884–1963). (Courtesy of ECU.)

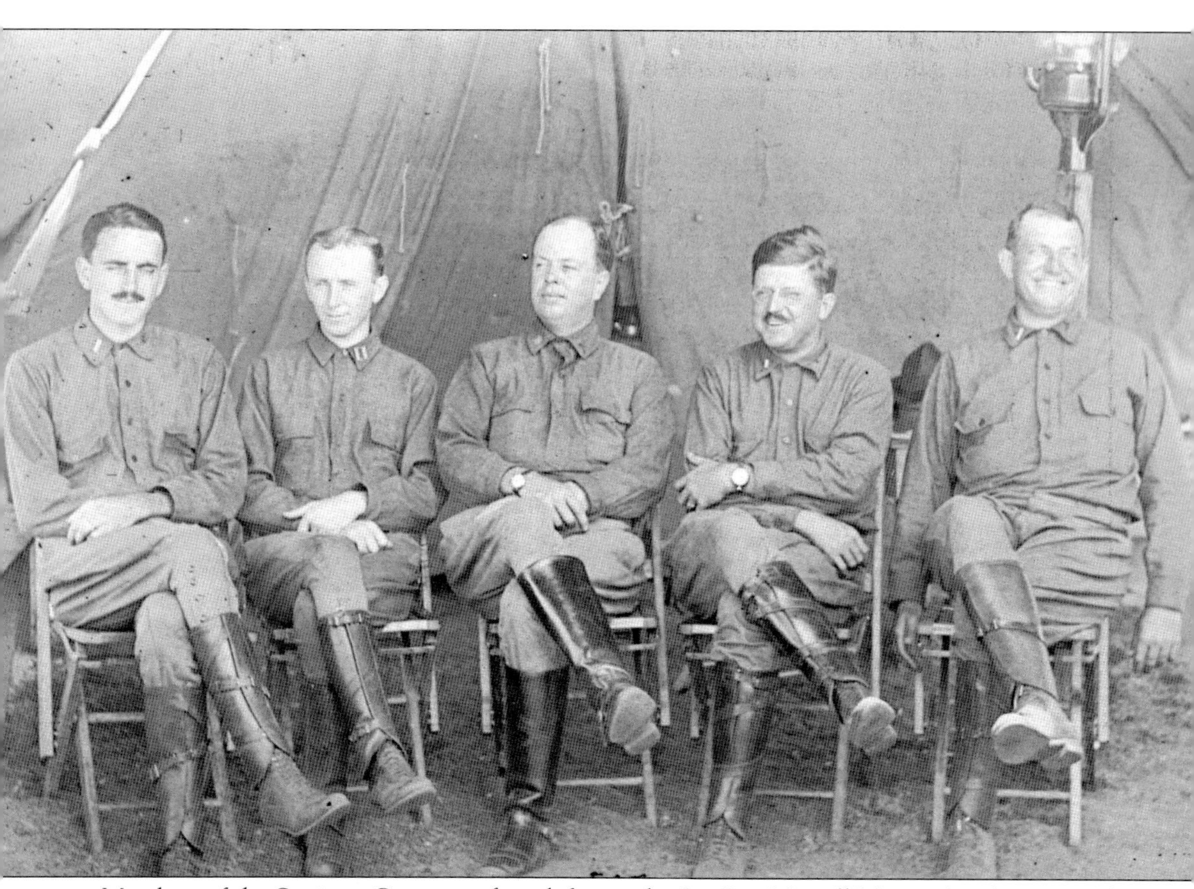

Members of the Sanitary Corps are, from left to right, Lt. Ben Morsell Meriwether (1892–1958), Ambulance Company No. 1, Canton; Capt. James William Tankersley (1882–1963), Sanitary Detachment, 1st Infantry; Lt. H.B. Hiatt; Maj. F.J. Clemenger, Commander, Field Hospital Company No. 1, Asheville; and Lt. John W. MacConnell. Clemenger and Meriweather were both members of the Buncombe County Medical Society. In the summer of 1908, Tankersley served as Morehead City's Atlantic Hotel's resident medical doctor as well as an officer in the NCNG. Later, after his military service, he operated a sanatorium in Wilmington, North Carolina. Hiatt served on active duty at Camp Glenn and Camp Stewart, Texas, during the Mexican Border War and was on staff at Guilford General Hospital in High Point and Sternberger's Hospital in Greensboro. MacConnell was a popular professor at Davidson College. (Courtesy of ECU.)

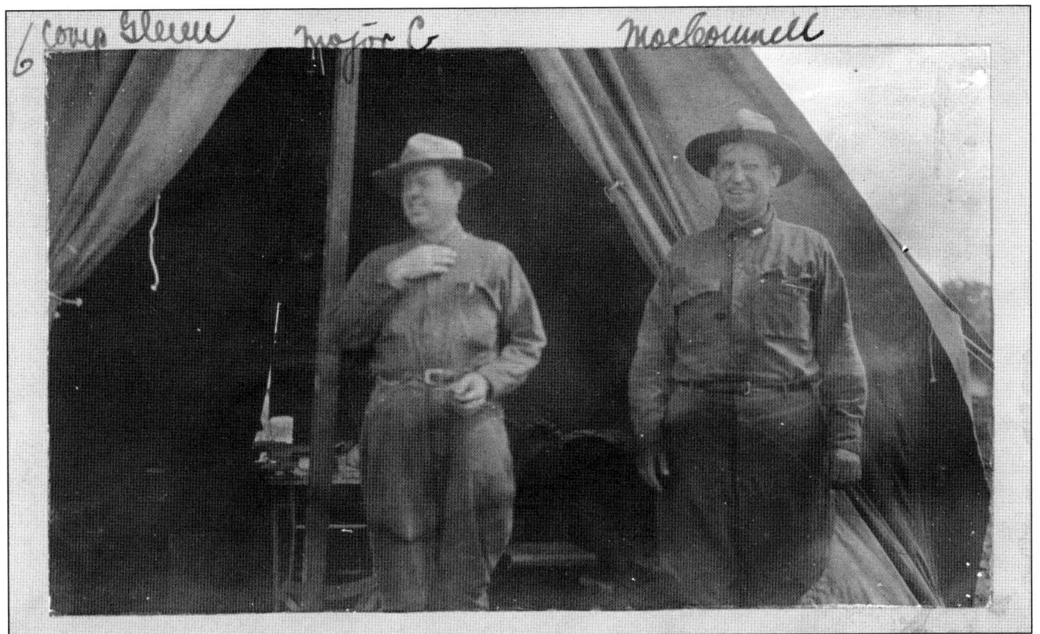


In 1916, Major Clemenger (left) leased a small boat that unfortunately sank when a stiff wind stirred up the sound. The local newspaper reported, "The little boat turned over on her side and remained there until a detail of field hospital men with buckets and ropes hauled her up and bailed her out by lantern light." Lieutenant MacConnell (right) is one of the hospital men. (Courtesy of ECU.)

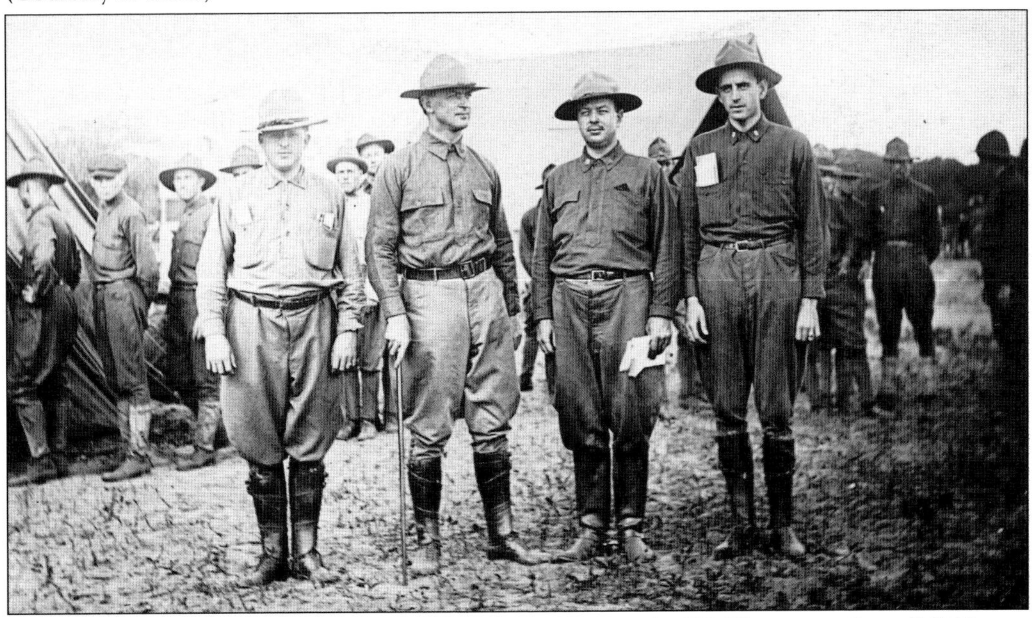

From left to right, Lt. H.B. Hiatt, Gen. Laurence W. Young, Maj. F.J. Clemenger, Capt. Bill Hunter are standing in front medical tents where soldiers in line are reporting for physical exams that included vaccinations for typhoid and smallpox. The exams were required for the first time in 1916 to determine whether or not soldiers would be accepted into US military service and sent overseas to fight in World War I. (Courtesy of ECU.)

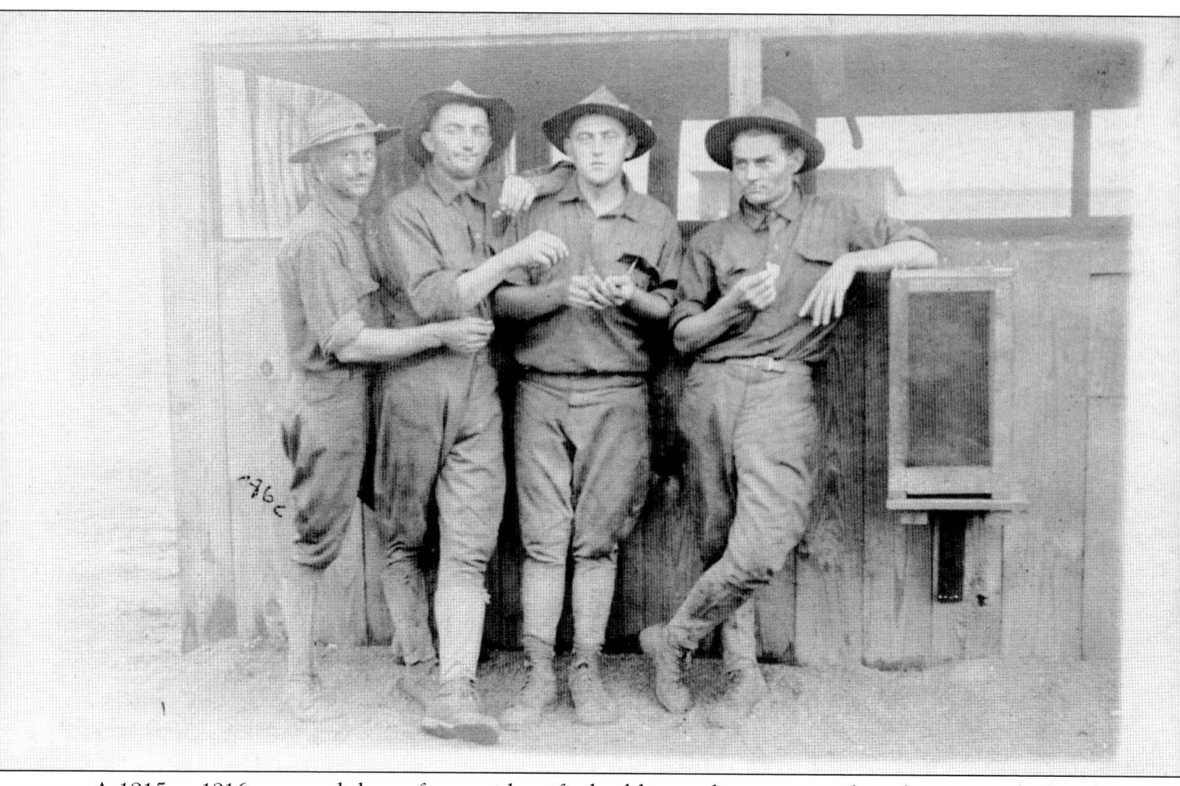

A 1915 or 1916 postcard shows four unidentified soldiers, who appear to be taking a smoke break, standing against a screened wooden building that is probably a mess building. During this period, the National Guard was advertising for young men to join its ranks in preparation for the trouble mounting along the Mexican border. North Carolina newspapers advertised the benefits of attending camps in an area known as a summer resort. Not only would soldiers acquire valuable experience during training, but they could also fish and surf bathe in the sound, and advertisements assured them there was time for both. Paid travel expenses were included, and according to their rank and number of days in camp, soldiers were paid for attending. Additionally, it was stressed that only steady and sober men should apply, and they should not look at this as an opportunity "to go a spree" during encampment. (Courtesy of North Carolina State Archives.)

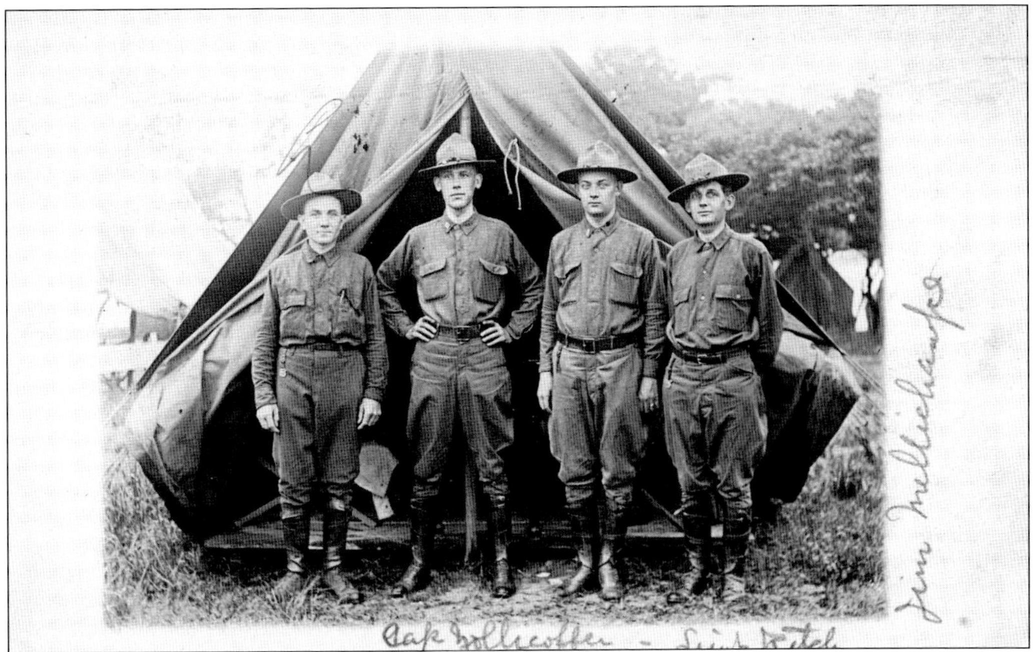


This postcard is dated July 23, 1915, and depicts, from left to right, Capt. Dallas Bancroft Zollicoffer (1887–1926), Lt. James W. Welch (1891–1966), and Lt. James H. Mellichampe (b1887) with Company M, High Point Rifles, 1st Infantry. Mellichampe and Welch placed as sharpshooters that year during encampment. Soldiers that qualified as marksman, expert riflemen, and sharpshooters received extra pay and a handsome medal to wear. (Courtesy of ECU.)

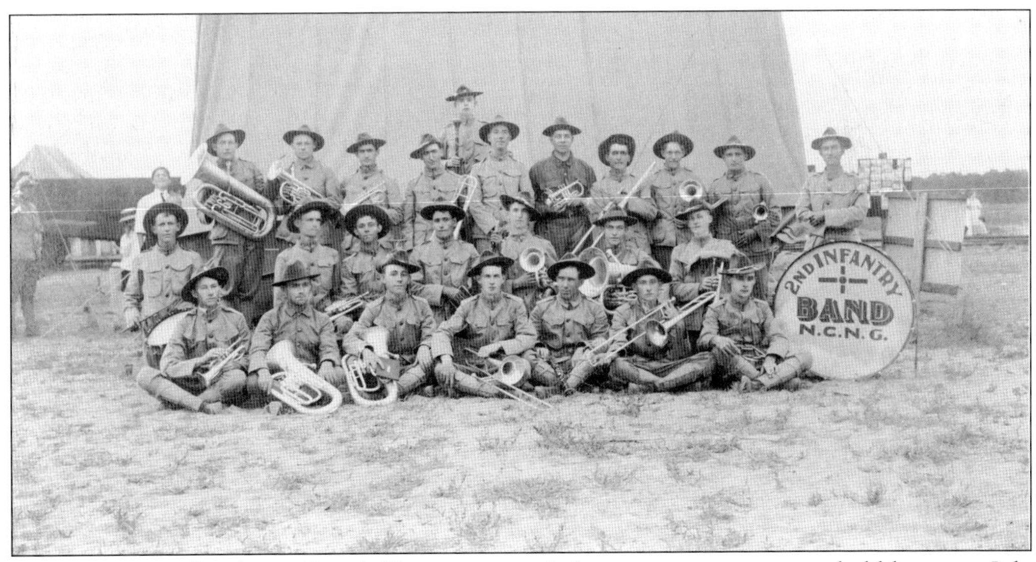


Company B, 2nd Infantry Band, Kinston, attended summer encampment held between July 8–15, 1909. Sgt. George Travis Skinner (1890–1987) (first row, fourth from the right) served two or more enlistments in the band. A soldier and several civilian children are peering on in the background. (Courtesy of North Carolina State Archives.)

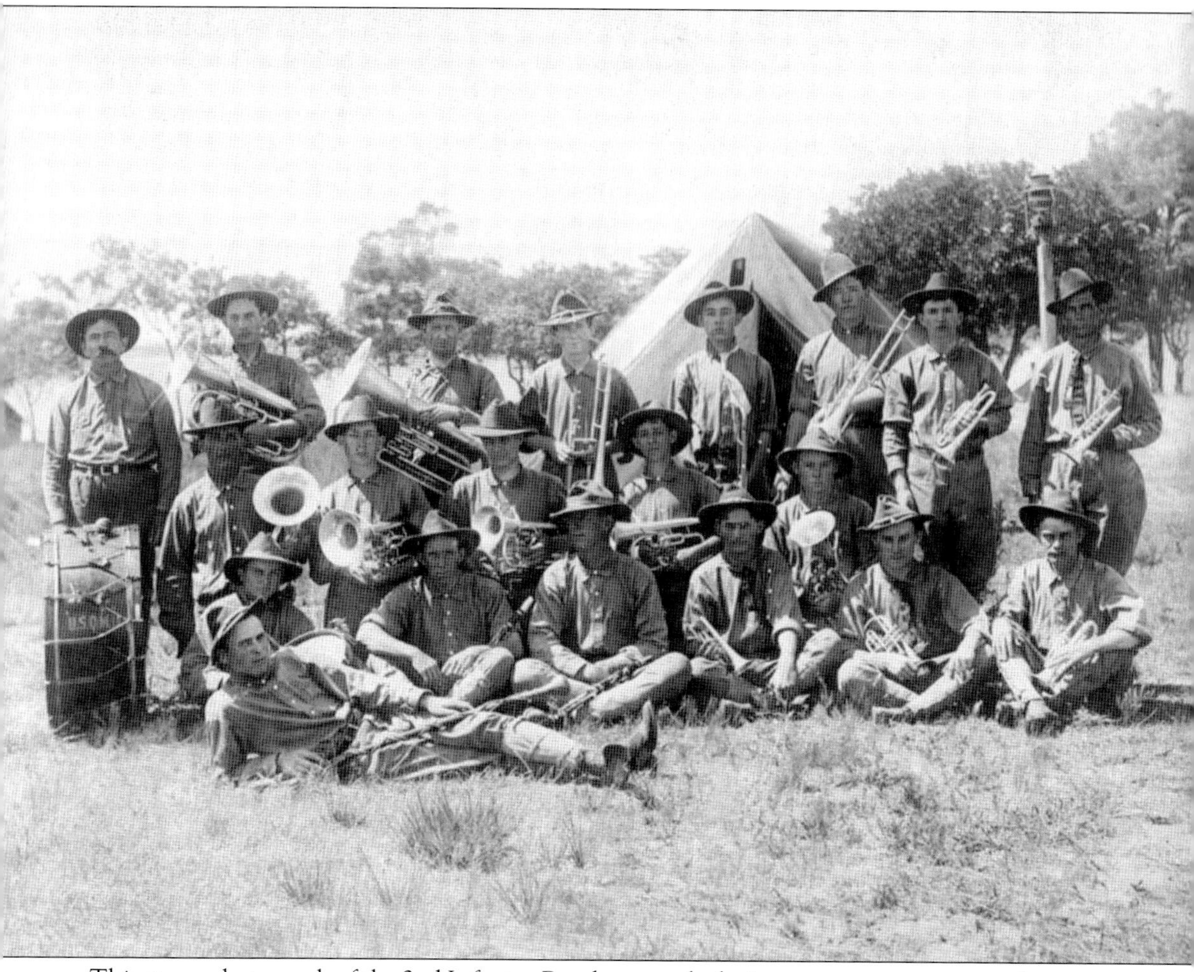

This group photograph of the 2nd Infantry Band was made during summer encampment between July 20–27, 1911. Later that year, the band was selected by the New Bern Fair Association to play for the November fair. The Kinston Band performed while marching in the parade and other events held. Sgt. George Skinner is believed to be standing, third row, sixth from the right. (Courtesy of North Carolina State Archives.)

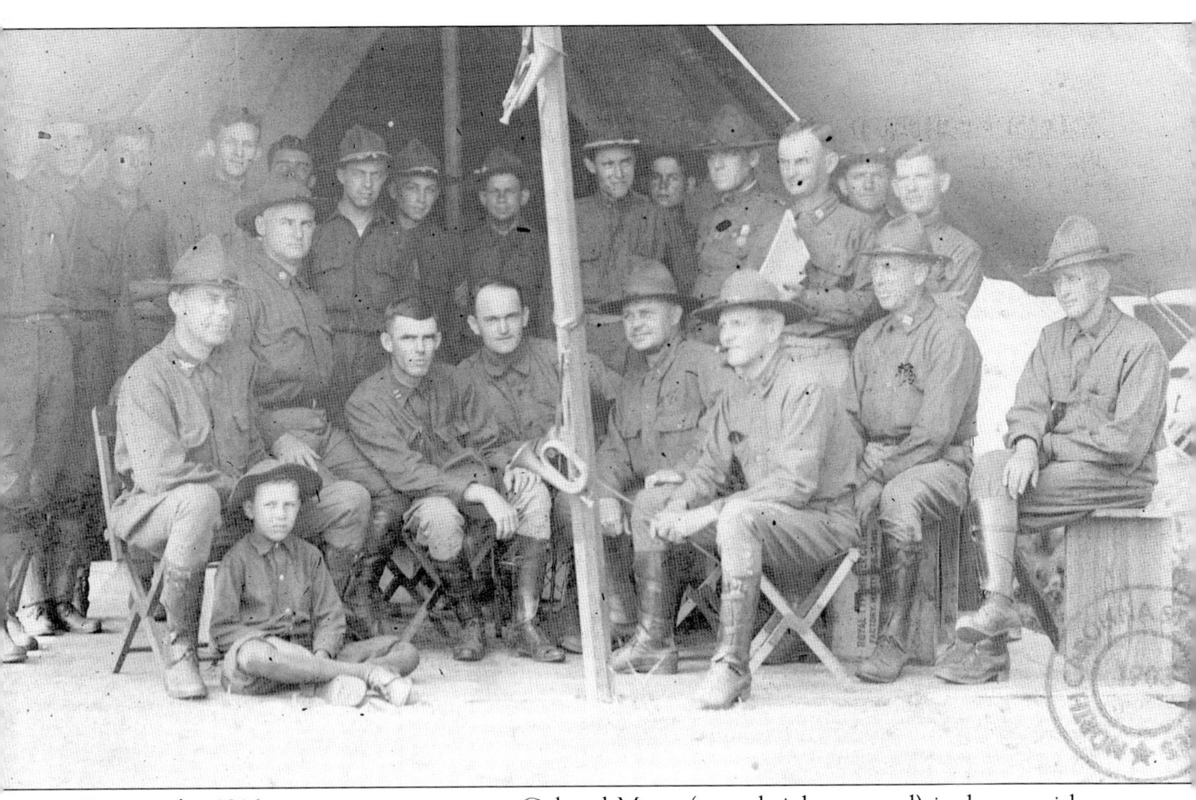

During the 1916 summer encampment, Colonel Metts (seated right, second) is shown with a group of soldiers in a tent. Metts served as adjutant general in World War I and, later, sought to build National Guard armories and housing facilities for soldiers under the Works Progress Administration. Though there were no immediate funds available, Metts had plans prepared and with local leaders' assistance, 28 armories were built. (Courtesy of North Carolina State Archives.)

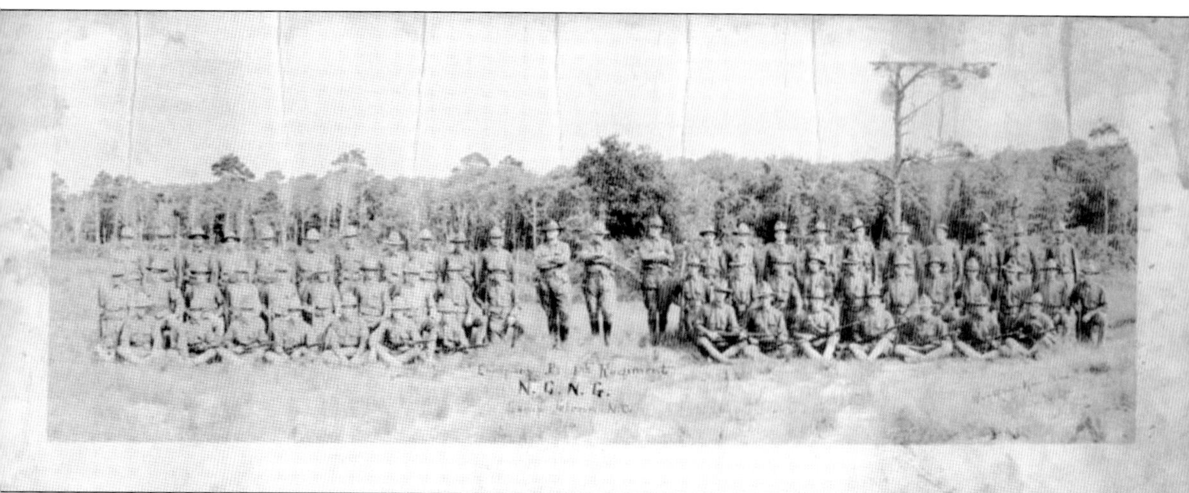


A 1916 group photograph shows Company B, 1st Regiment, Gastonia, at Camp Glenn during mobilization in preparation for the Mexican Border War. The Gaston Guards left Gastonia on the Seaboard Air Line Railroad in two sleeper tourist and one baggage cars June 24 at 7:00 p.m. and arrived in Morehead City June 25 at 7:30 a.m. Out of the 128 men who enlisted in Company B, 100 passed the rigorous physical examination that was given at Camp Glenn upon the troops' arrival. The 1st Regiment was the first to mobilize, with the other two following. Gaston Guards officers were Capt. John P. Reinhardt, 1st Lt. Clarence Spurgeon Stroup, 2nd Lt. Richard W. Rankin. The top-ranking enlisted soldier was 1st Sgt. Alfred B. O'Neil. (Courtesy of North Carolina State Archives.)

# *Two*

# Target Practice in the Pits

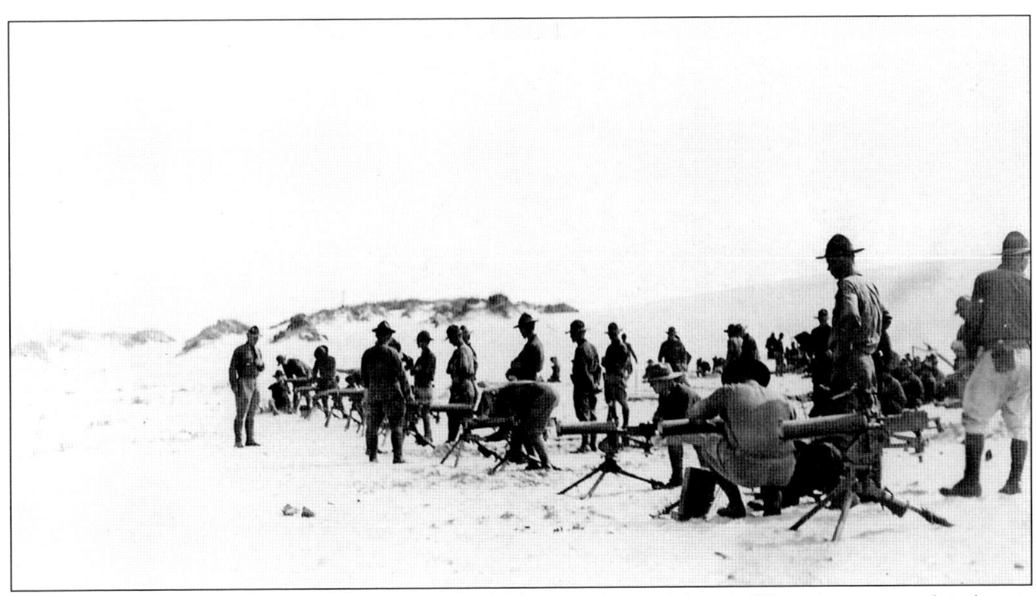

Machine gun and howitzer target practice took place at Camp Glenn's Class A range and Atlantic Beach. The camp commander, Col. Don E. Scott, noted in his 1923 report that "we should by all means have 1,000-inch machine gun range constructed at lower end of rifle range. It is very inconvenient to go to the beach for firing, and, in addition, it is more or less an expense and waste of time."

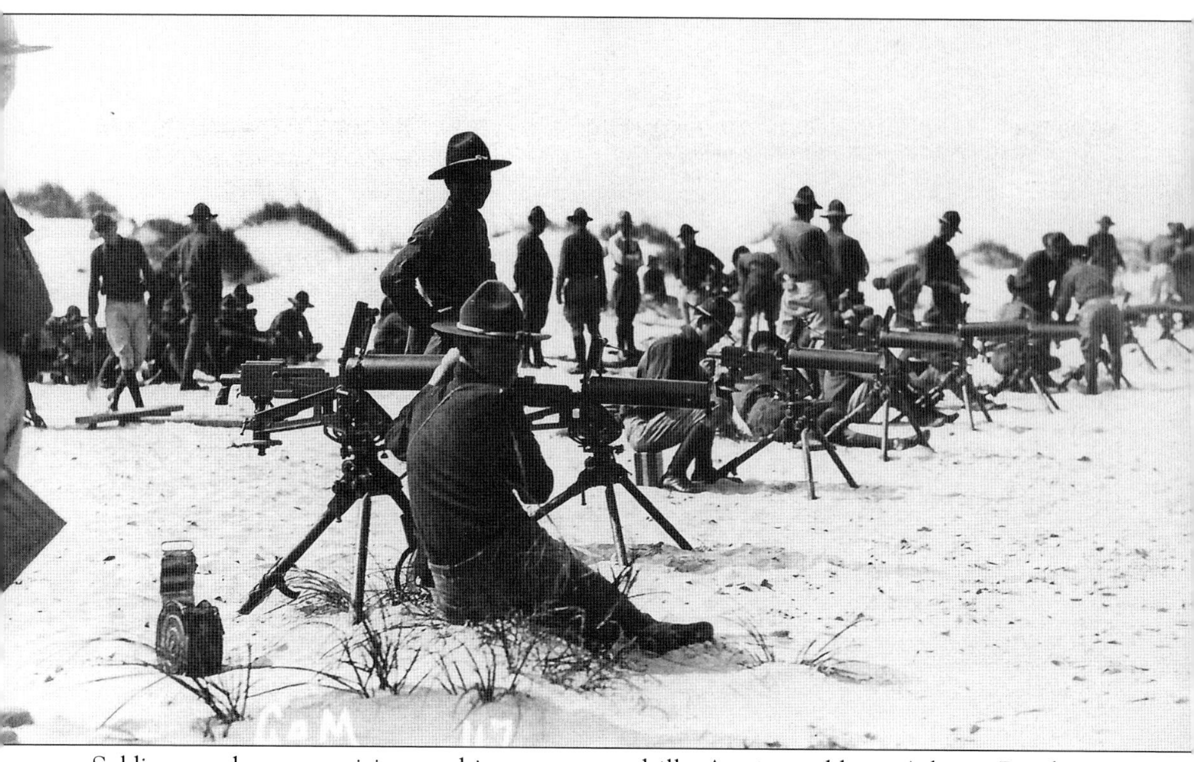

Soldiers are shown practicing machine gun target drills. As pictured here, Atlantic Beach was used as the practice range sometimes. Drill instruction included equipment care and adjustment, combat exercises, individual instruction, and lectures. Each NCNG regiment had its own machine gun company. During the 1921 summer encampment, there were 1,245 men in various units, and Capt. Carl Fitzhugh Batts (1885–1946), Machine Gun Company M, First Infantry, Wilson, commanded 65 men outfitted with four Browning machine guns of the improved type, shooting 425 times a minute; four mules; and four ammunition carts, carrying 400 pounds of ammunition each. Batts held weekly drills, and 90 percent of his men were present at each drill. The best shots in the machine gun company represented the state at the national target practice at Camp Perry, Ohio, in September.

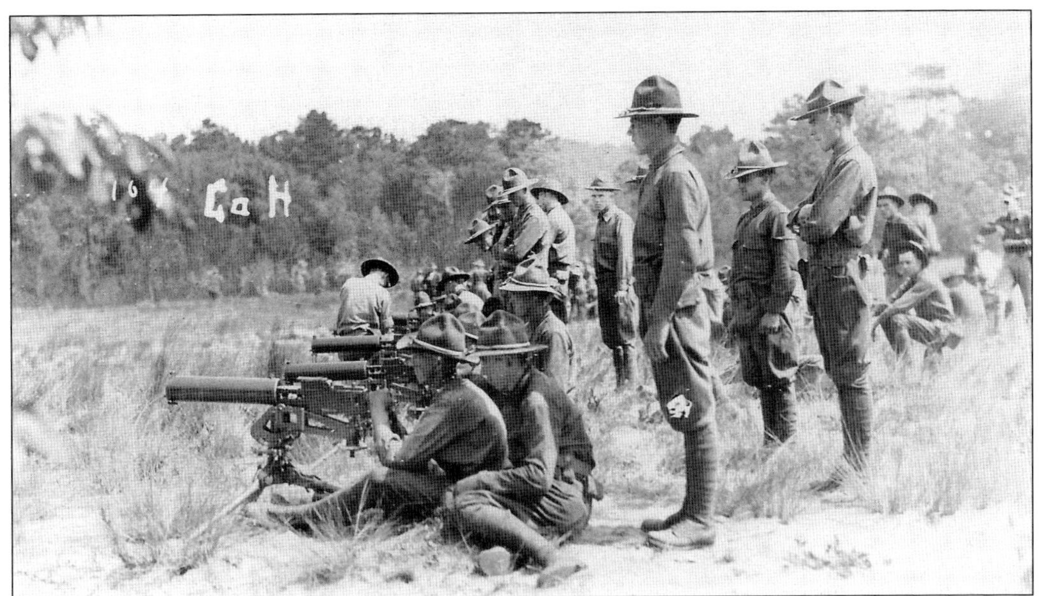


Company H soldiers are practicing firing machine guns on Camp Glenn's target field. The company's regiment is unidentified; however, the three Company H's regiments are as follows along with the soldiers who served in the three troops that scored high marks on the range in 1915: Pvt. Carl Miller, expert rifleman, 1st Infantry, Waynesville; Cpl. J.I. Gainey, sharpshooter, 2nd Infantry, Clinton; Sgt. D.M. Tate, sharpshooter, 3rd Infantry, Warrenton.

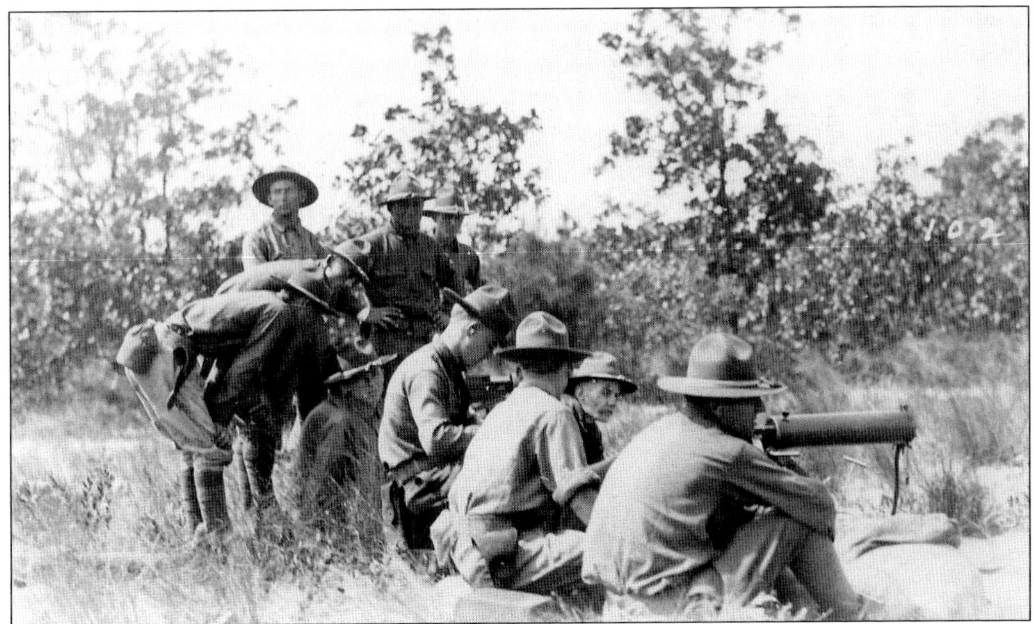


Soldiers seen here are receiving individual machine gun instruction as part of their daily drill routine. Machine gun drills were held daily, except Sundays, from 7:00 a.m. to 5:00 p.m. Noncommissioned officers were in charge training and reported the soldiers were "efficient and had good knowledge of the gun."

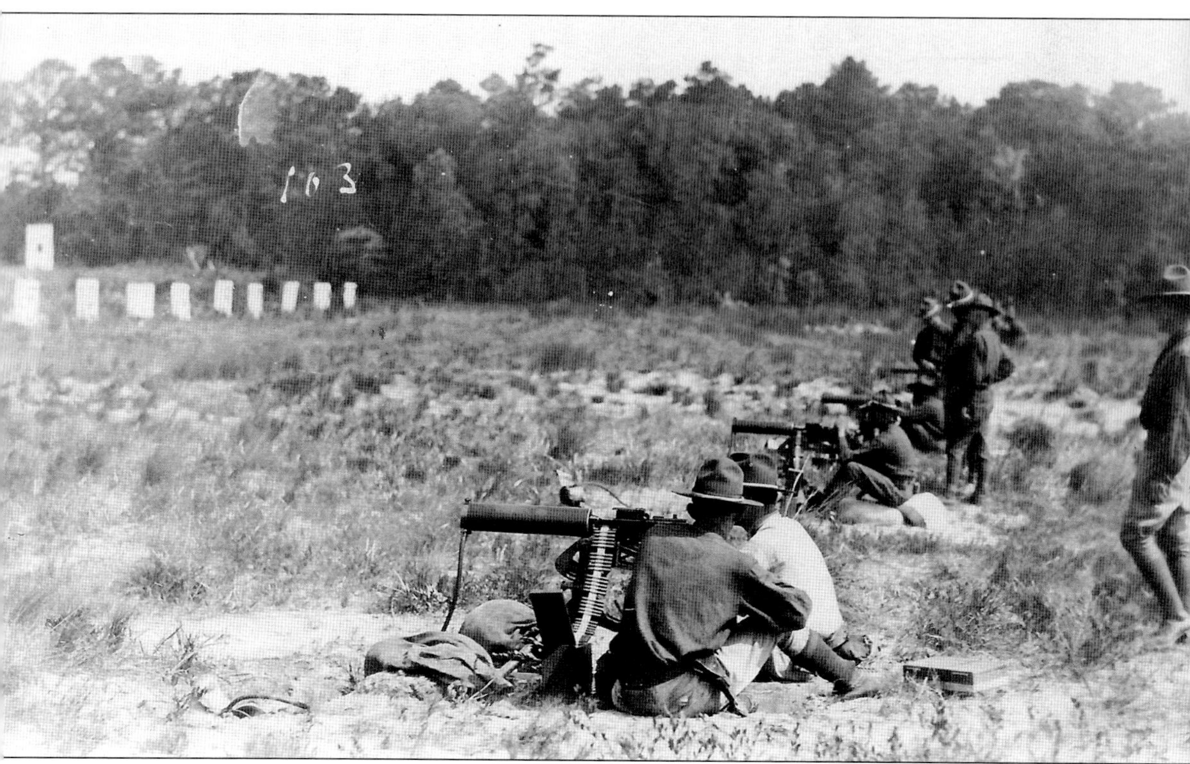

Soldiers seen here are practicing machine gun target drills in the target pit. In 1884, Hiram Maxim, an American-born British inventor, built the first effective machine gun, and his invention revolutionized modern warfare. On February 1, 1911, machine gun companies organized under the special authority of the Secretary of War. In 1916, each regiment had a machine gun company made up of 52 soldiers—two officers and 50 enlisted men. The NCNG's machine gun company consisted of 1 captain; 1 first lieutenant, 4 sergeants, 6 corporals, 47 privates, 71 horses; 1 combat wagon, 4 draft mules, 16 pack mules, 4 automatic machine rifles, 4 rifles, and 71 pistols. Some of the soldiers' duties included serving as signalmen and scouts, cooks, gun pointers, horse holders, range finders, ammunition carriers, and drivers. World War I was known as the "machine gun war" because of the weapon's standard issue.

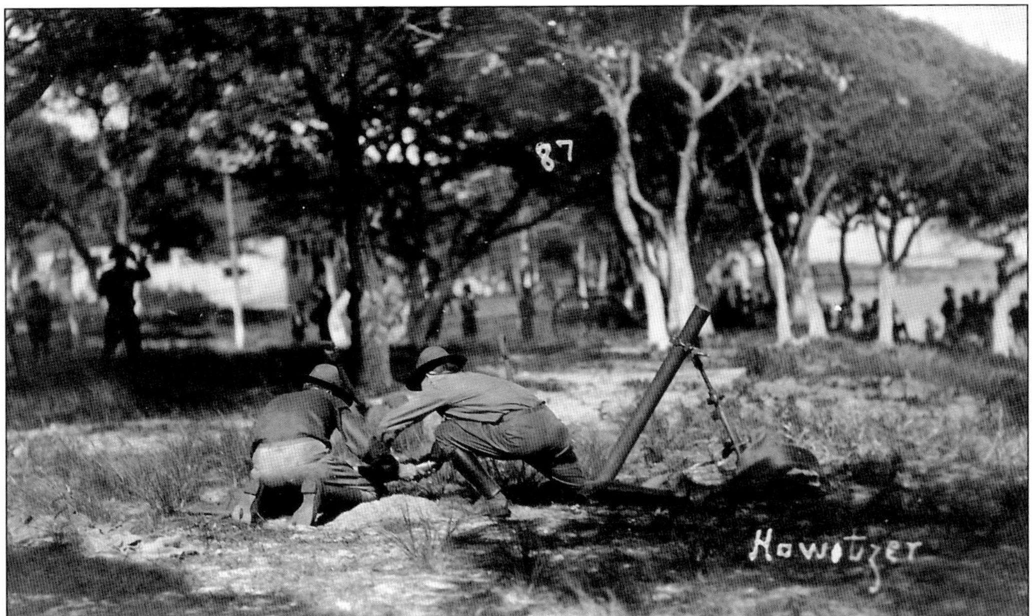


Crews were required to man the artillery weapons in trench warfare. Here, soldiers are seen loading a howitzer during a demonstration with people, buildings, and Bogue Sound in the background. The *1923 Adjutant General's Report* noted that the Howitzer Company put on a demonstration, "which was more than a surprise to all who witnessed it. Direct hits were not uncommon." Typically, howitzers' shots were fired across the sound.

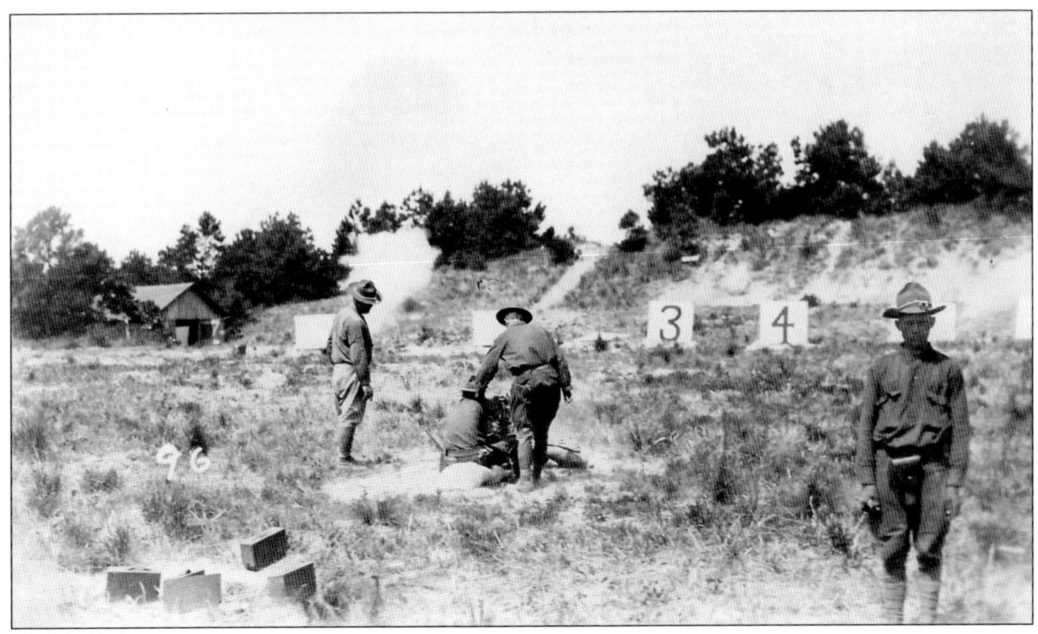


The target range's backstop was a 2-foot-thick, 30-foot-high, and 300-foot-long brick retaining wall. Sand was piled in front with a thickness of four feet at the top and sloped naturally. The storage building on the left was built in 1910 near the 500-yard range and was used to store targets, ammunition, and supplies.

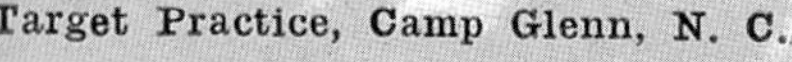


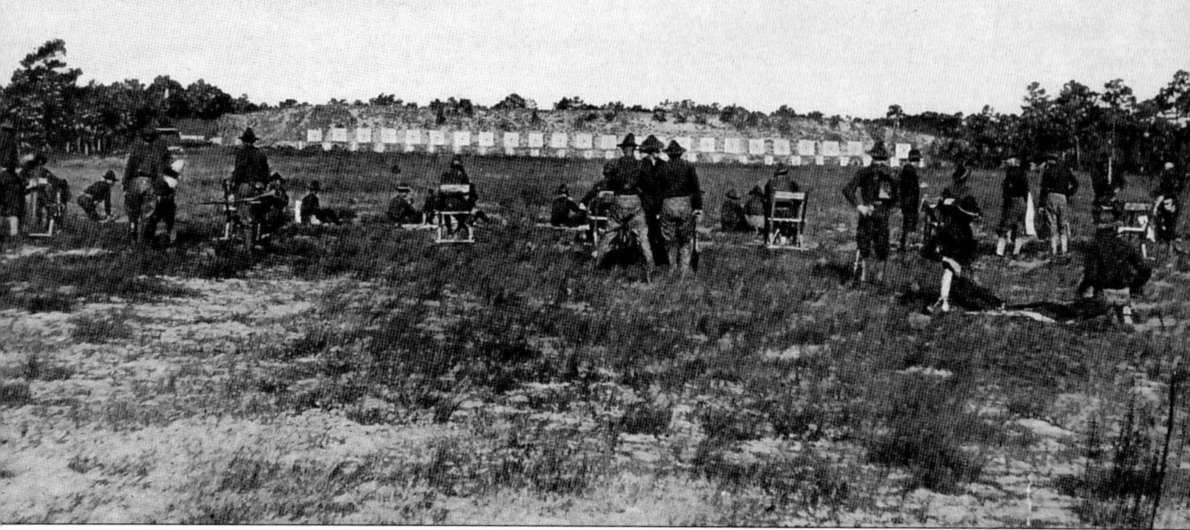

Soldiers are firing on the target practice field while scorekeepers watch closely. In 1914, Col. Thomas Stringfield (1872–1954) reported, "Interest in target and rifle practice still continues to increase, and the efficiency of the Guard along this line is increasing each year. Quite a number of companies have installed the Aiken treadle target at their home stations, and several others will be installed this year; so, in a very few years most all the companies, when such is practicable, will have their own ranges, which will be of invaluable aid to company commanders in instructing men and qualifying them in range practice." Colonel Stringfield was a medical doctor in Waynesville in civilian life. Multiple daily target practices were held because, as one officer reported, "Neither the State nor the War Department has any use for soldiers who can't shoot straight." (Courtesy of Linda Willis Sadler.)

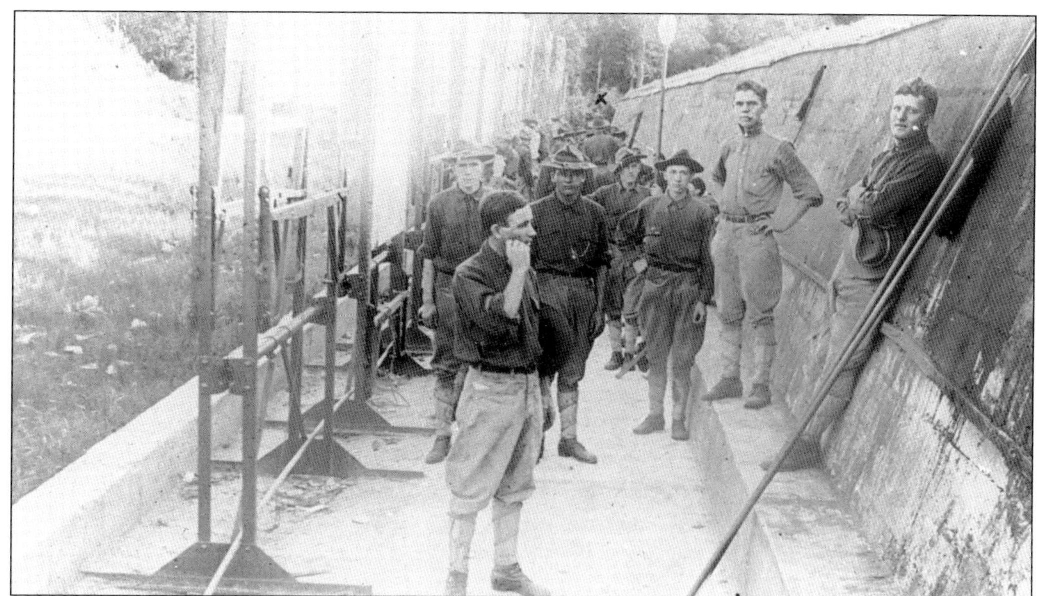

In 1912, Hickory soldiers stand in front of the rifle pit's concrete butt that stopped bullets fired in the range. After the range was built in 1906, Maj. Jesse C. Bessent (1885–1924) tested its safety by firing 25 bullets over Maj. W.L. McGhee and several local citizens' heads who were posted a half of a mile in the back. They reported hearing bullets pass 100 to 200 feet overhead before falling into Bogue Sound. (Courtesy of North Carolina State Archives.)

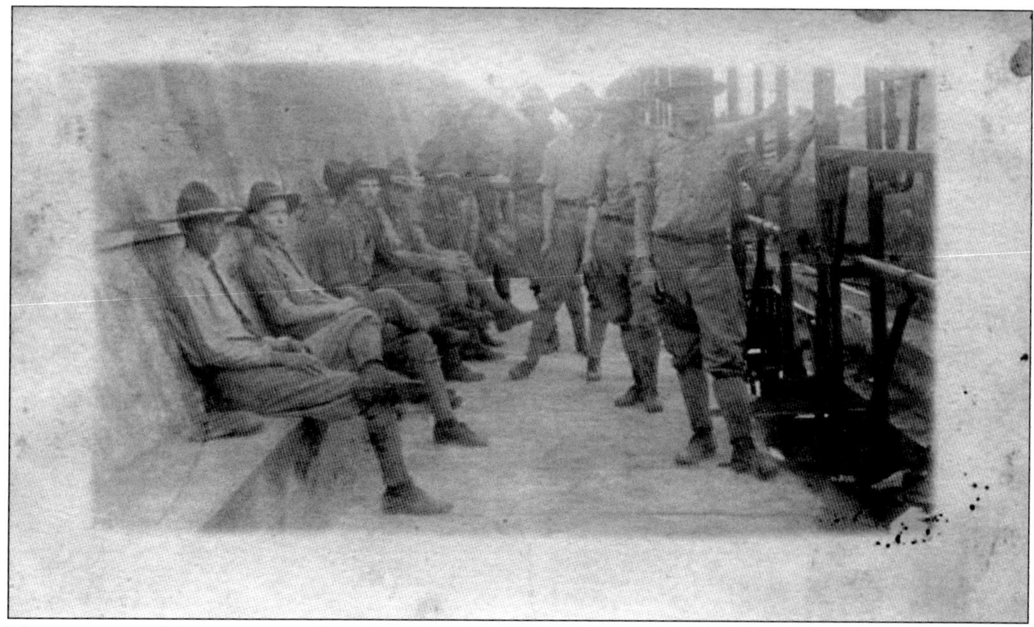

Here, some soldiers are standing at targets, and others are sitting on target butts. Targets had a steel frame support, two carriages, one pair of 6-by-12-foot wooden frames, and two pairs of 6-by-6-foot wooden frames. The coastal salt air rusted steel frames, so the frames were replaced frequently. Range officers in charge recommended painting the concrete butt green to prevent light reflecting in soldiers' eyes as they shot. (Courtesy of North Carolina State Archives.)

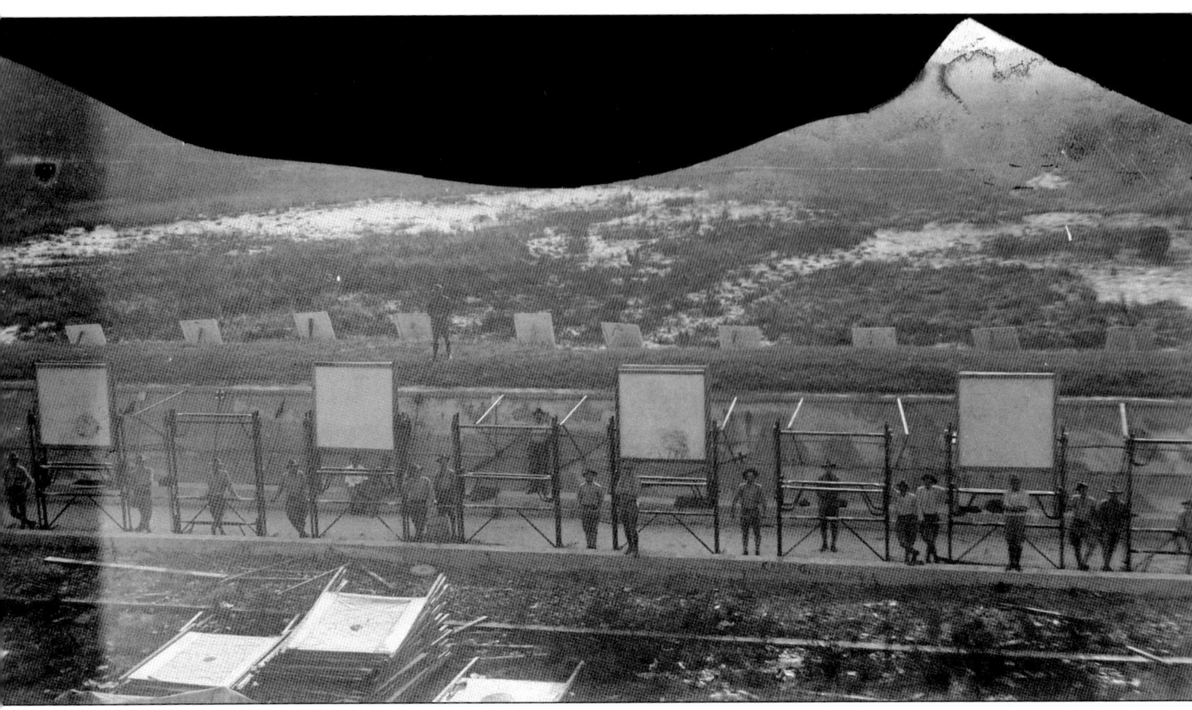

A 1908 broken glass plate negative shows the some of the 25 Aiken treadle targets used on the practice field. Aiken targets replaced the revolving Texas target. In 1906, chief engineer Charles Pearson, of the Contracting and Engineering Company, Morehead City, was hired to survey and lay out the range. Soldiers cleared 25 acres, building target butts or impact mounds with a backstop on a slight rise. A 1-foot-thick, 8-foot-high brick wall that was 300 feet long backed the target butts and were topped with 6 feet of sand that sloped to the bottom. The target pit had a brick and cement floor that drained. A water well was supplied, and a shed that ran the full length of the butts was built to protect the markers from the sun and weather. The cost of the target pit was estimated to between $8,000 and $10,000. (Courtesy of the University of North Carolina at Chapel Hill.)

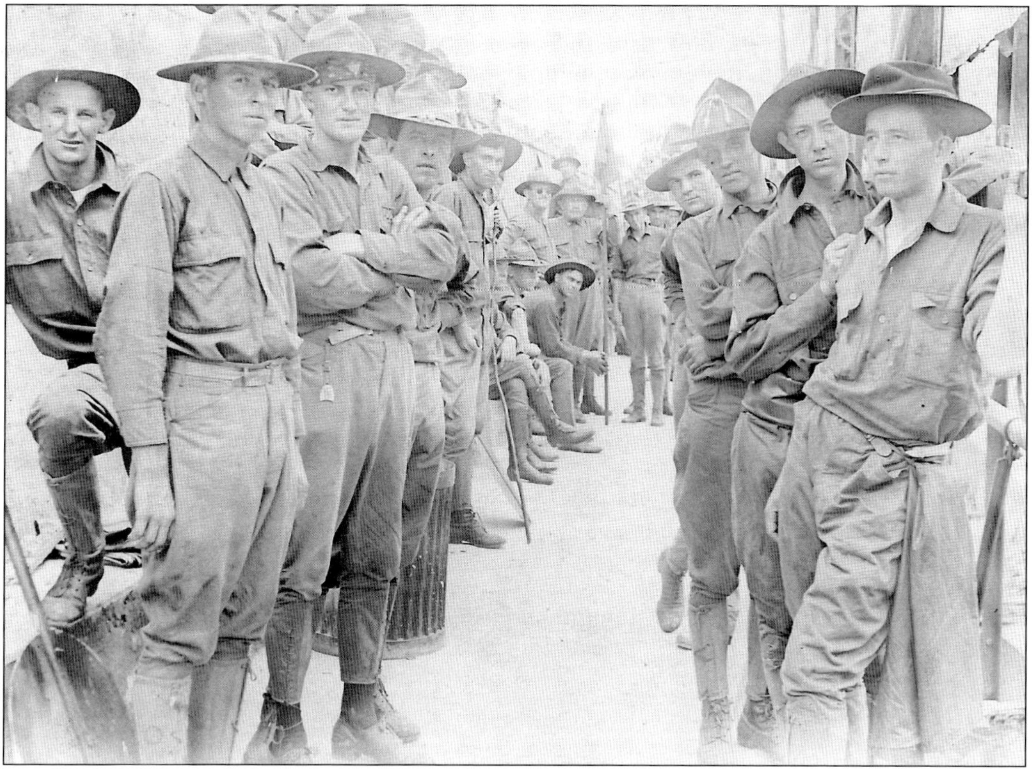

Unidentified soldiers are seen standing in front of the posted daily shooting reports. In 1911, Major Bernard was responsible for putting up shooting reports every day, posting each man's name and score before night. His promptness "was appreciated by both officers and men."

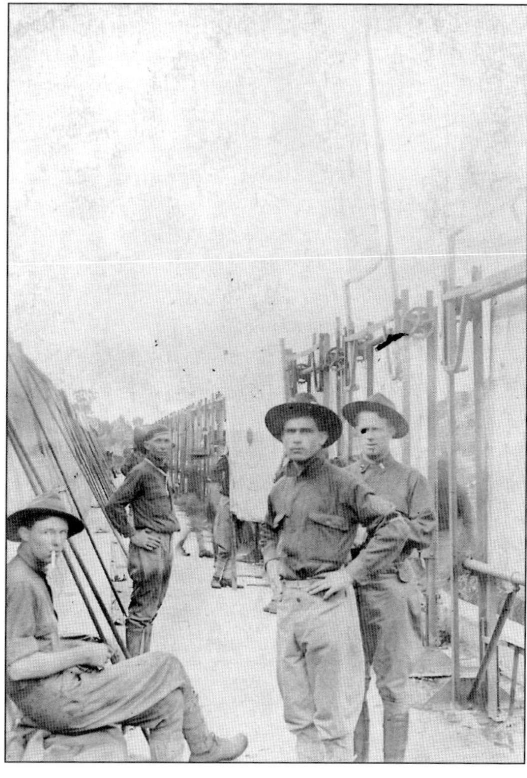

In the *1906 Adjutant General's Report*, Col. Wyatt Lemuel (W.L.) McGhee (1848–1920) reported, "The target pit will be equipped with twenty-five Aiken targets, sufficient to allow fifty men to practice at the same time. They are the latest models, are not affected by sun or rain. Any boy can work them. I will also state that I purchased this car of targets, etc., at $250 less than they were sold to the State by the manufacturers."

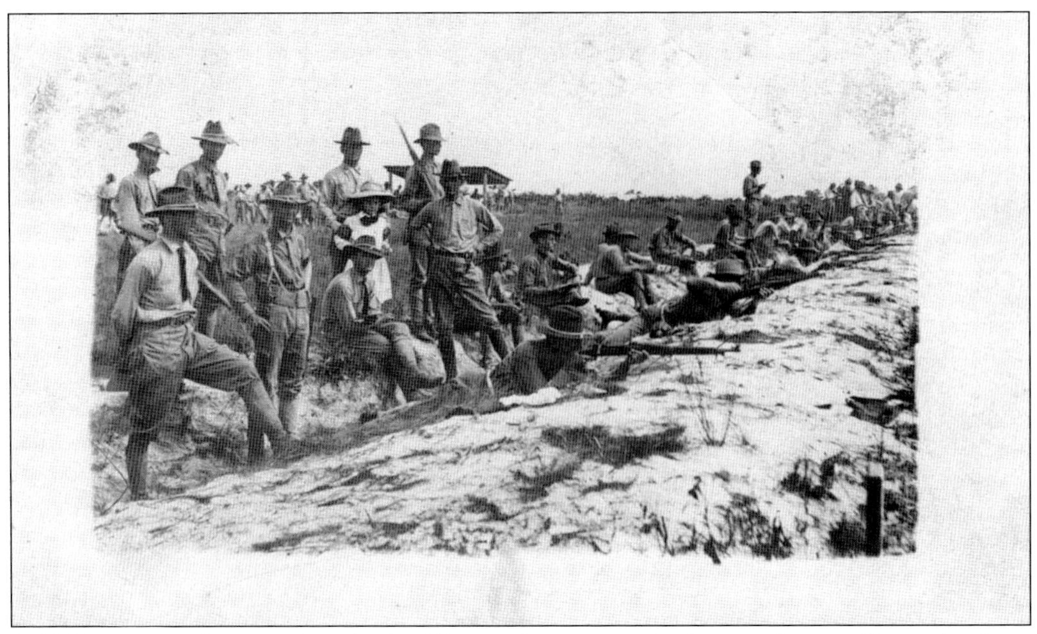

A 1909 postcard shows unidentified soldiers and a young girl, who may be an officer's daughter, looking at the photographer during a rifle practice. Other soldiers can be seen in the background, and some are under a shelter. Soldiers' families were frequent visitors during summer encampment, getting firsthand looks at drills and participating in Camp Glenn activities. (Courtesy of the University of North Carolina at Chapel Hill.)

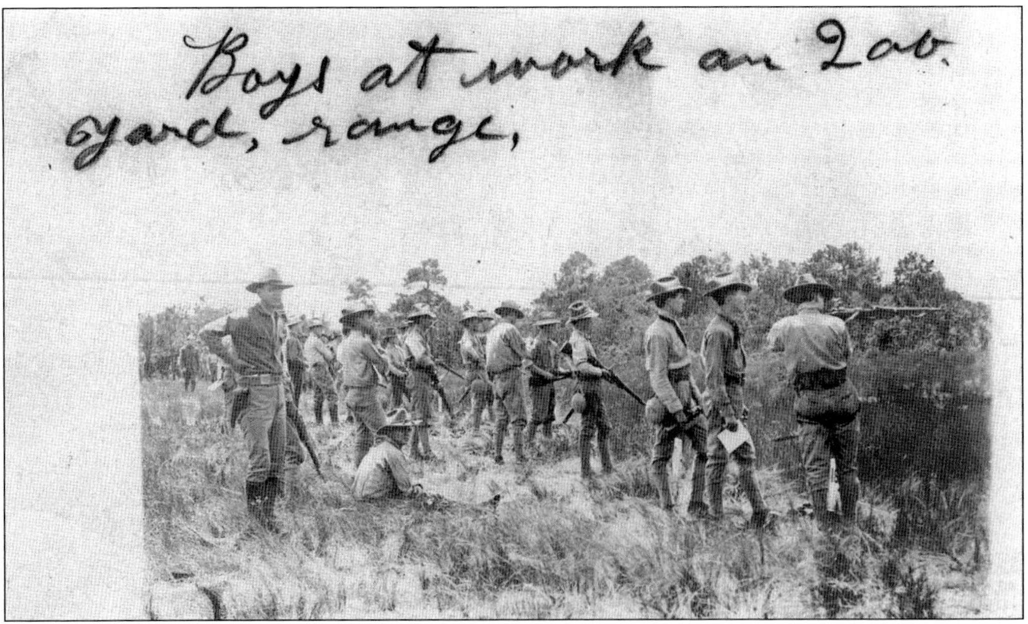


The 200-yard range was the first target practice range constructed when Camp Glenn was established in Morehead City in 1906. The site averaged about 200 yards wide by 1,100 yards long and adjoined the drill grounds. The 1906 report noted, "It was convenient for practice at all times without endangering any part of the drill-grounds." (Courtesy of the University of North Carolina at Chapel Hill.)

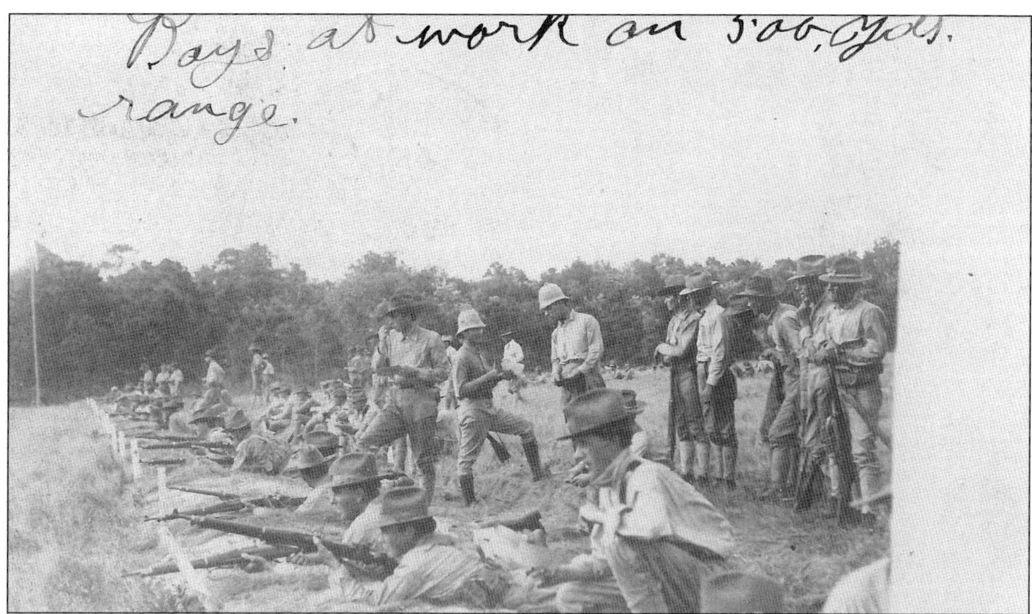


The 500-yard range was constructed in 1907 and outfitted with signal and danger flags and a bathing pool in the pits. No sighting shots were allowed during the target practice, except at the 500-yard firing point. This postcard was sent from Pvt. Will O. Wyckoff, Company H, 3rd Regiment, Warrenton, to his mother in 1908. Two US Army soldiers, wearing summer helmets, were detailed to make the inspection that year. (Courtesy of Linda Willis Sadler.)

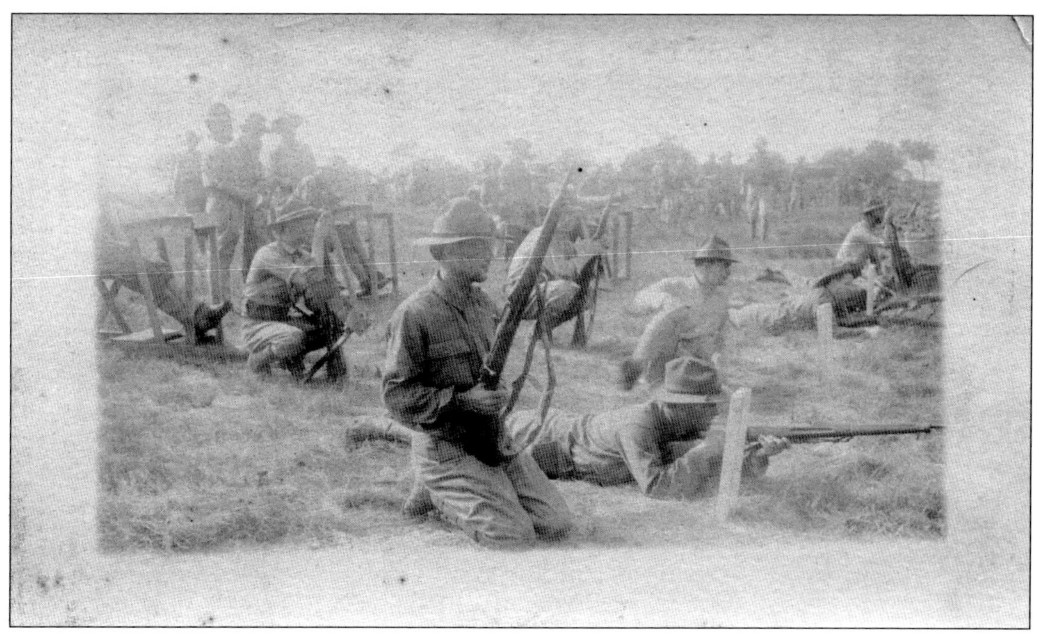

Several Louisburg soldiers are shown lying in a prone position while practicing rifle shooting. Note the other soldiers observing and recording scores. Cpl. Thomas C. Alston was a Company D soldier serving at Camp Glenn when this c. 1915–1916 photograph was taken. Alston may be in the photograph; however, he is unidentified. (Courtesy of North Carolina State Archives.)

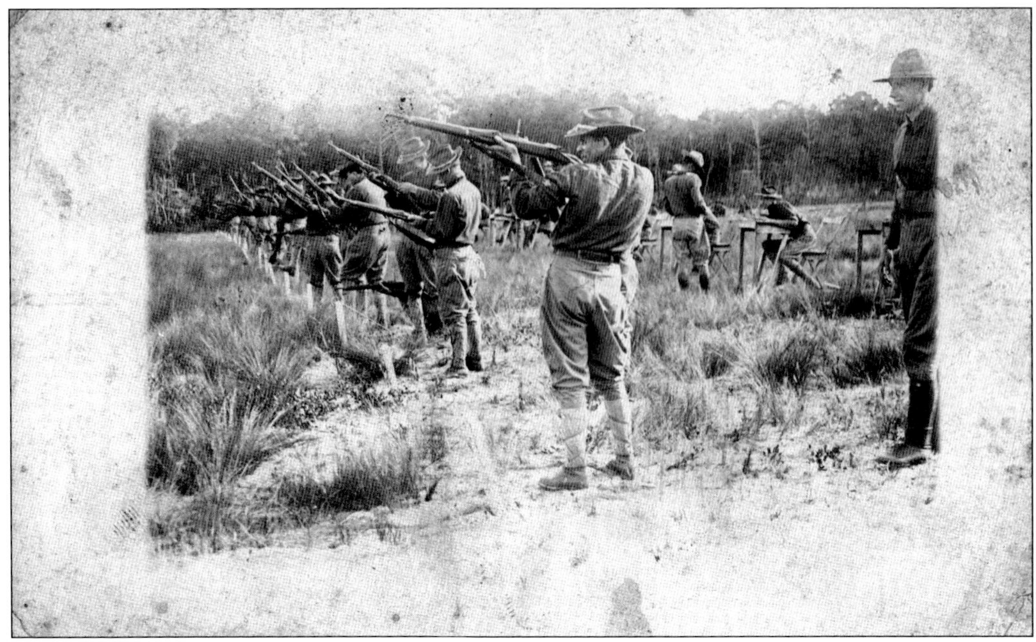

Lt. George Huffman (far right), Company A, is seen smiling, obviously pleased with his troop's performance on the rifle practice range during the 1912 encampment. Two different types of drills were held that year—target firing and company firing. In both drills, the Hickory Rifles led with 17 marksmen qualifying. (Courtesy of North Carolina State Archives.)

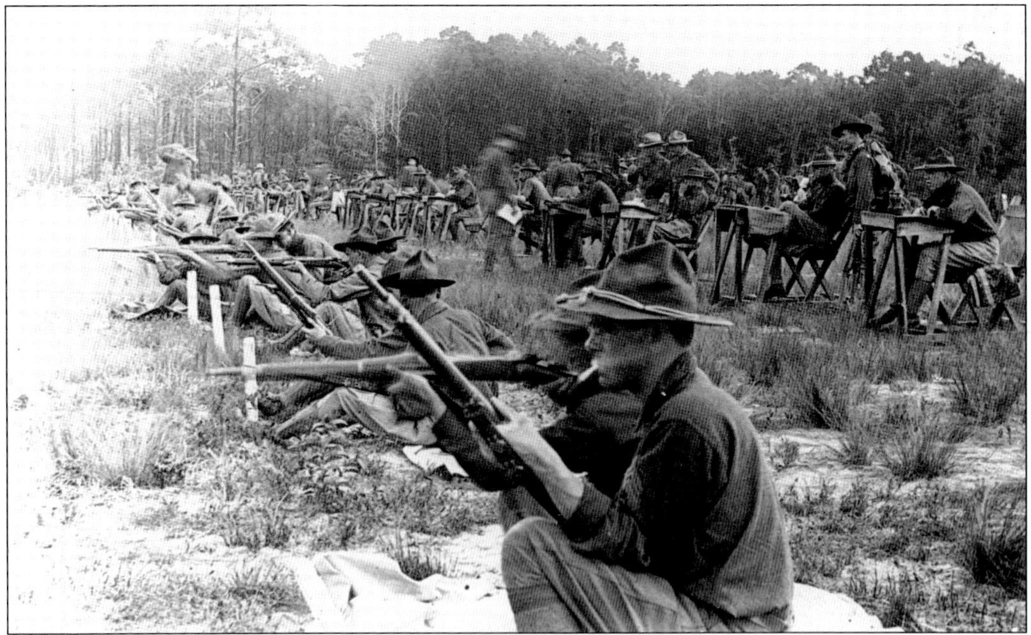

Aptly named the Hickory Rifles, Company A, 1st Regiment soldiers were known for having the highest scores on the practice field. In 1911, Sgt. H.R. Triplett, Company A, received a marksman badge from the US War Department for his score in target shooting. The soldiers with the best shooting scores represented the NCNG at the National Target Practice Competition held every September at Camp Perry, Ohio. (Courtesy of North Carolina State Archives.)

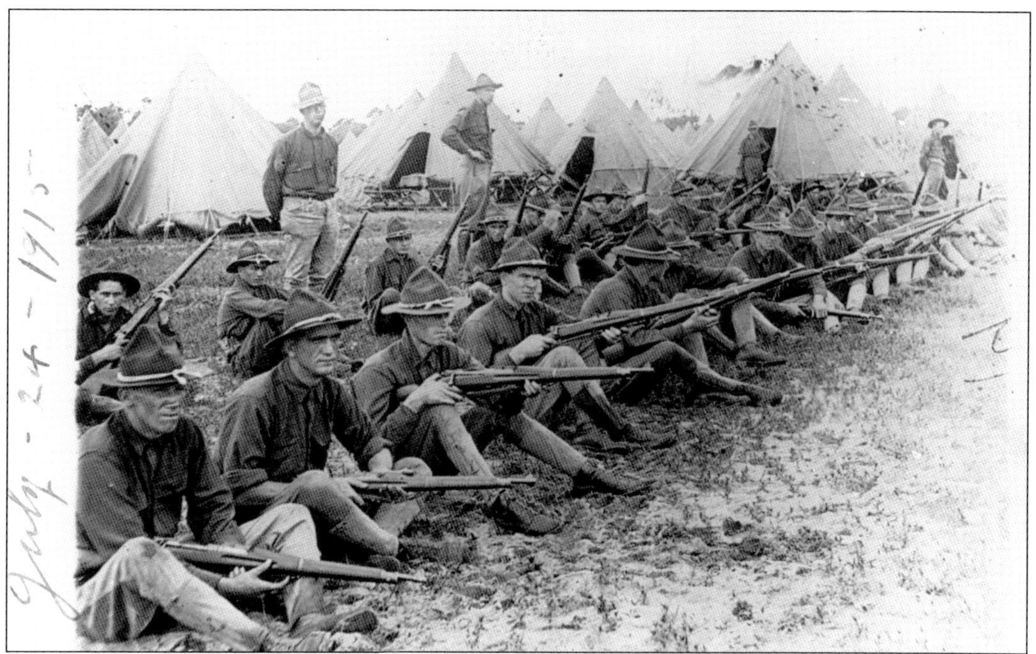


In 1915, Company A, Hickory, led the entire 1st Regiment on the shooting practice range, setting the target practice field record. Out of the 27 men that shot over the course field, eight qualified as expert riflemen, nine as sharpshooters, three as marksmen, and seven as second-class riflemen. (Courtesy of North Carolina State Archives.)

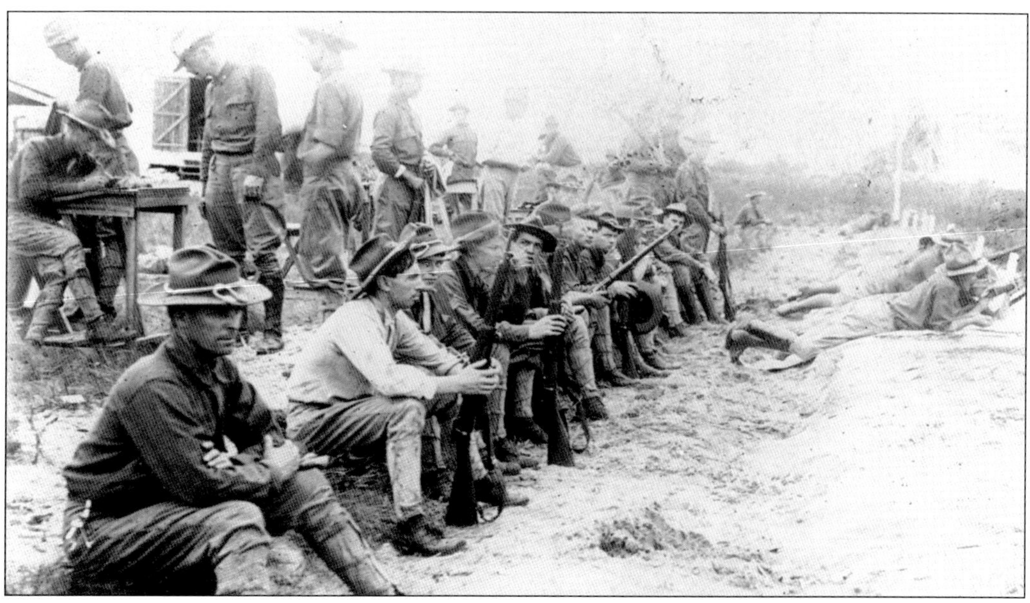

Hickory Rifle soldiers are sitting behind their fellow troop members lying while firing on the range. The 1910 summer encampment was held August 3–10, and it was reported that "in the target practice the marksman's record course, Special Course 'C,' should be followed, and troops should carry sufficient supply of 'Three in One' oil for cleaning rifles and revolvers." (Courtesy of North Carolina State Archives.)

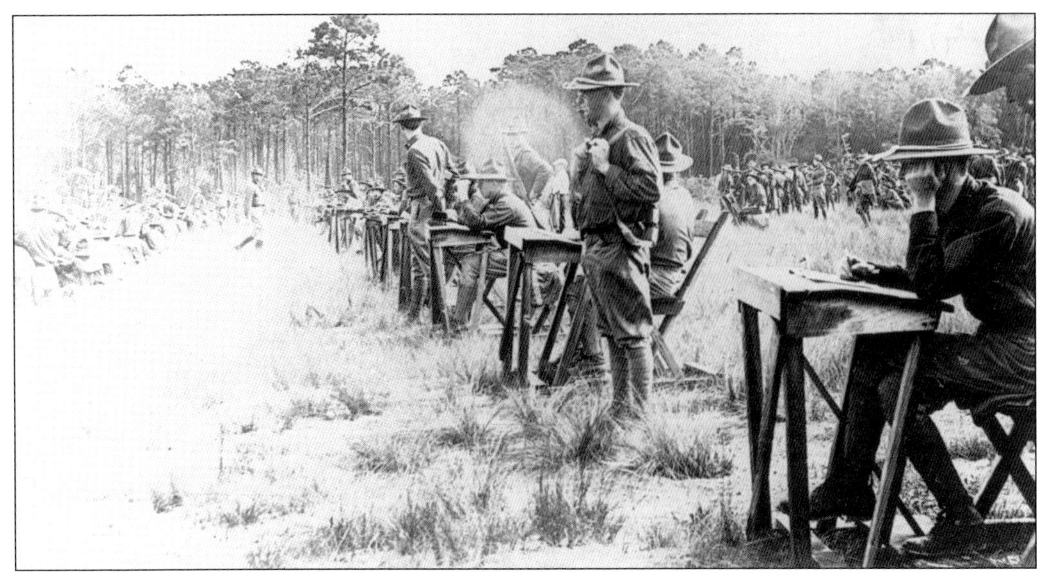

Target scorers are recording Company A's practice results. During the July 1915 encampment, Cpl. W.A. Elrod led Company A, Hickory, with a score of 227, out of a possible 250. The Hickory Rifles first tried out on the instruction course range, and soldiers were required to make 150 points out of a possible 225 in order to be eligible to take part in the record course. (Courtesy of North Carolina State Archives.)

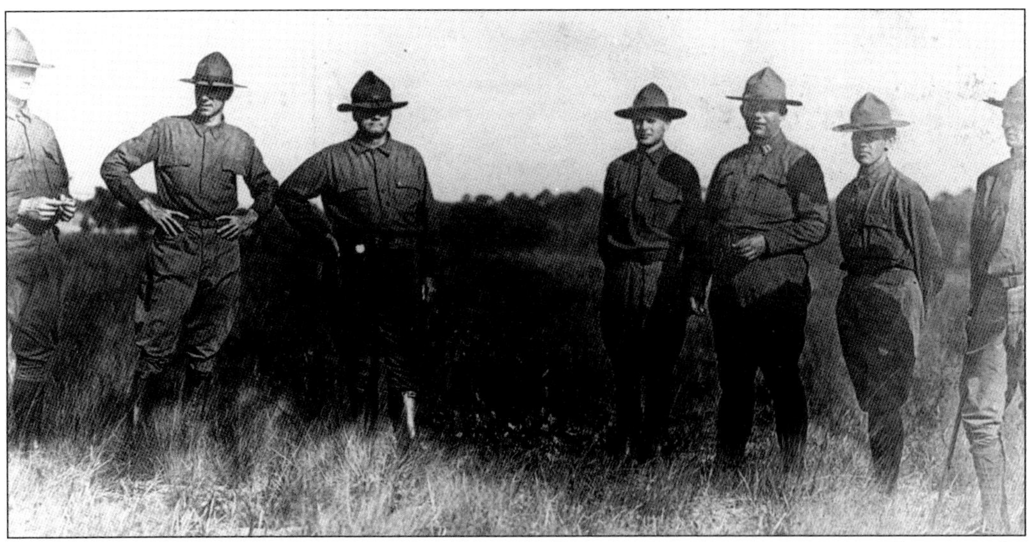

Lt. George Huffman (second from the left) is seen along with other Company A officers on the target practice range. Hickory Rifle officers were very proud of their soldiers for outscoring other companies on the target practice field during some encampment periods. In 1912, Hickory's Board of Aldermen awarded to the troop for outshooting all other companies during summer encampment. (Courtesy of North Carolina State Archives.)

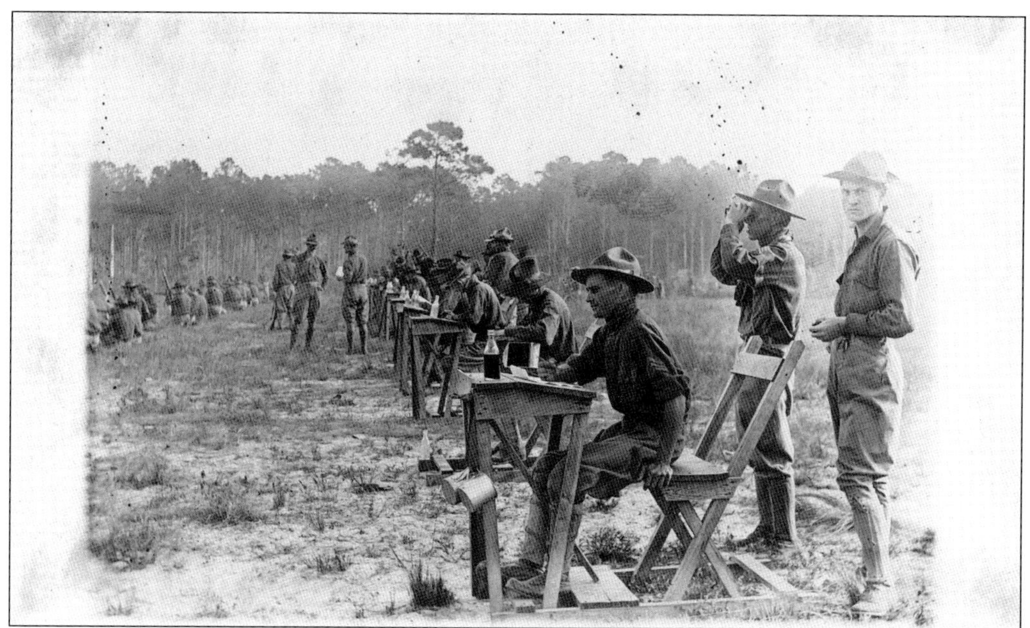

Seen sitting at score tables, soldiers are recording target practice results. One soldier uses field glasses to view target scores, while soldiers farther down the field review marksmanship results. After target practices were completed, competitive shooting was held, and soldiers scoring the highest marks were awarded badges and trophies. (Courtesy of the University of North Carolina at Chapel Hill.)

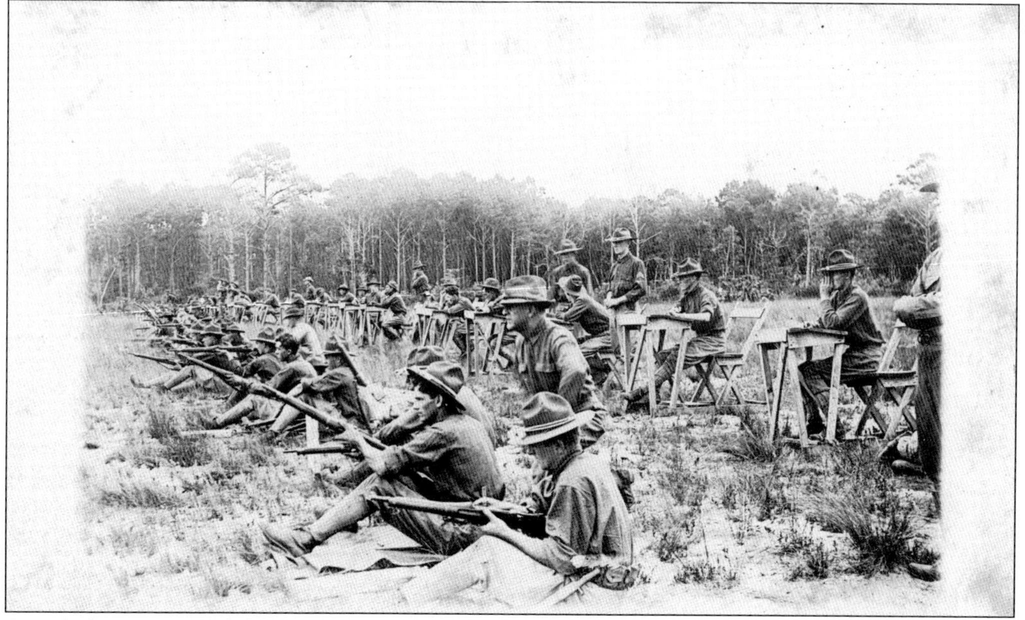

A real-photo postcard shows Company A, 1st Regiment, soldiers sitting on the target practice field while target scorers record results during the 1912 marksmanship training. It was noted that the Hickory Rifles "stood first in field firing at moving and disappearing targets." The target tables shown are some of the 25 tables made during Camp Glenn's 1910 improvement period. (Courtesy of the University of North Carolina at Chapel Hill.)

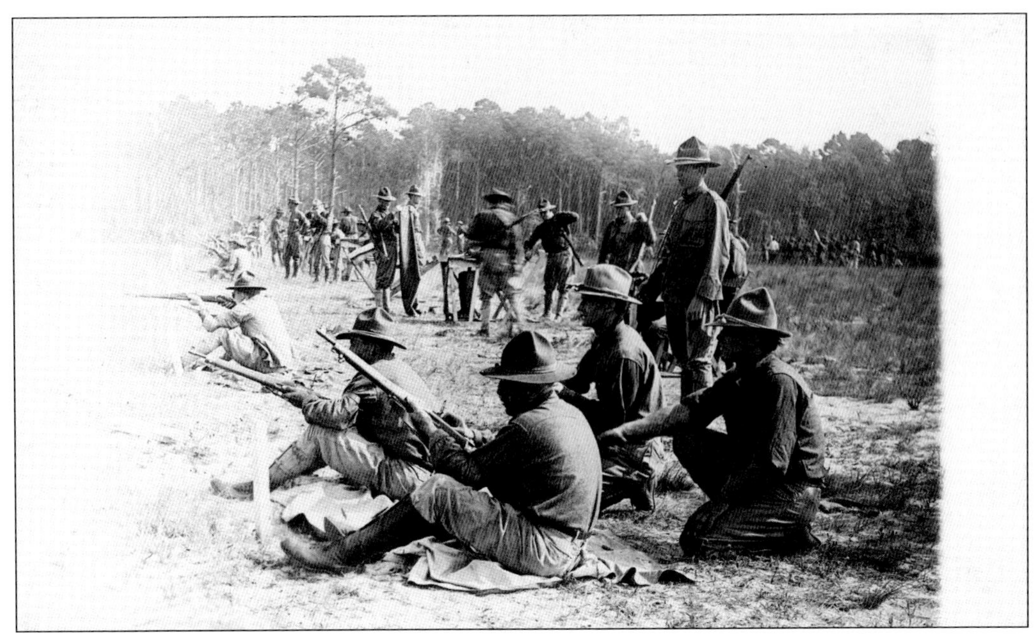

In 1906, Col. W.L. McGhee, in charge of the rifle range, reported 30 percent of the 1st Regiment placed as second- and first-class marksmen in Special Course C, an accomplishment for a first trial. After completing instruction practice, soldiers who qualified as first classmen were eligible to fire on the Qualification Course, Organized Militia, or the Qualification Course, Regular Army. (Courtesy of the University of North Carolina at Chapel Hill.)

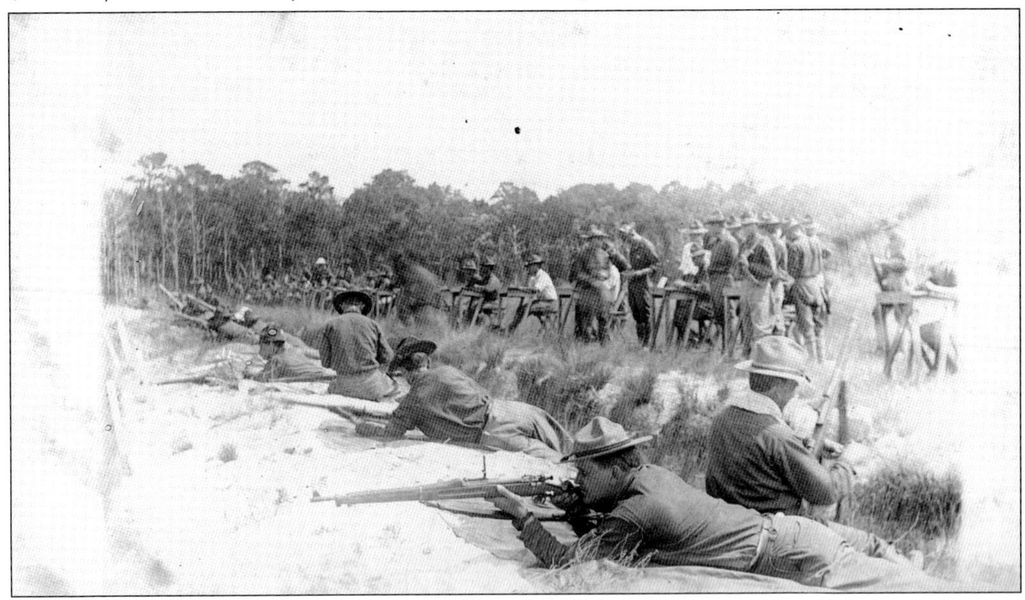

Soldiers are prone practicing with rifles equipped with telescopic sights. The prone position and long-distance shooting were part of trench warfare used during World War I. In 1913, a rifle camp of instruction was established for the three infantry regiments to teach soldiers how to shoot rifles with telescopic sights. Only soldiers who qualified as experts and sharpshooters were allowed to take part in long-distance rifle practice. (Courtesy of the University of North Carolina at Chapel Hill.)

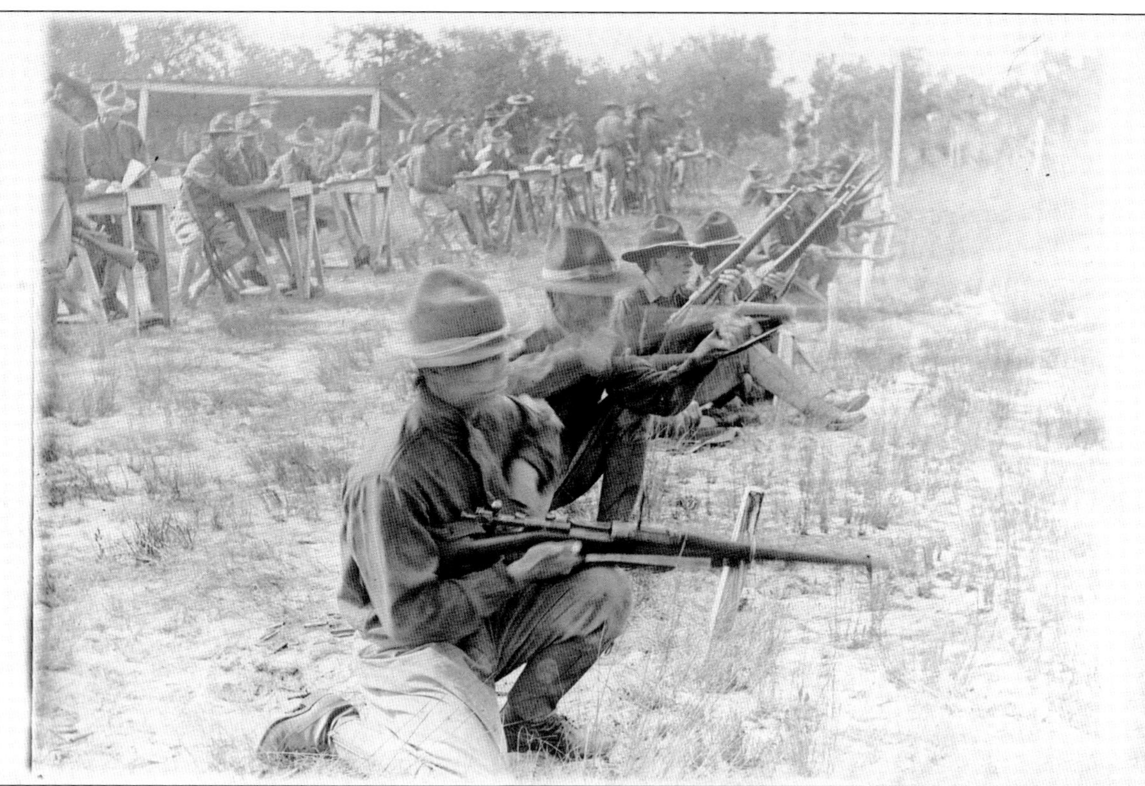

A blurred photograph shows soldiers in action on the range. During encampment, gallery practice where soldiers fired small weapons with a reduced ammunition charge was held first, requiring soldiers to fire until they scored at least 90 points out of a possible 150. Soldiers then advanced to target range practice, and when completed, they advanced to competitive shooting. Teams of one officer and nine enlisted men from each infantry participated in competition on Special Course C. The DuPont Trophy was the chief trophy awarded at competitive shoots held at Camp Perry, Ohio. In 1911, the trophy was won first by the team from Company B, 3rd Infantry, Raleigh. Company L, 2nd Infantry, Lumber Bridge, led the teams of the 2nd Infantry. Company K team, 1st Infantry, led the teams of the 1st Infantry. (Courtesy of the University of North Carolina at Chapel Hill.)

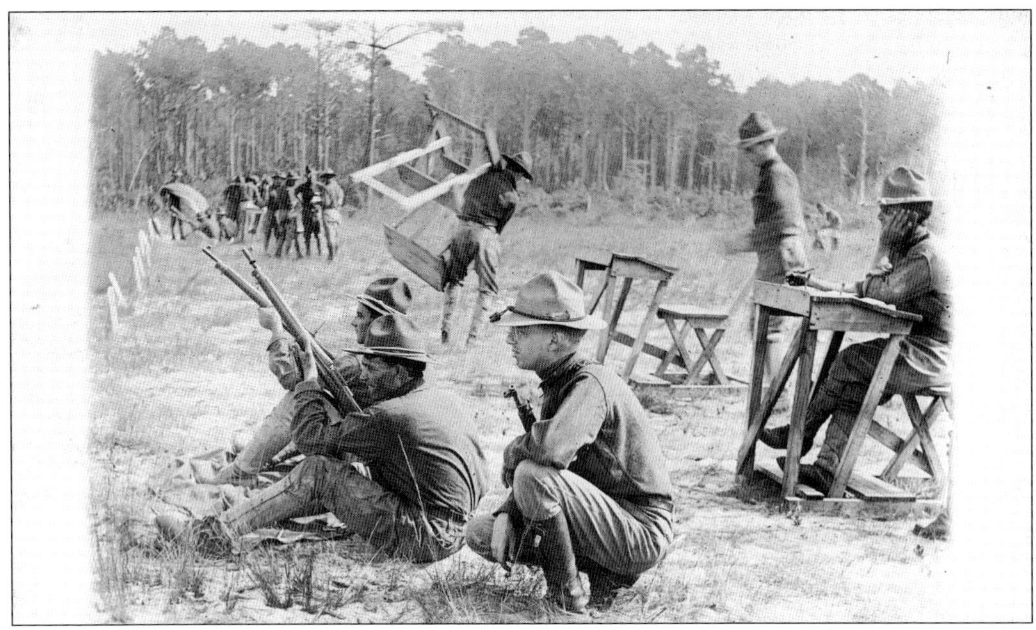

The 1913 report noted, "That on no morning was there a delay in beginning this practice of more than ten minutes, and the course was completed satisfactorily in the time allotted for the purpose. The Range Officer and his assistants, and the Statistical Officer and his assistants performed their duties in a manner entirely satisfactory to the undersigned. They were at all times courteous and zealous in the performance thereof." (Courtesy of the University of North Carolina at Chapel Hill.)

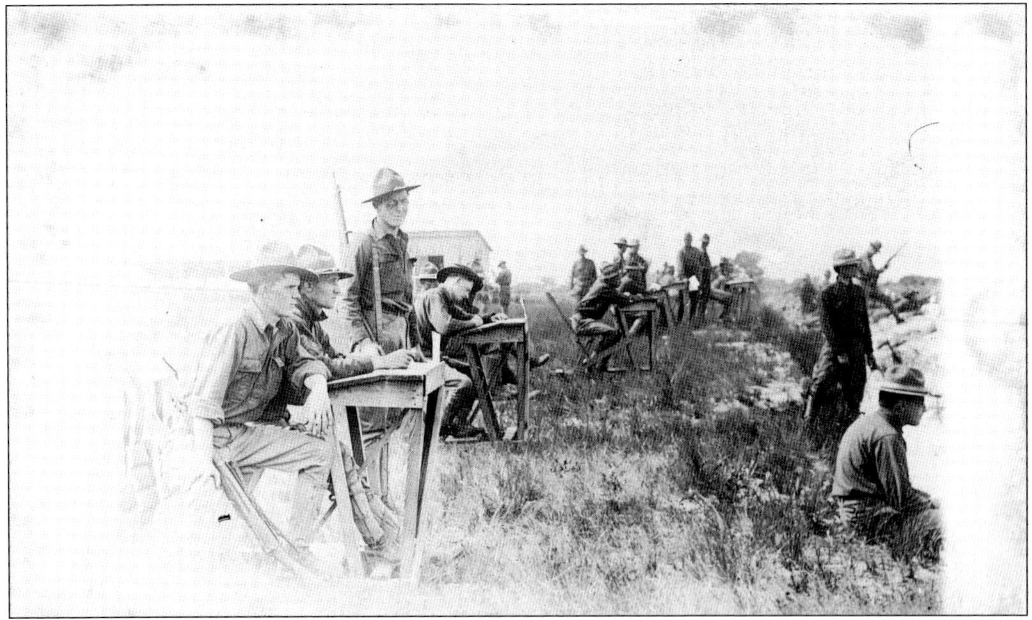

Regimental commanders required field, staff, line officers, and noncommissioned officers to fire and qualify with rifle and revolver, and enlisted men had to fire with rifle and complete the marksman's course on Special Course C. The regiment's statistical officer on duty submitted a report giving a complete record of all firing to the adjutant general's office at the close of each regimental encampment. (Courtesy of the University of North Carolina at Chapel Hill.)

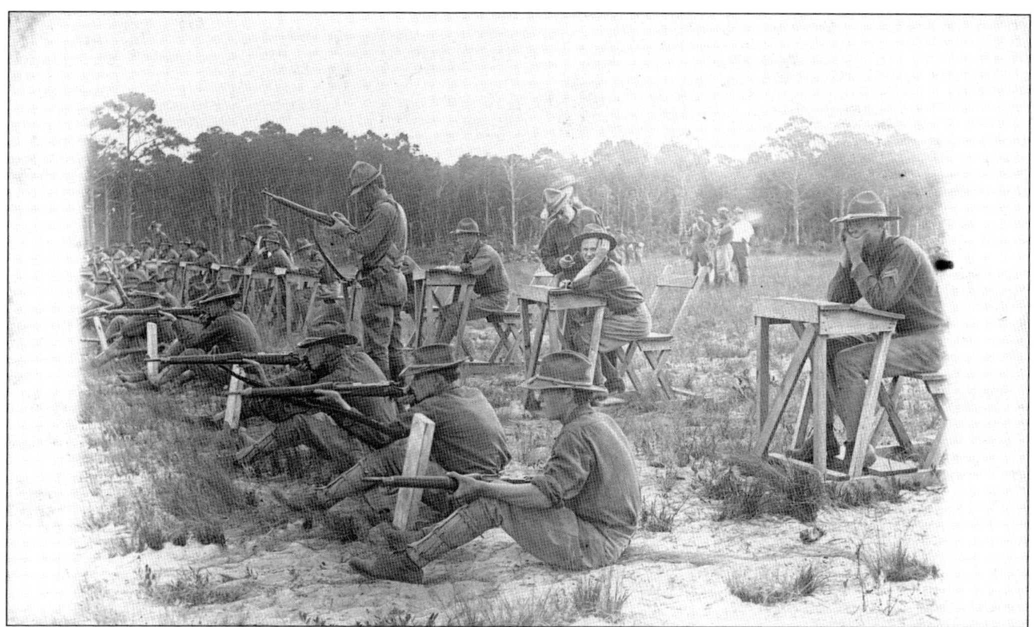

A company commander prepared a list of members before leaving his home station. Immediately after arriving in camp, the commander requisitioned scorecards books from the statistical officer. Commanders prepared scorecards and inspected rifles for each company member present for duty. Pit officers, scorers, and target tenders were detailed to the range to ensure prompt and efficient service. (Courtesy of the University of North Carolina at Chapel Hill.)

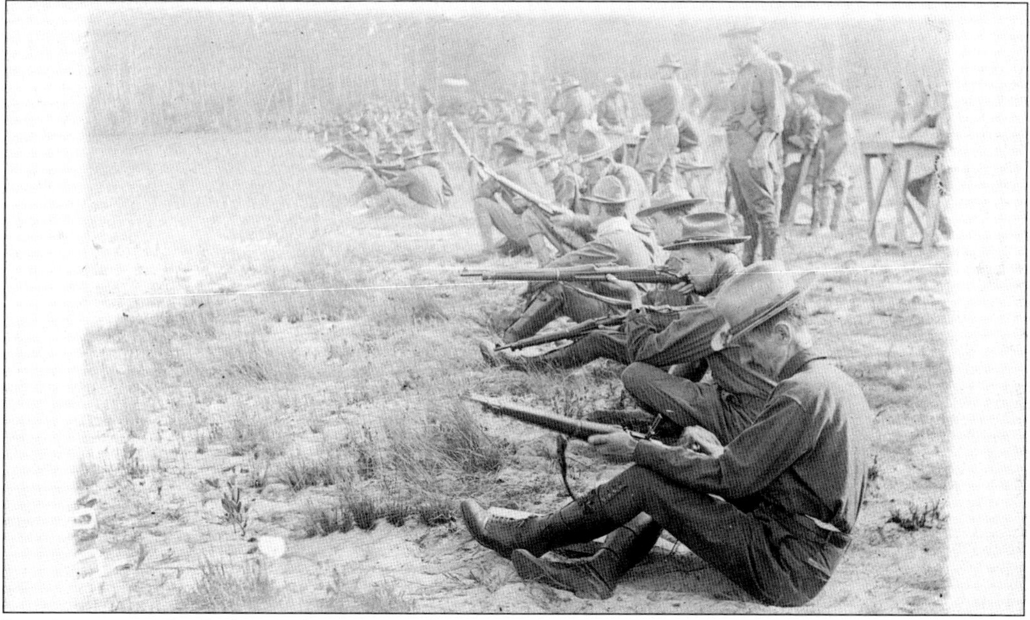

In 1911, a total of 454 marksmen, 2 sharpshooters, and 20 expert riflemen qualified on an updated rifle range and target practice field. Col. W.E. Gary (sitting in the foreground) is on the rifle practice field taking part in the drill. In 1907, the colonel was assigned to special duty and accompanied the 1st Infantry to the Jamestown Exposition's Camp of Instruction. (Courtesy of the University of North Carolina at Chapel Hill.)

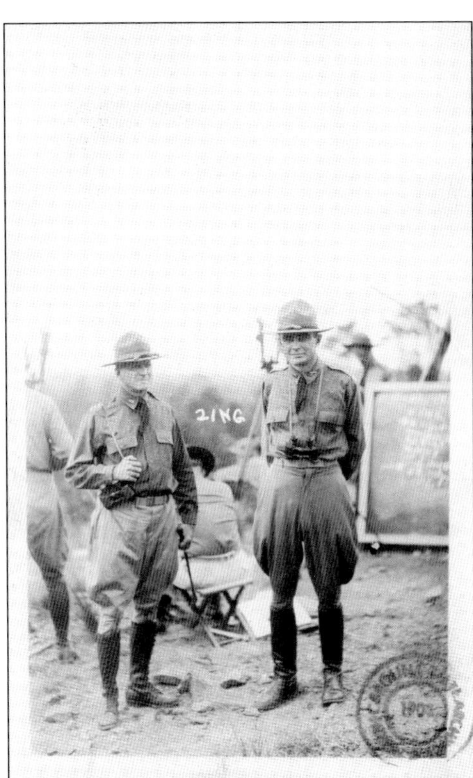


A 1916 real-photo postcard shows Col. John Van Bokkelen Metts (left) and an unidentified officer with the 2nd Infantry, North Carolina National Guard, standing on the target practice range. A soldier is sitting at a score table behind them. This photograph was taken when mobilization training was held at Camp Glenn. (Courtesy of North Carolina State Archives.)

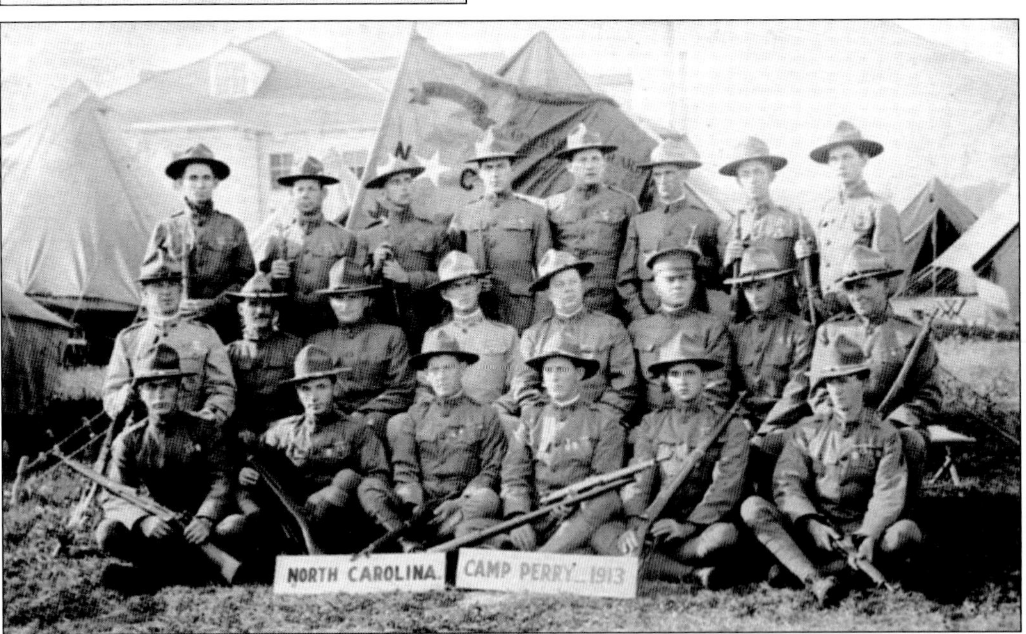


In 1913, Sgt. H.R. Triplett, Company A, 1st Regiment, and Sgt., Joseph M. White (third row, far left), Company L, 3rd Regiment, Thomasville, were selected to compete in the National Shoot held at Camp Perry, Ohio. The soldiers left for Ohio August 17, and the *Hickory Democrat* reported, "This is one of the highest honors that can be paid a National Guardsman." (Courtesy of North Carolina State Archives.)

# *Three*

# Drills, Marches, and Dress Parades

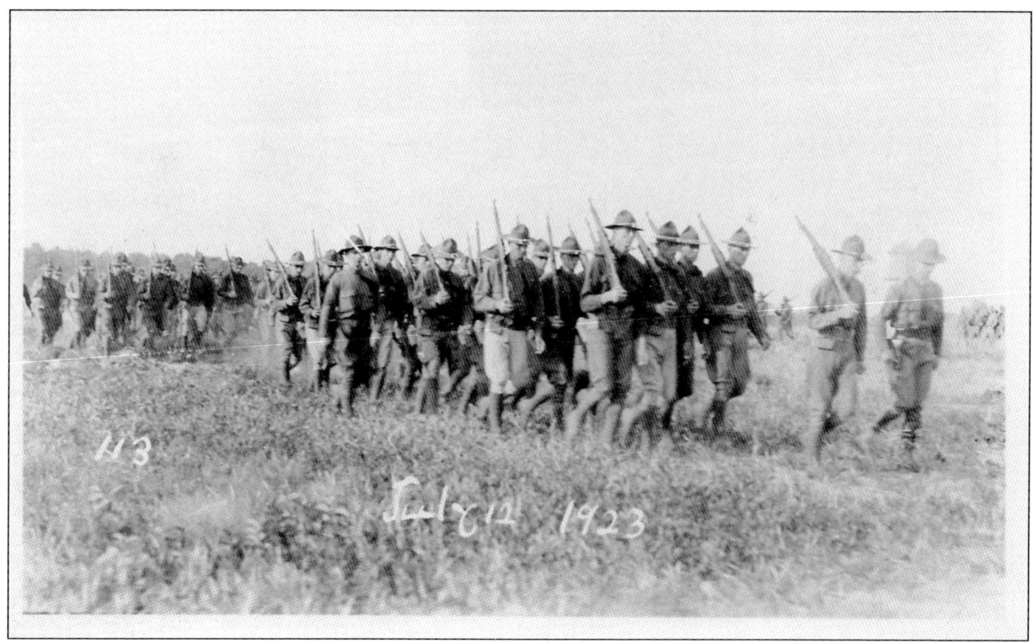


Encampment drills took place during July and August 1923, with about 2,700 soldiers attending. The *1923–1924 Adjutant General Biennial Report* noted, "The various drills covering School of Soldiers, School of Squad, School of Platoon, and company were very good; steadiness of men in ranks was excellent. The appearance of the organization as to neatness and soldierly bearing was very good."

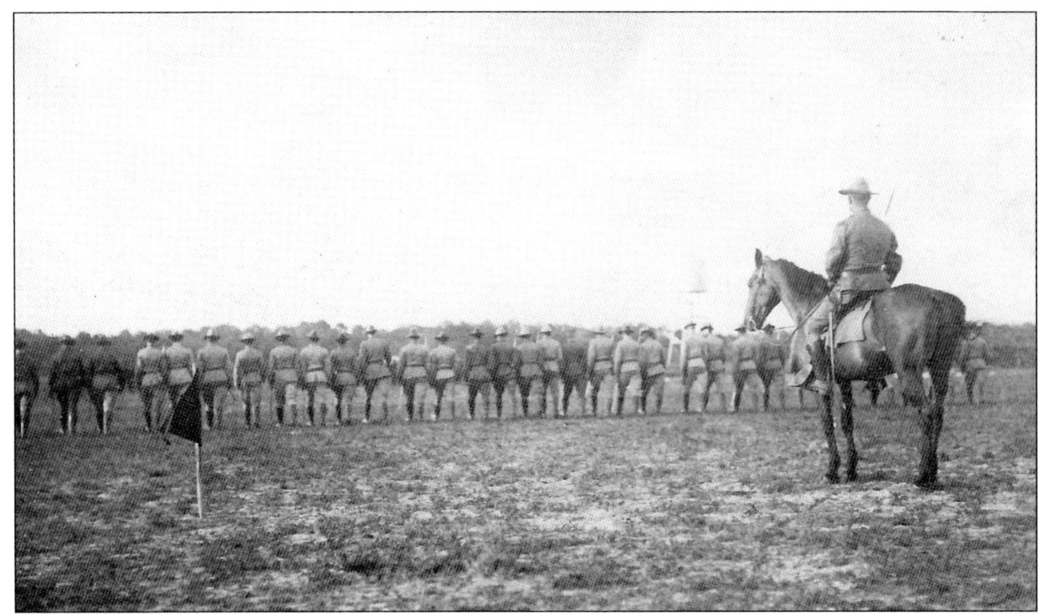

In this real-photo postcard by Wootten Studio, New Bern, Company A, 1st Regiment, Hickory, is shown in formation holding swords as a mounted officer observes. Parades and reviews were held as a part of regular inspection by organization commanders and visiting dignitaries, and both officers and enlisted men were required to appear in the blue or dress uniform. One of the parade grounds also served as a rifle range.

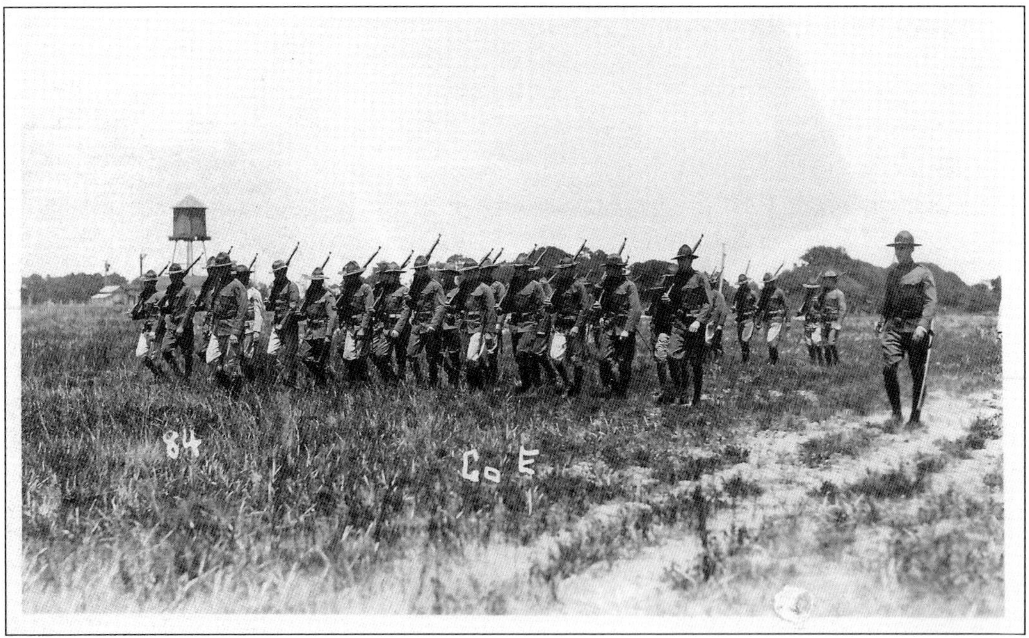


Company E's regiments were 1st Infantry, Statesville; 2nd Infantry, Goldsboro; and 3rd Infantry, Oxford. Soldiers practiced drilling from 7:00 a.m. to 11:00 a.m. and then again in the afternoon for 2.5 hours. Inexperienced soldiers who performed poorly during drills improved in their maneuvers with practice. During their time off from drilling and chores, soldiers enjoyed recreational activities such as baseball, boxing, volleyball, wrestling, boating, swimming, and fishing.

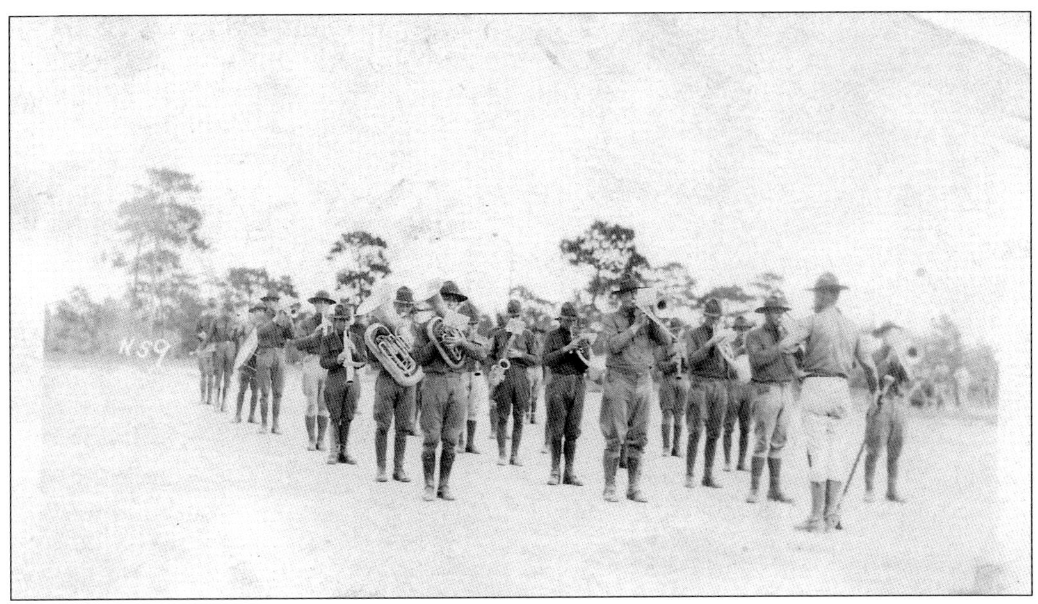


First day beginning drills for regimental bands were in the school of the soldier and military courtesy under the sergeant-instructor. On the following days, the first drill hour was on first-aid instruction under the medical inspector-instructor. Bands practiced daily and attended battalion inspections, parades, and reviews. Field musicians accompanied their companies on the target range and on the drill ground, except on drill days when service calls and signaling instruction were given.

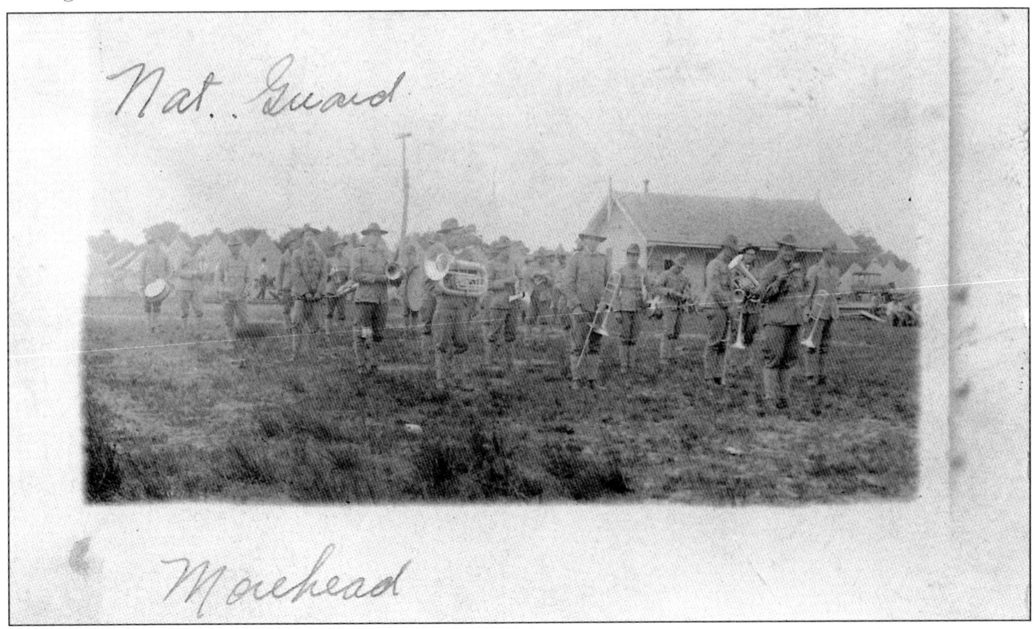


Each of the three regiments had its own band with conductors leading members playing cornets, clarinets, saxophones, trombones, basses, and snare and bass drums. The band practiced each morning, and members performed for guard mount, battalion parades, and other military occasions. Regimental bands held public concerts and town parades for local citizens during encampment periods.

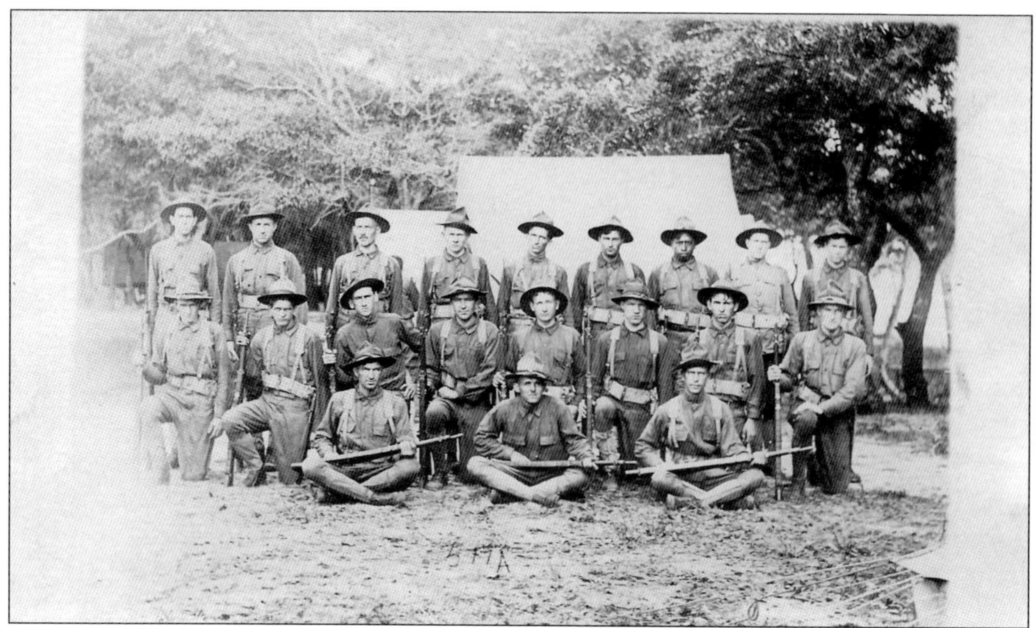

Soldiers outfitted for drilling are holding rifles that appear to be Springfield rifles. Rifle belts carried ammunition in pouches and had holsters for weapons. Uniform clothing was made of either cotton or wool depending on the season and consisted of underwear and socks, olive drab shirt and trousers, puttee leggings typically called "leggins," hobnailed trench shoes, the service coat or "blouse," and a trench coat for winter weather.

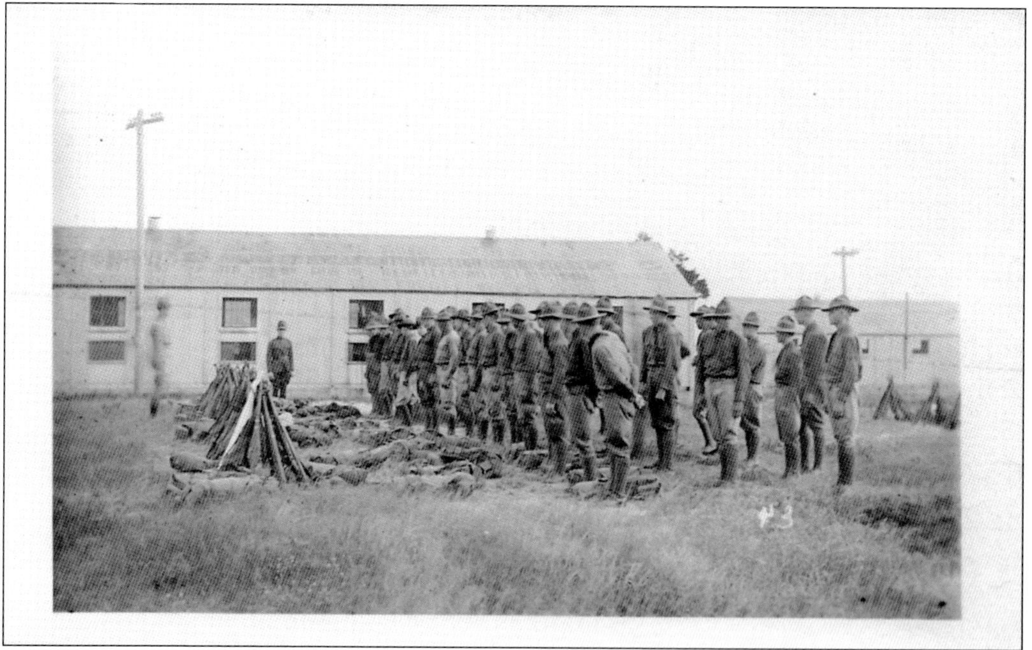

Weapons and equipment is seen lying on the ground as a group of soldiers listen to instructions from the blurred figure of an officer. Drill lectures and instructions were given on the use and care of soldiers' issued equipment. Storage warehouse buildings are shown in the background along with telephone or telegraph poles and wires.

Port arms, a two-count movement, is a procedure for executing the manual of arms in individual and unit drill movements. Two unidentified soldiers are holding their rifles according to the second count, which means to hold the rifle diagonally across the body, about four inches from the waist, with the right forearm horizontal and the elbows close to the sides.

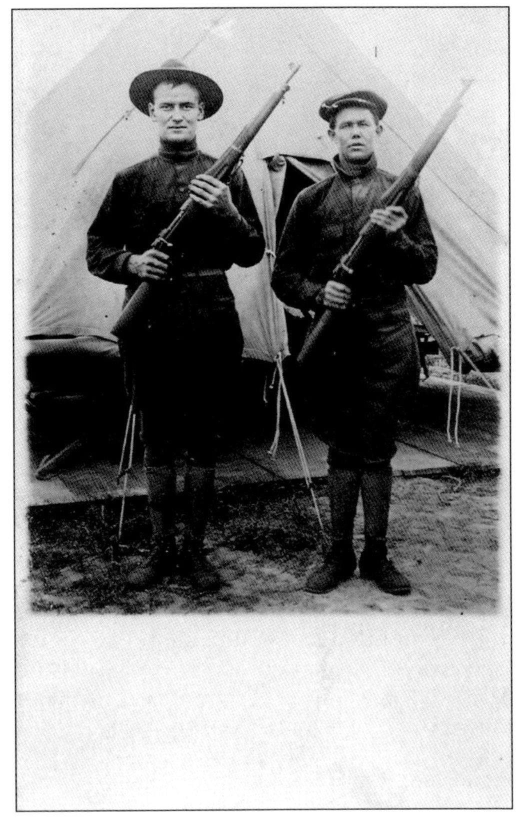

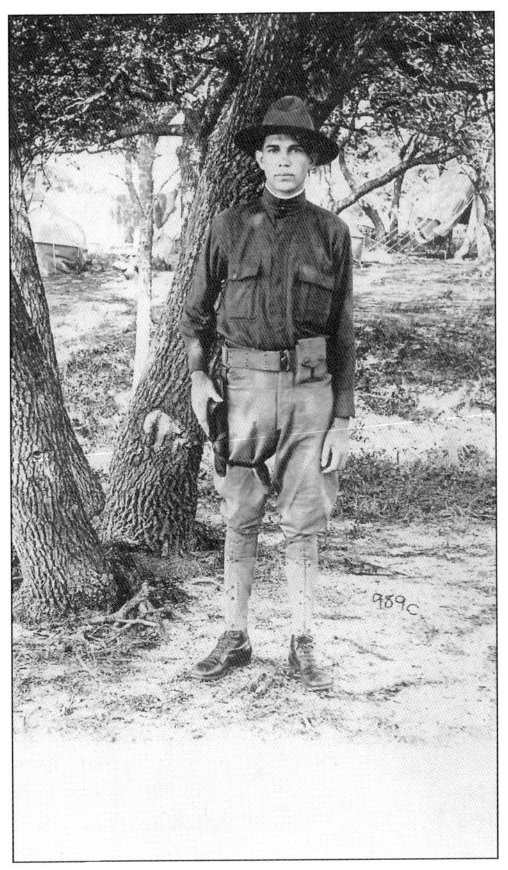


An unidentified soldier, carrying a holstered pistol, is standing in front of a live oak tree. During training exercises, teams of officers and enlisted men held competitions during pistol practice on the range. Soldiers performing well were awarded marksman or expert titles according to their scores and traveled to Camp Perry, Ohio, to compete with other states' National Guard regiments.

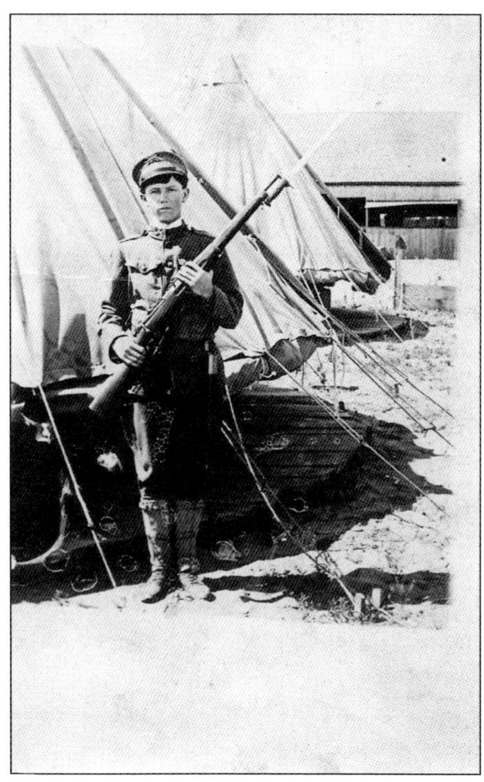

Holding his rifle with bayonet, a soldier is standing in front of a tent. Bayonets were used in hand-to-hand fighting, and its use, or the threat of it, often drove the enemy from his position, causing him to surrender. A commanding officer noted, "The fact should be appreciated that bayonet exercise is of value not only in the physical development of the soldier, but in creating fighting morale."

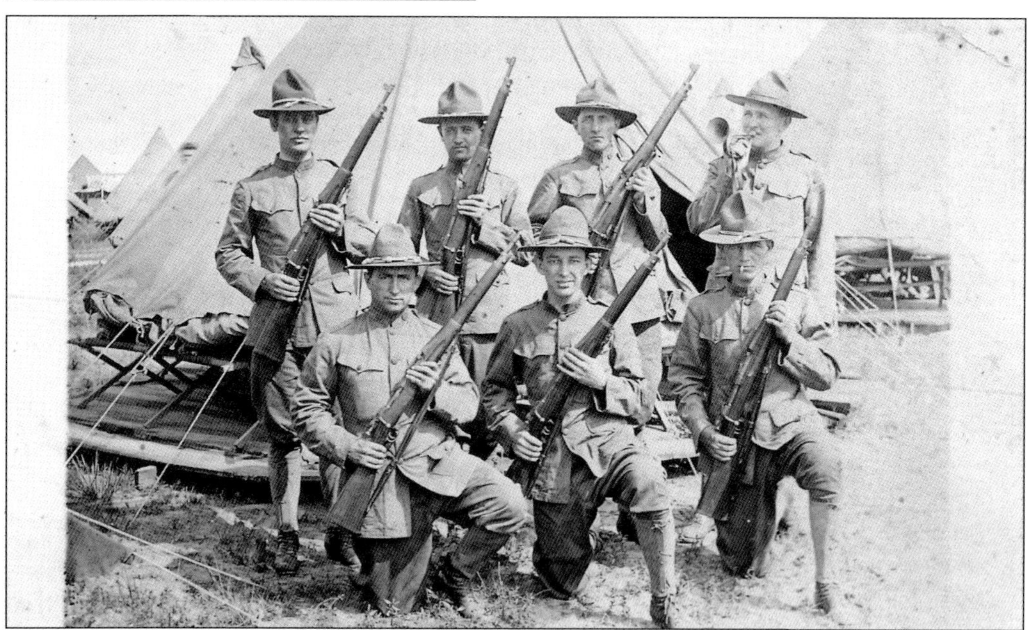

Holding their rifles at their shoulder, soldiers are kneeling and standing. One soldier is playing a bugle. This is not an actual drill because one soldier is seen smoking a cigarette. In 1915, MCW sent this postcard to J.B. Waddell, of Selma, with a message that reads, "In front of our tent." In 1915, Sgt. Maurice Charles Waddell (1886–1962), Company C, 2nd Regiment, Rocky Mount, was at Camp Glenn. (Courtesy of Linda Willis Sadler.)

An unidentified officer displays a light cavalry saber worn by officers in troop ceremonies. The 31-inch curved-blade saber was attached by a scabbard chain to a belt and was worn facing the rear on the left side of the body. Hometown civic organizations were known to hold military sword ceremonies in recognition of a soldier's accomplishments, at which a soldier was presented with a fine sword inscribed with his name and rank.

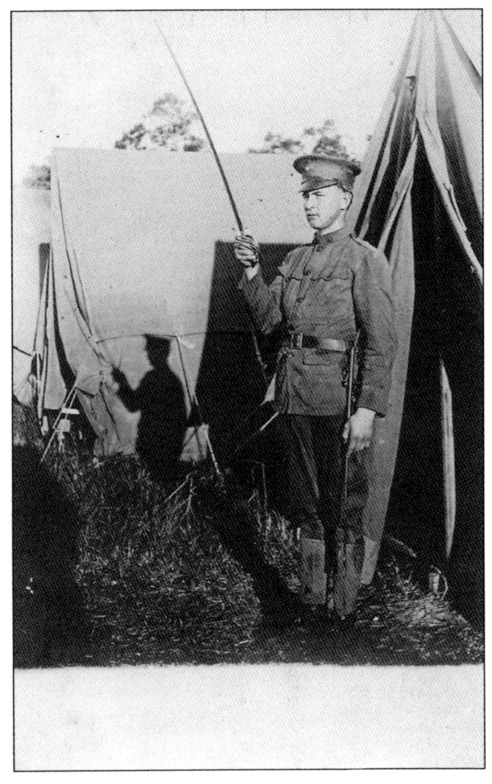

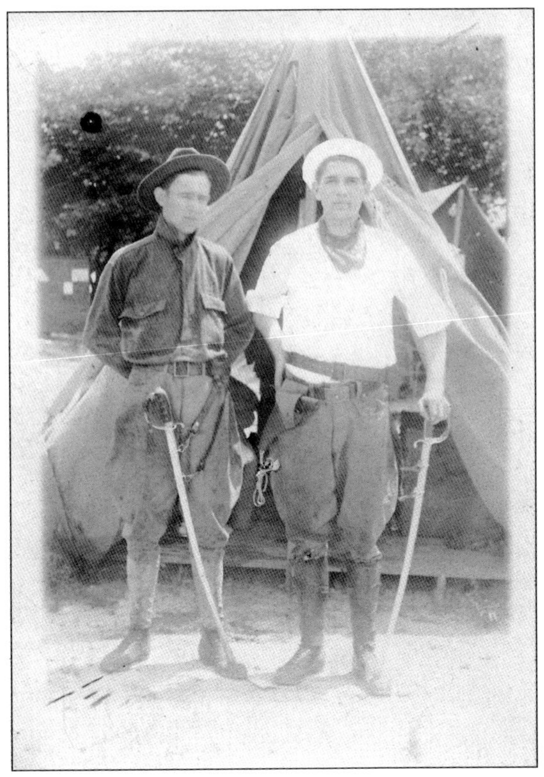

Infantry and Coast Artillery soldiers are pictured with sabers while standing in front of a tent. In 1906, a sword cost $5.18, scabbards were $2.59, and saber slings and knots were purchased from military supply stores. Soldiers were issued a cotton khaki uniform and a blue dress uniform consisting of a hat, shirt, and leggings or puttees. Uniform costs were as follows: hats $1.56; leggings 41¢; shirts 61¢: blue uniforms $4.81; and khaki uniforms $2.79.

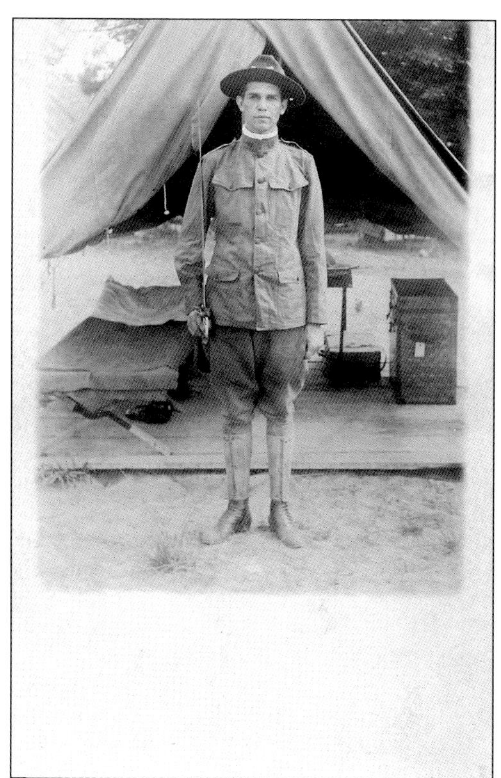

An unidentified officer is holding his sword in the position of carry sword. The *Manual of the Sword* states that, on the command of execution of the sword, it is pulled out of the scabbard and held in the position of carry sword. The sword should be held with the inner blade/edge riding in a vertical position along the forward tip of the right shoulder.

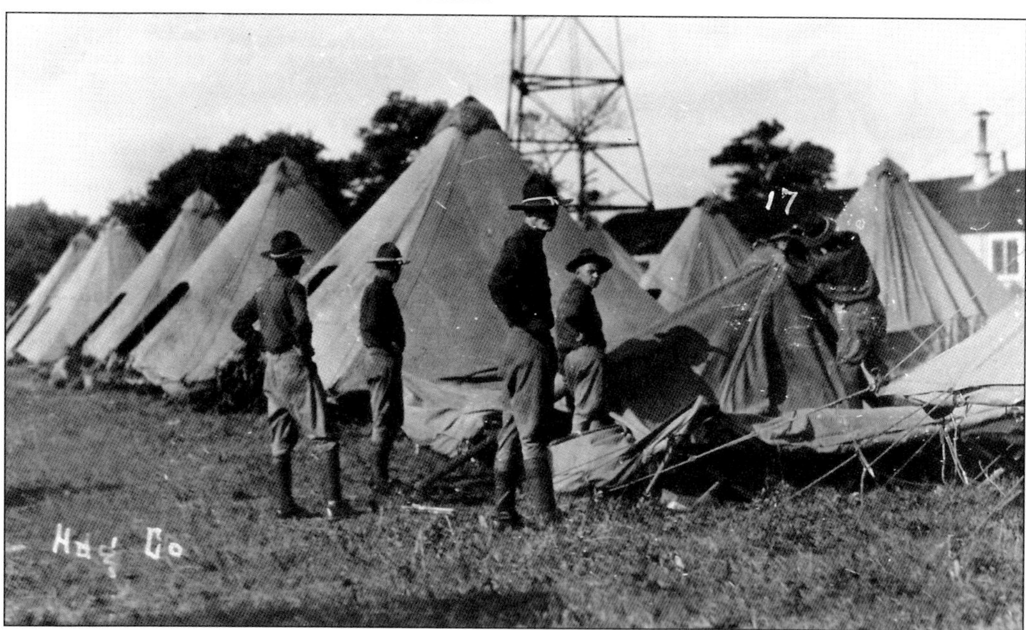

Personal equipment and tent pitching drills were part of practice drills during encampment. This image shows conical headquarter tents for officers, who are looking at the photographer as others are pitching tents. Soldiers arriving by train at night pitched tents in the dark. In 1916, the *Franklin Times* reported that weary soldiers were reminded that a good breakfast would follow, spurring men to "put in the last stob" so they could "get busy about the meal."

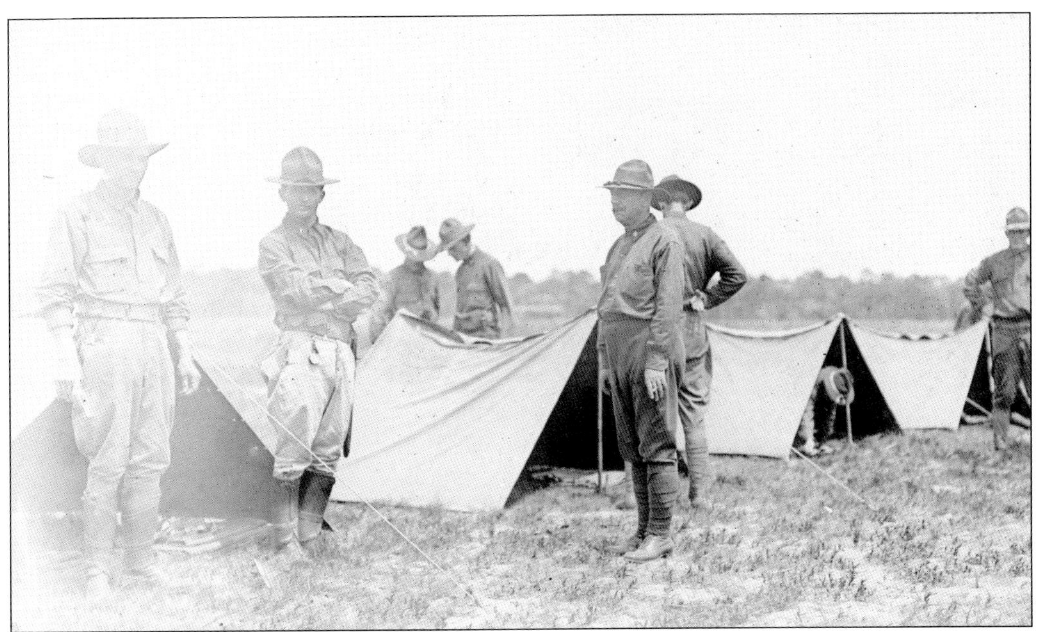

A 1914 report stated, "Each officer below the grade of major was furnished with one shelter tent complete from equipment furnished to the organization." Each company held shelter, or dog tent, pitching drills with a display of equipment during encampment. According to an earlier report, soldiers who did not practice these drills could spend a "a miserable night in the rain in a tent poorly pitched." (Courtesy of the University of North Carolina at Chapel Hill.)

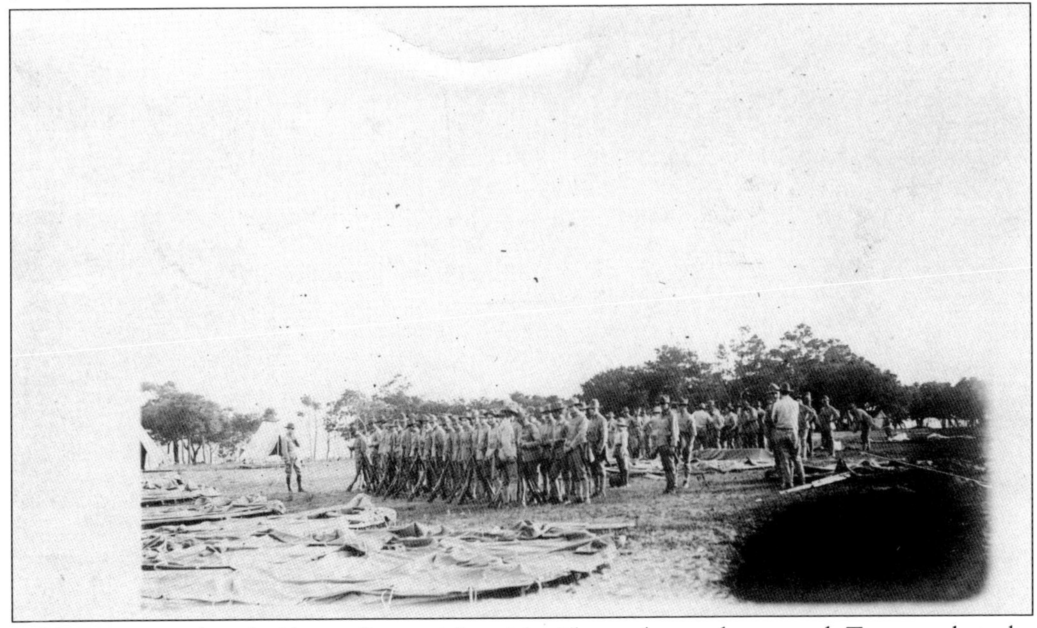

Soldiers are standing holding rifles upright with rifle stocks on the ground. Tents ready to be pitched are on the ground. Soldiers' duties on the first day were to make camp, which included setting up tents and putting the camp in order. In training that day, companies were instructed in the school of the soldier and military courtesy under the sergeant-instructor. (Courtesy of the University of North Carolina at Chapel Hill.)

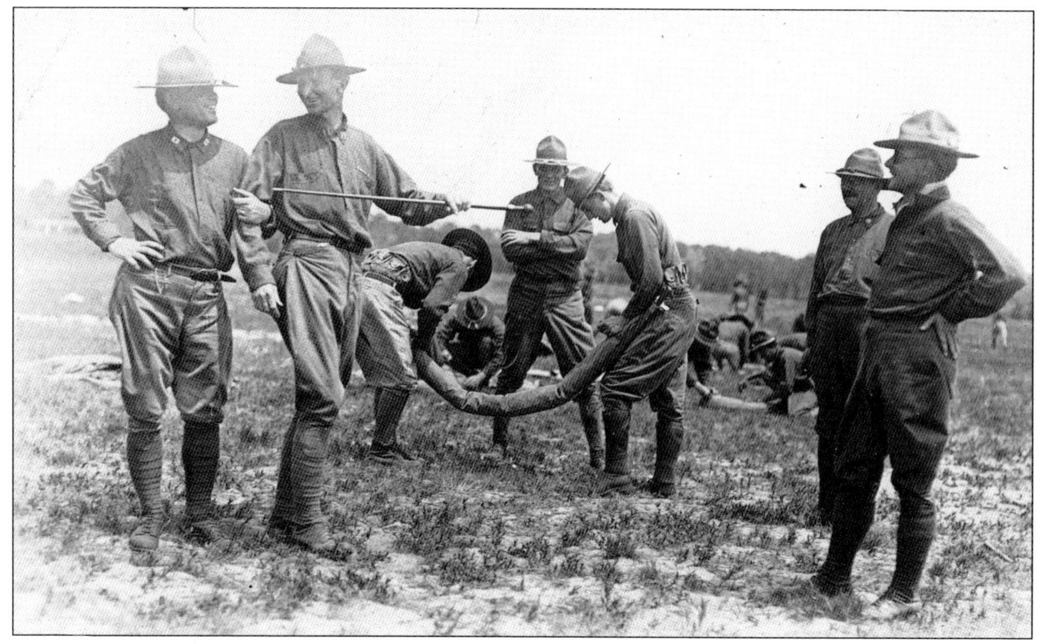

Arm-in-arm unidentified officers, with one holding a baton, are seen marching to something, perhaps, more like a period dance rather than a military drill. Officers observing the show appear to be amused. Seen in the background, soldiers are busy practicing a blanket roll drill. (Courtesy of the University of North Carolina at Chapel Hill.)

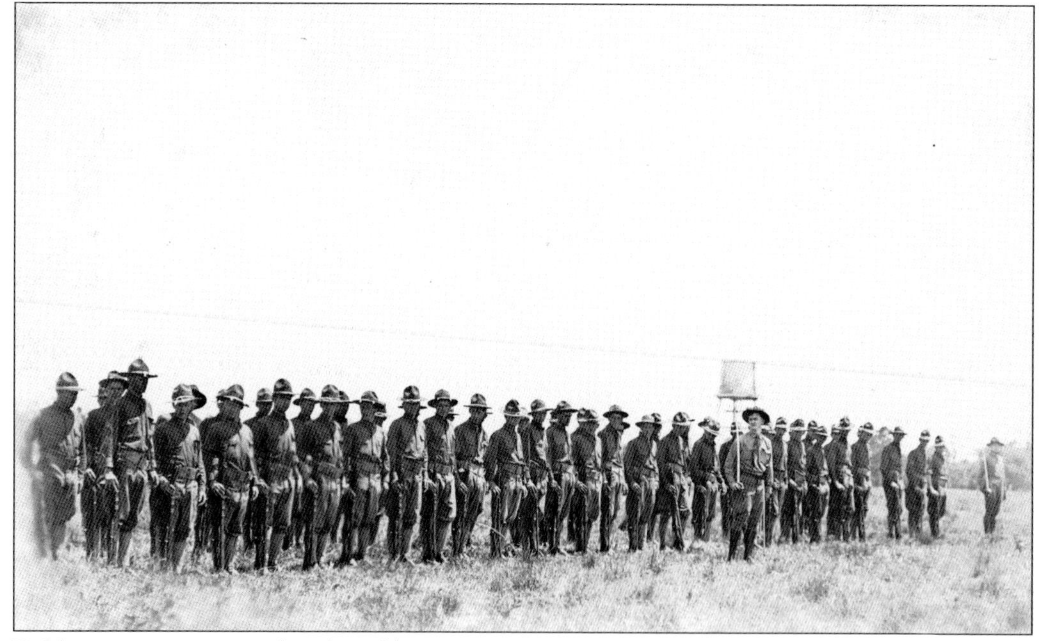

Field instruction is paused as the soldiers' attention is diverted from the drill to the photographer. Soldiers are lined up in formation with two officers in front. Promptness in falling in was an important part of drilling. Being late for a drill or patrol meant that the soldier would be left behind when the troop departed on their march or patrol. (Courtesy of the University of North Carolina at Chapel Hill.)

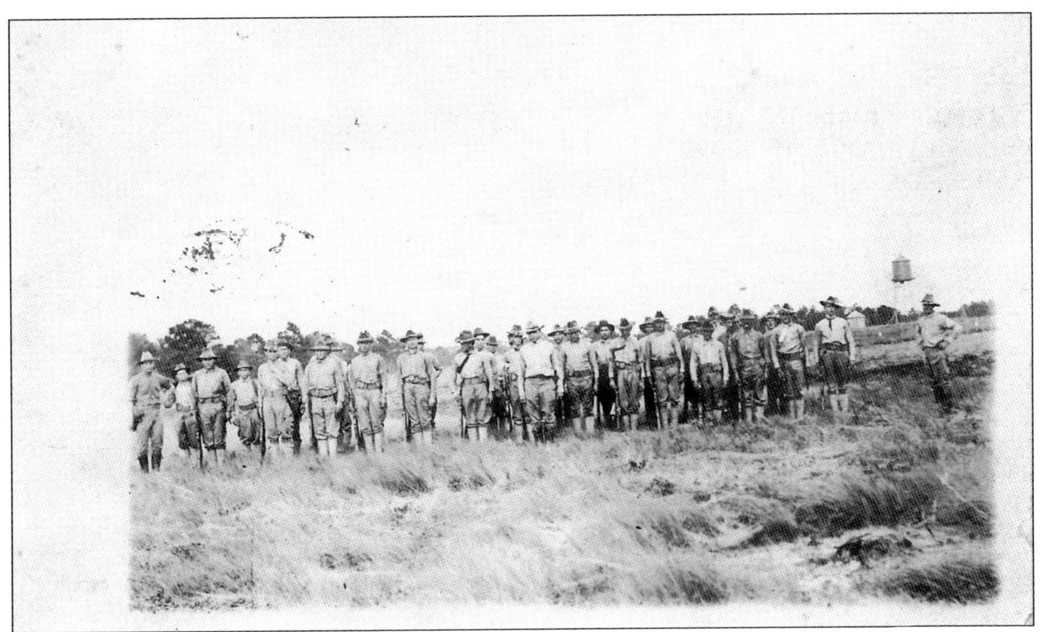

Company E, 3rd Regiment, Oxford, soldiers are in formation in mostly two columns with a third column off to the right. The company commander is on the far right. This postcard was dated on August 7, 1908, and read, "From Bunyon Morehead North Carolina to Miss Ethel Dickerson, R., #3 Oxford, N. C." If Bunyon was Dickerson's suitor, the romance failed as Ethel Dickerson and Will Blackwell, Oxford, were wed in November 1914.

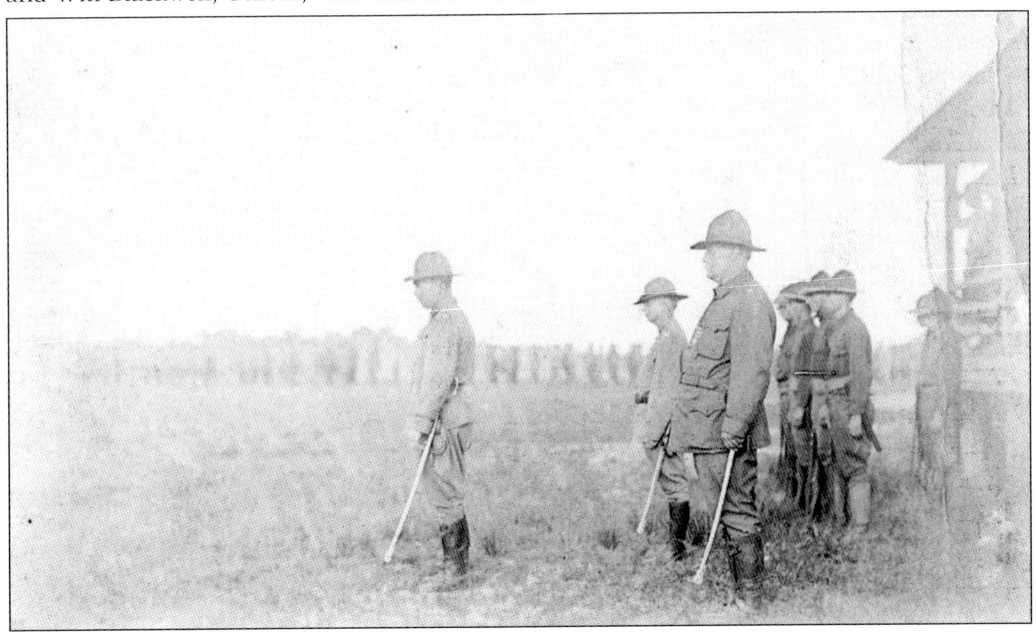

Lieutenant Colonel Bessent (second row, front) is with soldiers on the drill grounds. In 1906, General Armfield recommended the following in his report, "As soon as possible, the grounds, including the campsite, drill-ground and rifle-range, should be leveled and grass sowed, or some method used to secure a turf. This should be done this fall or winter to permit the ground to become settled and a turf formed before the time for the next encampment."

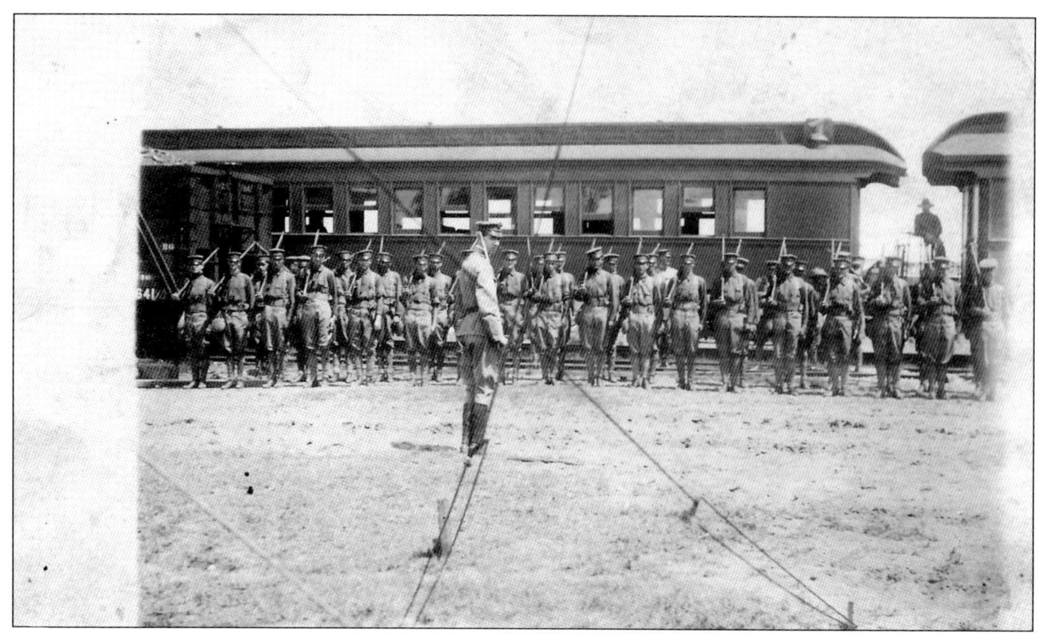

Soldiers are standing at attention in front of an Atlantic & North Carolina Railroad train that provided transportation to Camp Glenn. In 1905, the *News & Observer* reported the railroad agreed to "construct a platform, sidings, and other facilities necessary for the safe and convenient handling of troops and their equipment and to erect some buildings." The railroad also agreed to maintain a short trunk service between the Camp Glenn and Morehead City.

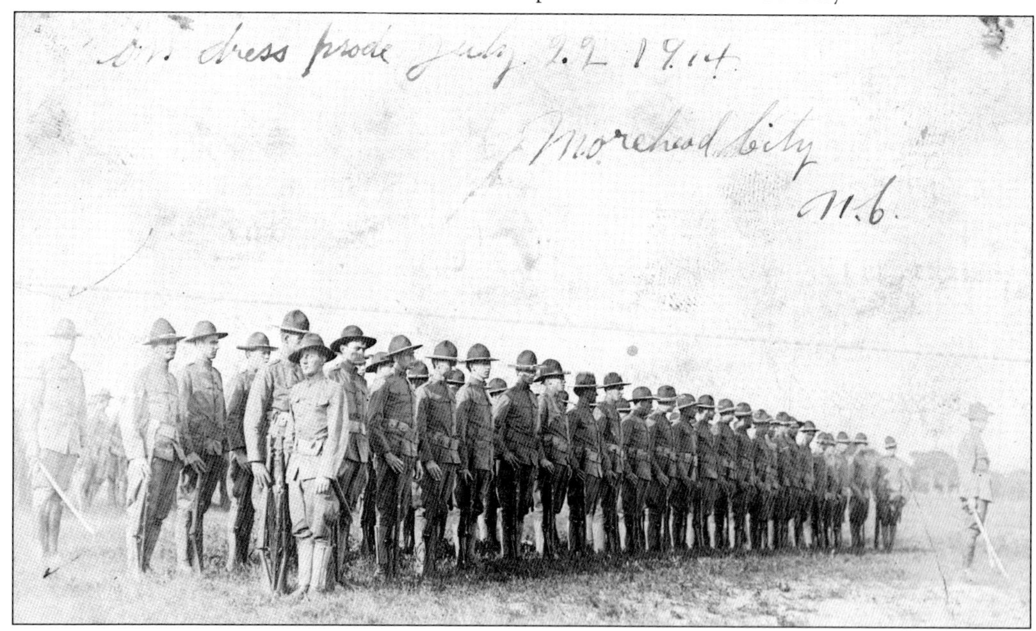


Gov. Locke Craig visited Camp Glenn for the day during summer encampment held July 21–30, 1914. The governor spent the day in camp, touring and giving speeches, and in the afternoon, he reviewed the troops in a dressed parade. Company A, 1st Regiment, Hickory, Col. Junius Tazewell (J.T.) Gardner (1860–1925), commander, are shown here on the parade grounds "dressed within an inch of their lives." (Courtesy of North Carolina State Archives.)

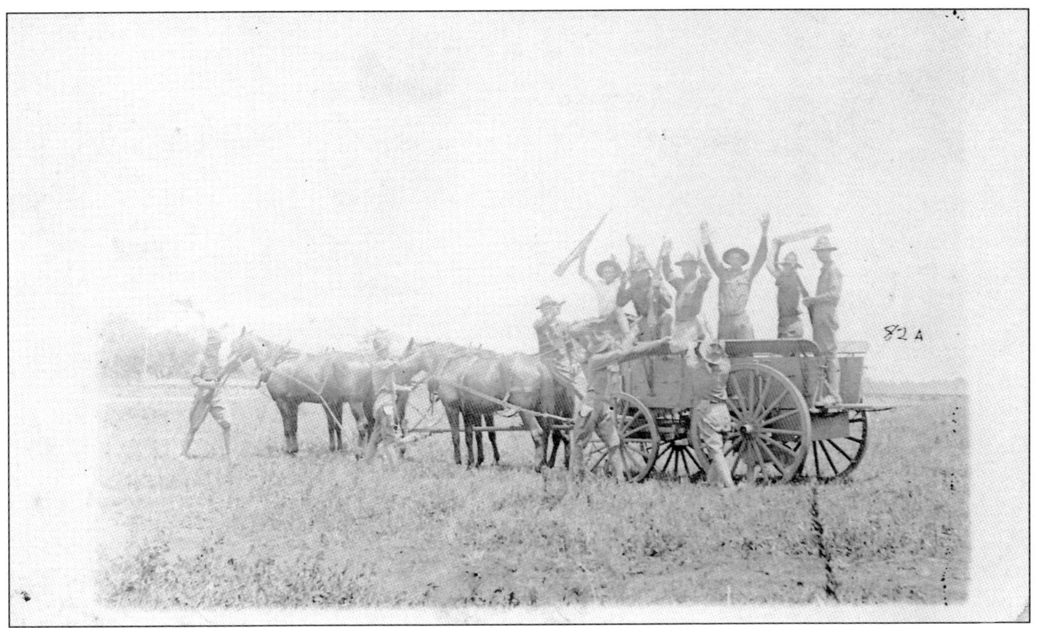


In July 1911, Camp Glenn's soldiers held their first sham or mock battle at the end of a three-day march. Wagon trains loaded with ammunition and supplies were prime targets for "enemy soldiers." During one sham battle that summer, a company commander's "capture" by two "enemy" soldiers failed when the soldiers turned after hearing a sound and were captured by their prisoner whom they had not disarmed.

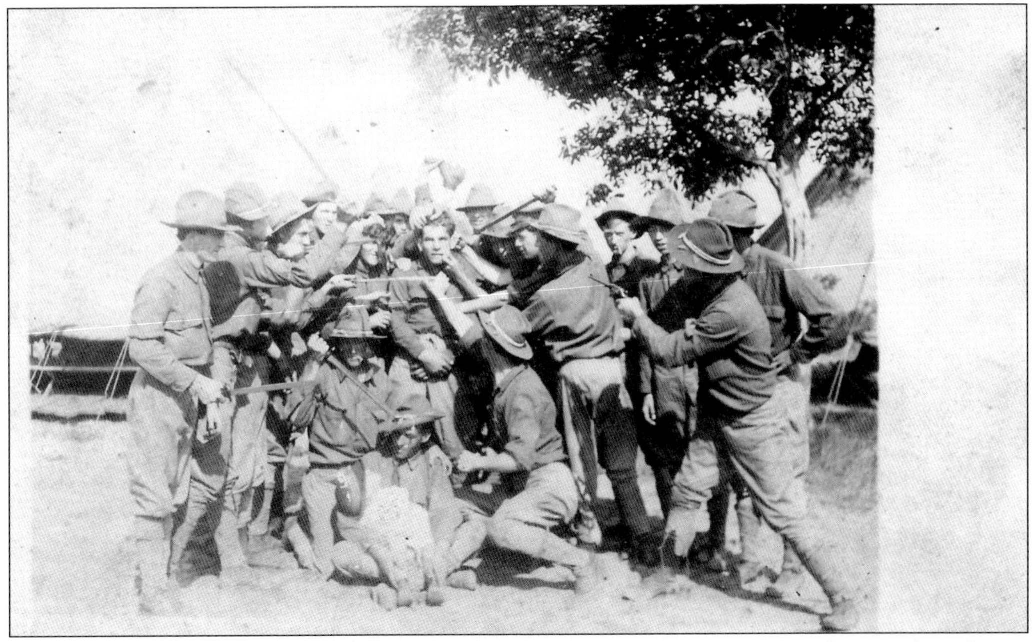

The two soldiers with guns and swords drawn on them may be "prisoners of war" taken during a mock war campaign or sham battle drill. It is unclear if the young girl is amused or terrified at what is going on. It is also not known if the little girl's mother is nearby and watching what is taking place.

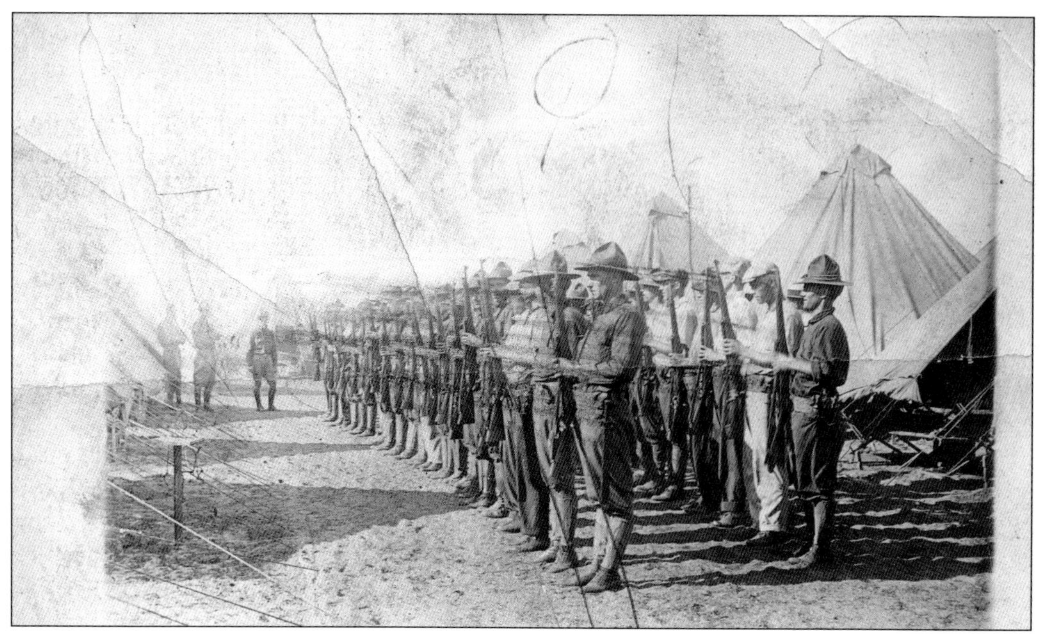

Both postcards seen here were sent from Sgt. Luther Albert Jackson (1890–1977), Company C, 3rd Infantry, in 1916 to Melville G. Evans in Henderson and shows an inspection in a company street upon the soldiers' arrival at Camp Glenn. In the photograph above, soldiers are holding rifles while standing in formation. Below, soldiers are standing in front of tents with clothes lying on the ground. A young boy and a dog look on, and Bogue Sound is seen in the background. The message on this postcard reads, "Hellow old Boy. how are you get on *[sic]* We haven't left here yet and don't know when we will leave" Jackson was referring to leaving for the Mexican border to take part in the Mexican Border War. (Courtesy of North Carolina State Archives.)

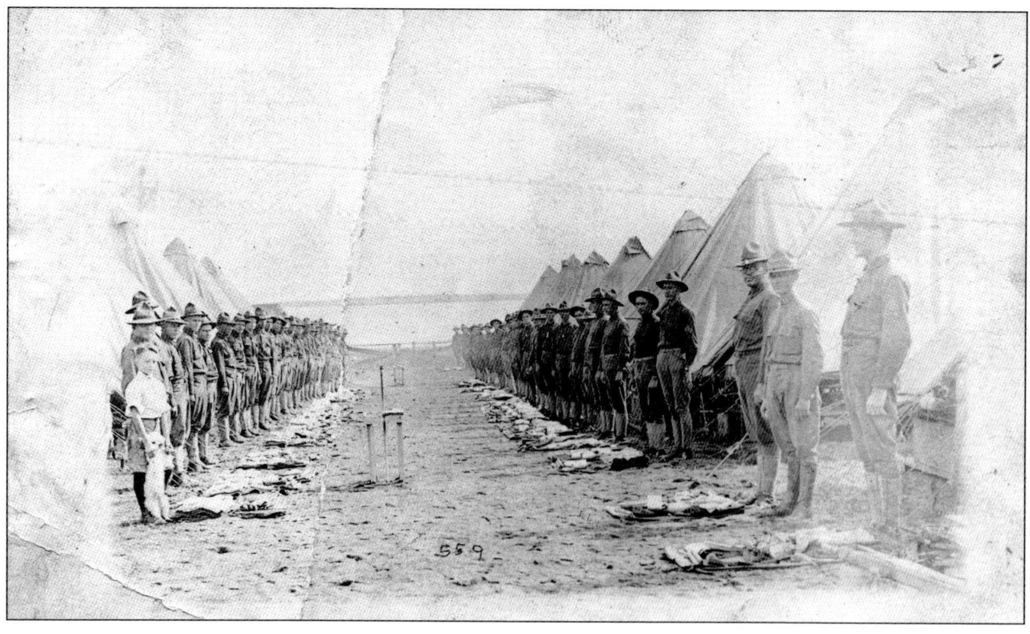

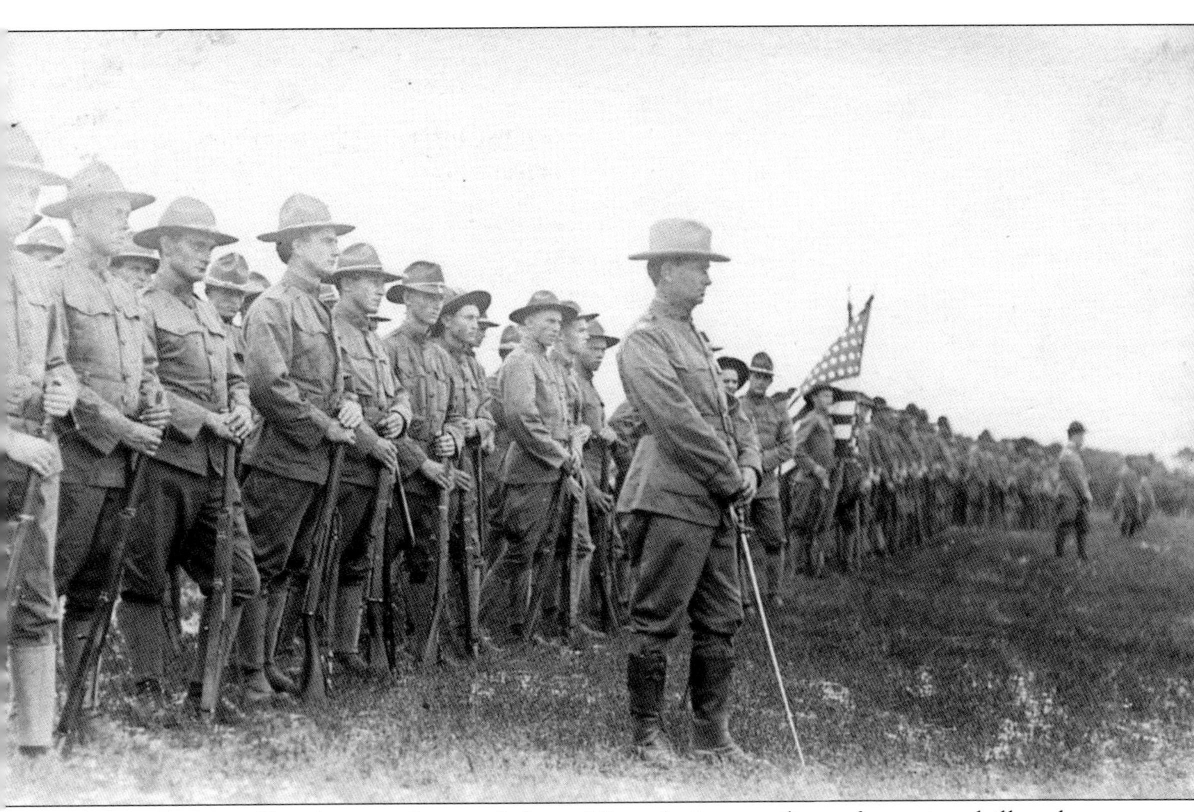

General Young (front) is standing with his soldiers during a military formation drill and an American flag is seen in the front line's center. This photograph was taken in 1916–1917 when NCNG troops mobilized at Camp Glenn, in preparation for war during the Punitive Expedition against Pancho Villa, led by Gen. John Joseph "Black Jack" Pershing (1860–1948). Young was a popular commander with soldiers and state leaders. An article about Young in the *Roanoke Beacon*, on July 21, 1916, describes the general as standing "all of six feet two in his socks" and "was found at most places almost any time of the day but hardly ever at brigade headquarters." A direct and decisive man, Young was described as, "inviting suggestions and remarks from the lowest ranking officer and his talks were few, brief, and filled with meaning," and was quick to decide but could change his mind if "shown." He was also known to consider ideas and suggestions and use good judgement in his decisions. (Courtesy of North Carolina State Archives.)

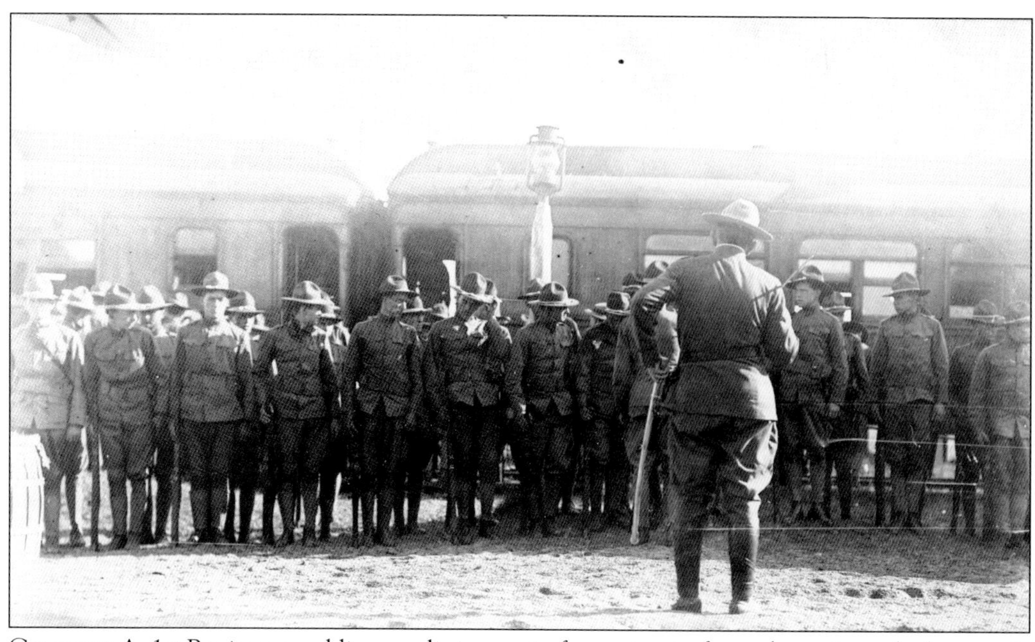

Company A, 1st Regiment, soldiers are lining up in formation in front the train and a lamp pole after their arrival at Camp Glenn. There may be some confusion going on as some the men seem to be looking down the line at a soldier in the center of the front line. Part of the train depot is seen at the edge of the photograph (left). (Courtesy of the University of North Carolina at Chapel Hill.)

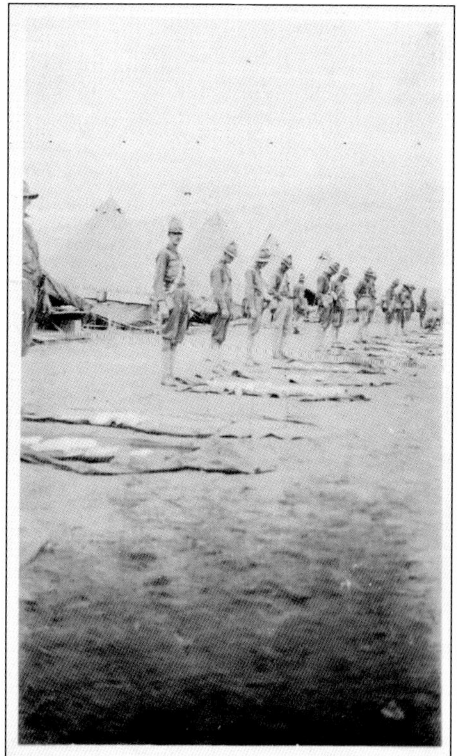

Soldiers are standing in formation for inspection in a company street. Some men are looking at the photographer while others are looking down at their bed or blanket rolls. A soldier's bedroll consisted of the following: a shelter half, set shelter poles, guy rope, poncho, blanket, pair socks, comb, toothbrush, piece of soap, set blanket-roll straps, housewife (pocket sewing kit), towel, and five shelter pins. (Courtesy of ECU.)

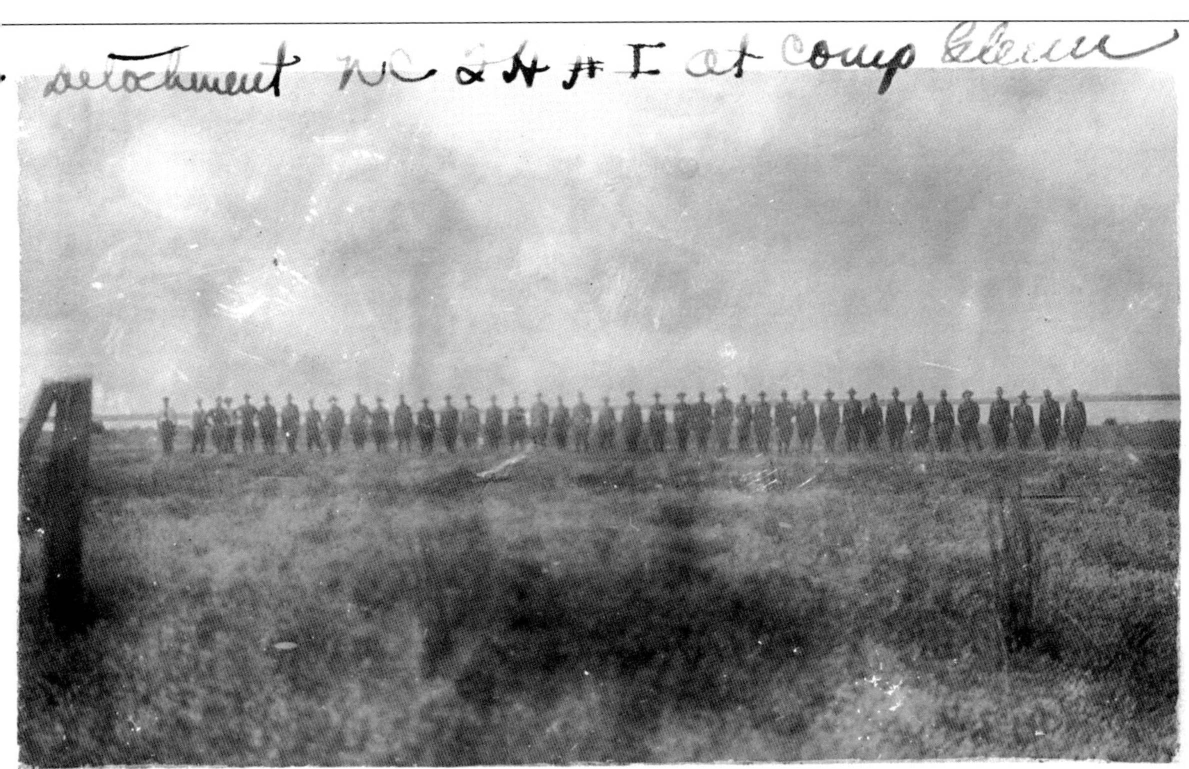


Companies F, Asheville; H, Waynesville; I, Mount Airy, 1st Regiment soldiers are lined up in formation along Bogue Sound's shore at Camp Glenn during the 1916 mobilization. Capt. Frank Erwin Walker (1887–1964), Company I commander, was the first to leave with his soldiers on the train for Camp Glenn on June 24, 1916, with Capt. William F. Swift and his soldiers of Company H and Capt. Charles I. Bard, Company F, leaving shortly after. The captains spent three weeks recruiting for soldiers to join the ranks in order to fight on the Mexican border, and their efforts were hampered by a disastrous flood that occurred in the western part of North Carolina. The flood required extra labor from men and slowed recruitment of soldiers. Eventually, 90 soldiers were enlisted, and all left for training at Camp Glenn.

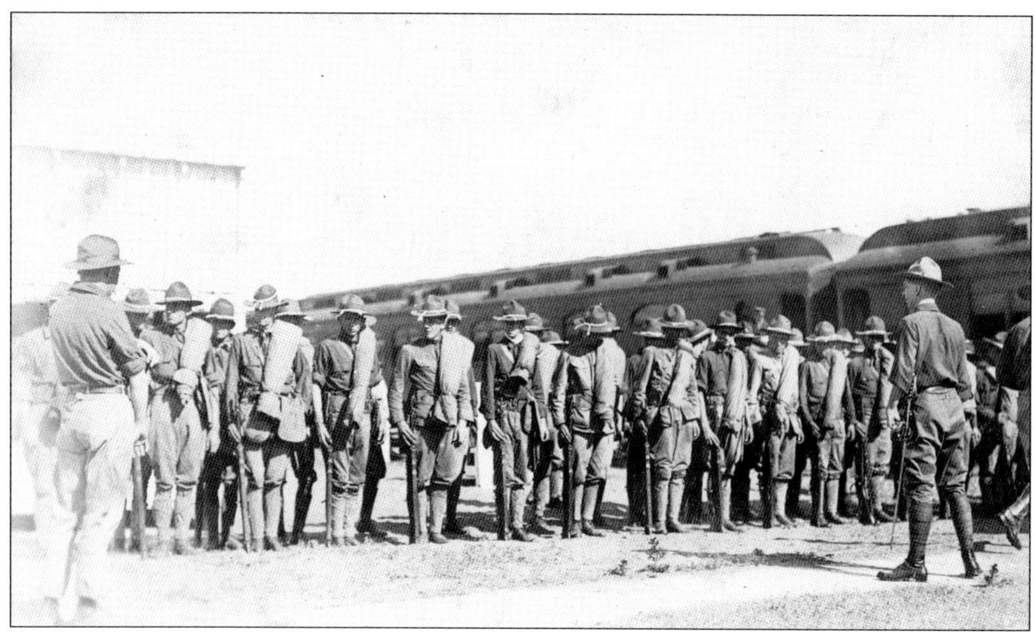

Company members are in formation with bedrolls on their shoulders and rifles at their side on their arrival at Camp Glenn. The train depot is seen behind the soldiers. Meals and coffee were provided for the men who traveled by train to camp. Company commanders were responsible for making the travel arrangements, and costs were not allowed to exceed 75¢ per man. (Courtesy of the University of North Carolina at Chapel Hill.)

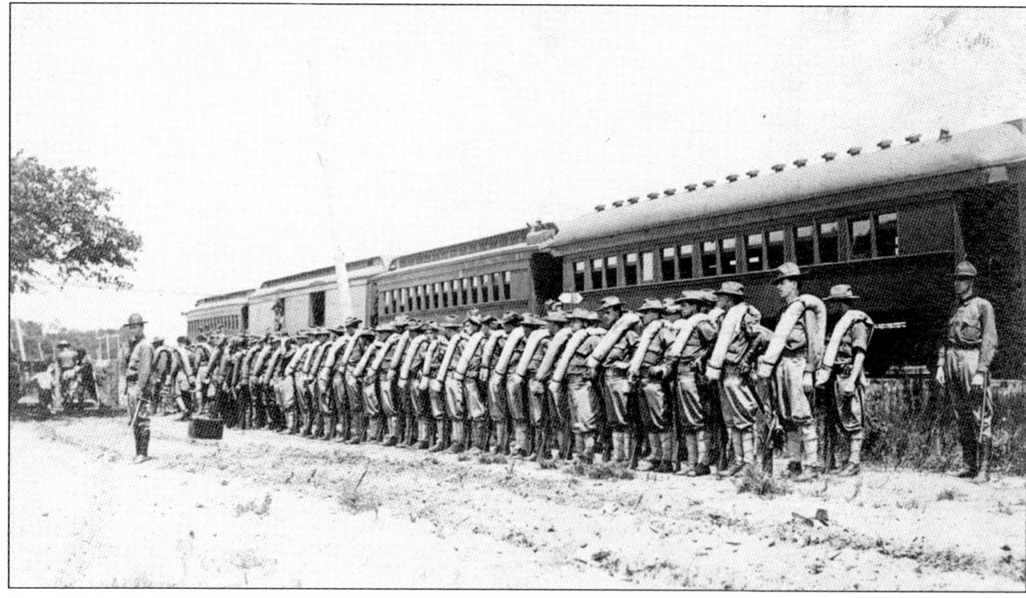

Company A, 1st Regiment, left Hickory July 15 and returned July 26 from the 10-day encampment. The Hickory Rifles had three commissioned officers and 56 enlisted men, making it the largest Hickory company to go to camp. In 1916, the *Hickory Daily Record* reported that under the command of Capt. George L. Lyerly, who was said to be "capable and energetic," the company was considered one of the best in the NCNG. (Courtesy of the University of North Carolina at Chapel Hill.)

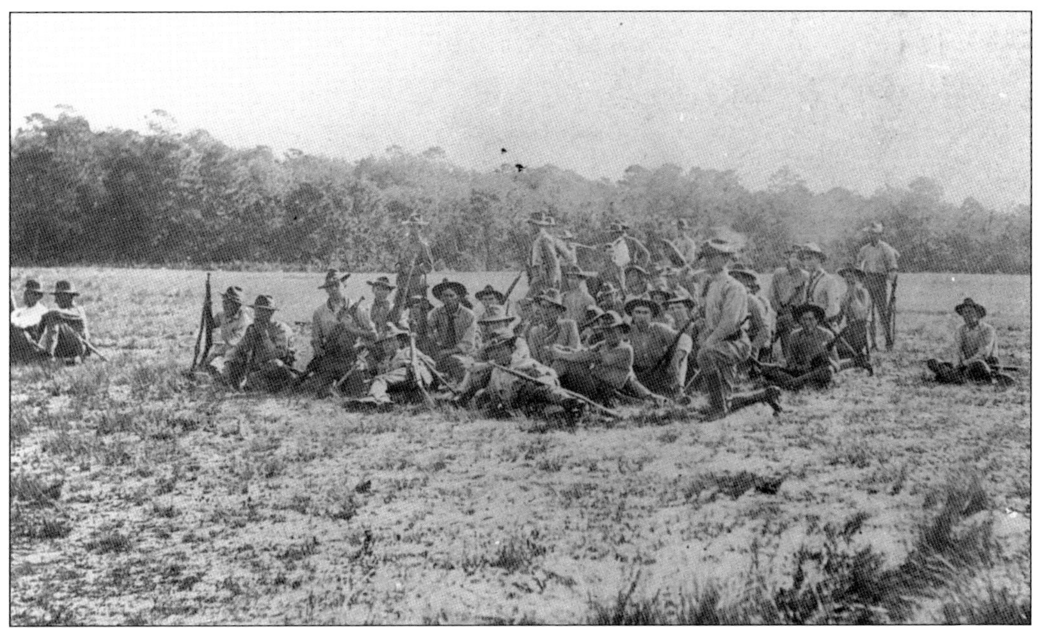

The Hickory Rifles, Company A, 1st Regiment, is seen here in a field in a c. 1910 photograph. Company and battalion field movements were added to rifle practice that year, and commanding officers found results very satisfactory. Though the amount of work was double that of the previous year, it was performed with the "same amount of cheerfulness on the part of participants." (Courtesy of North Carolina State Archives.)

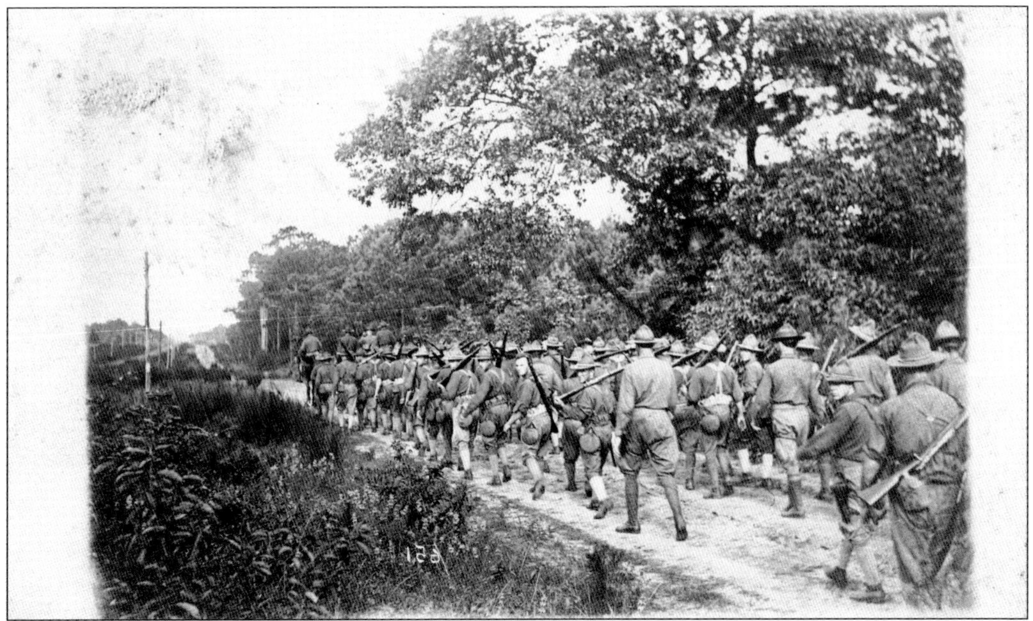

During the 1916 mobilization, the Hickory Rifles are seen here marching three miles from Camp Glenn to Crab Point. After arriving at Crab Point, a sham battle took place from 9:00 a.m. to 3:00 p.m. These hikes prepared the men for the movement of the brigade to the border, with a commanding officer stating, "They will be toughened to the work of a soldier." (Courtesy of North Carolina State Archives.)

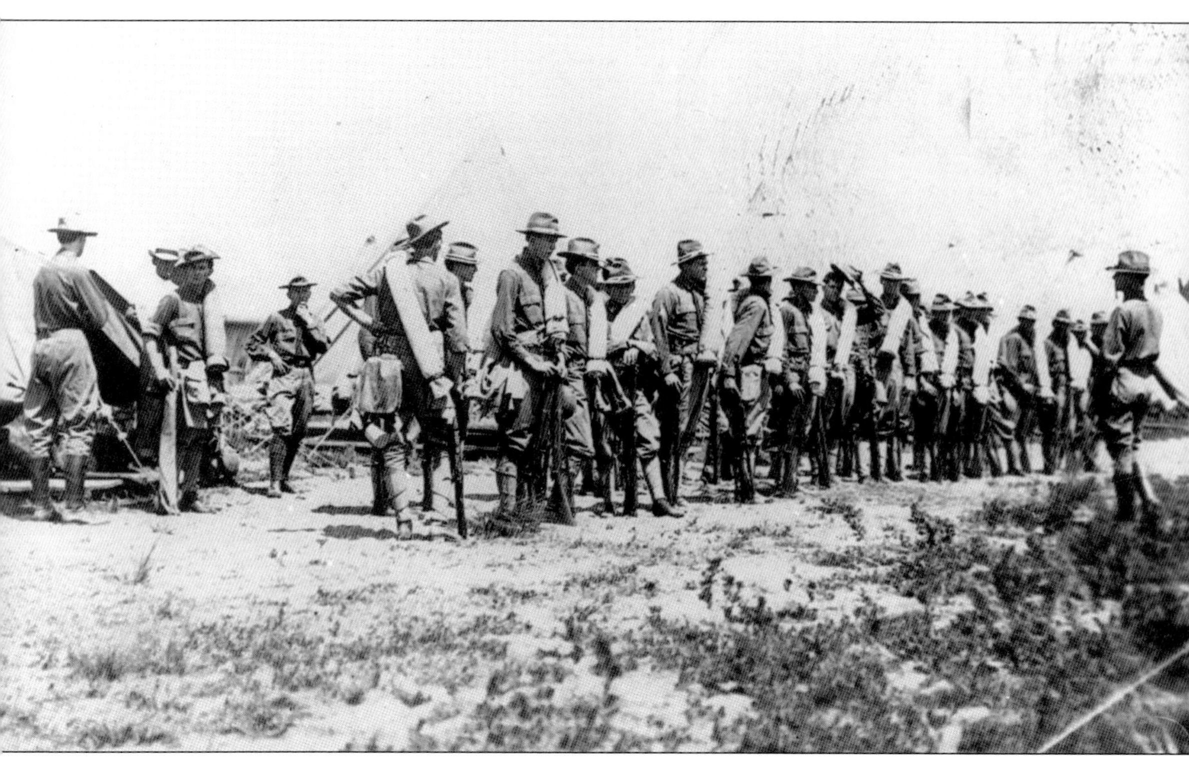

Drill marches or hikes lasting one to three days were part of military training at Camp Glenn. Soldiers carried full field equipment, including a shelter tent, canvas bedding roll, olive drab wool blanket, and canteen. They also carried a haversack, a small, sturdy canvas bag with rations. The maximum authorized weight of bedding and clothing rolls for general officers in campaign was 100 pounds and 50 pounds for all other officers. The men prepared their own meals and slept in shelter halves. At the end of the march, the soldiers engaged in a mock battle dividing up into two teams—the brown team and the blue team. Along the way, there were trains of wagons loaded with ammunition and supplies that were targets that soldiers attempted to capture. Soldiers found these exercises beneficial and enjoyable; however, the best part was the march back to camp and more comfortable conditions. (Courtesy of North Carolina State Archives.)

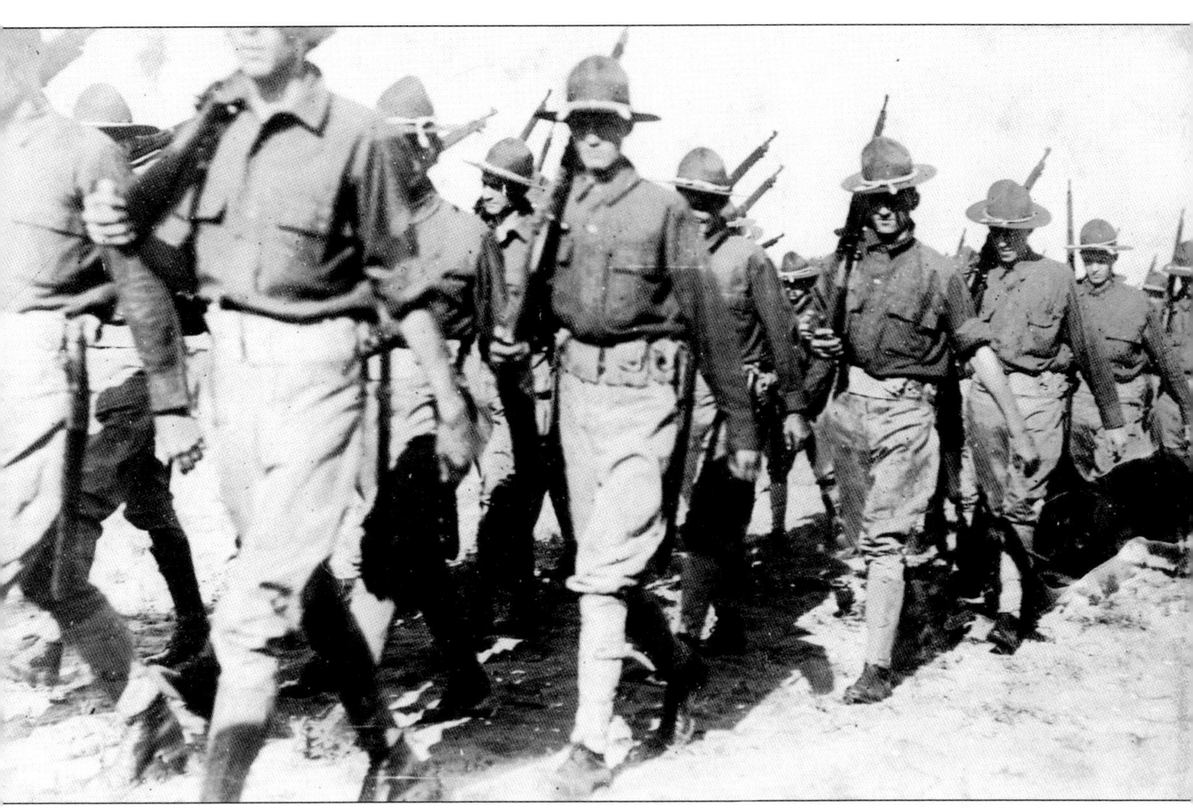

The 1910 report notes the following: "The First Regiment went into camp at Morehead City, August 2-10, for instruction in rifle practice and field movements. . . . The drill began with the company the first day, then battalion drill, regimental parade, and on the last day a march and sham battle. With the exception of one morning, all officers and men reported for duty at the pit or drill field on time." All troops were required to march, and sometimes, the march's distance would be 12 miles or more. Venomous snakes were a danger, as well as sharp sandspurs. To protect against these and other hazards, each soldier was issued one pair of serviceable leather shoes and a pair of woolen socks. The Joseph M. Herman & Co., Boston, Massachusetts, supplied the army russet marching shoe for $3.10 per pair. (Courtesy of the University of North Carolina at Chapel Hill.)

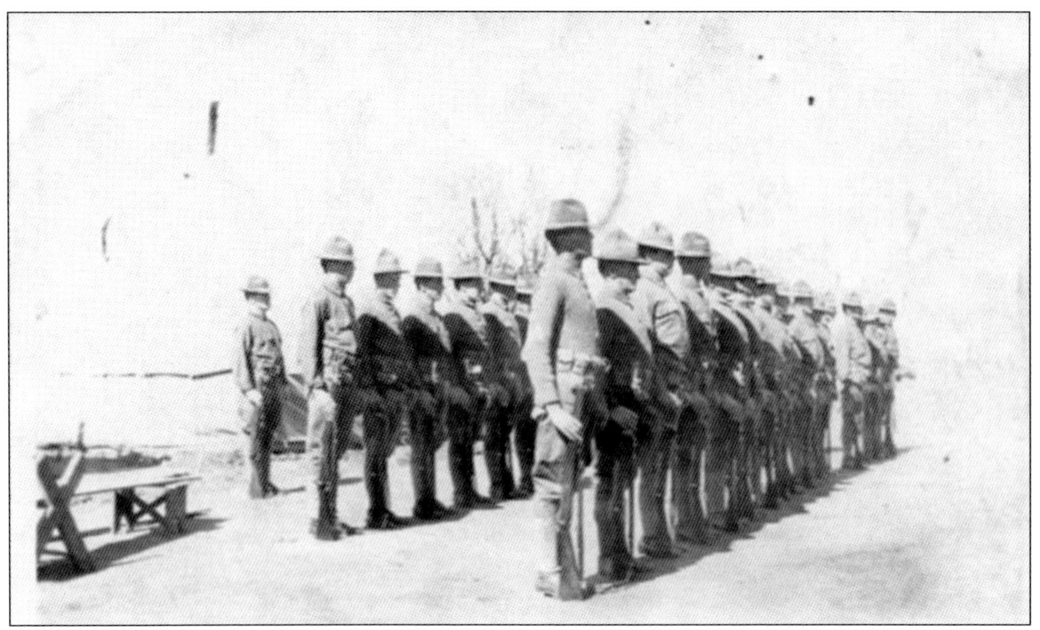

Lt. Elmer Nelson Griggs (1890–1975) and his fellow soldiers of Company F, 1st Regiment, Asheville, are lined up for inspection in a company street. Known as the "Rough and Ready Guards" during wartime, Capt. Edward Fulton Jones (1889–?) was company commander, Griggs served as first lieutenant, and John W. Hunnicutt (1893–?), a lawyer from Asheville, served as second lieutenant. (Courtesy of North Carolina State Archives.)

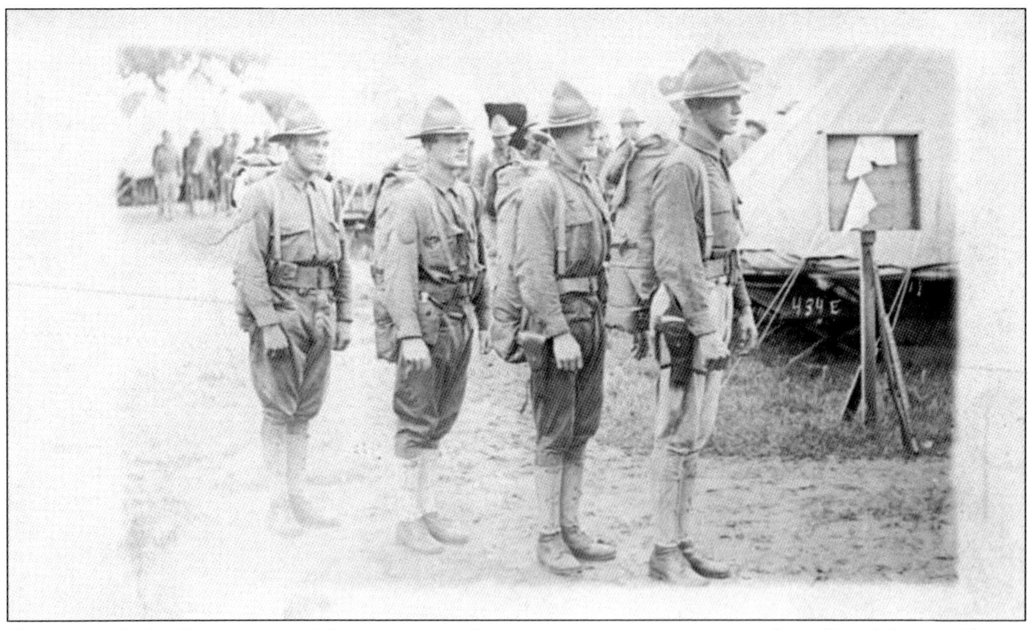

Company F, 1st Regiment, soldiers are standing in a company street and outfitted for a military hike. Sergeant Griggs (second from left) is one of the troop members. Griggs fought in World War I and was promoted to lieutenant while serving. Griggs was gassed in 1919 while fighting overseas, and after a long recovery in an overseas hospital, he returned home to Asheville and civilian life. (Courtesy of North Carolina State Archives.)

*Four*

# Camp Life

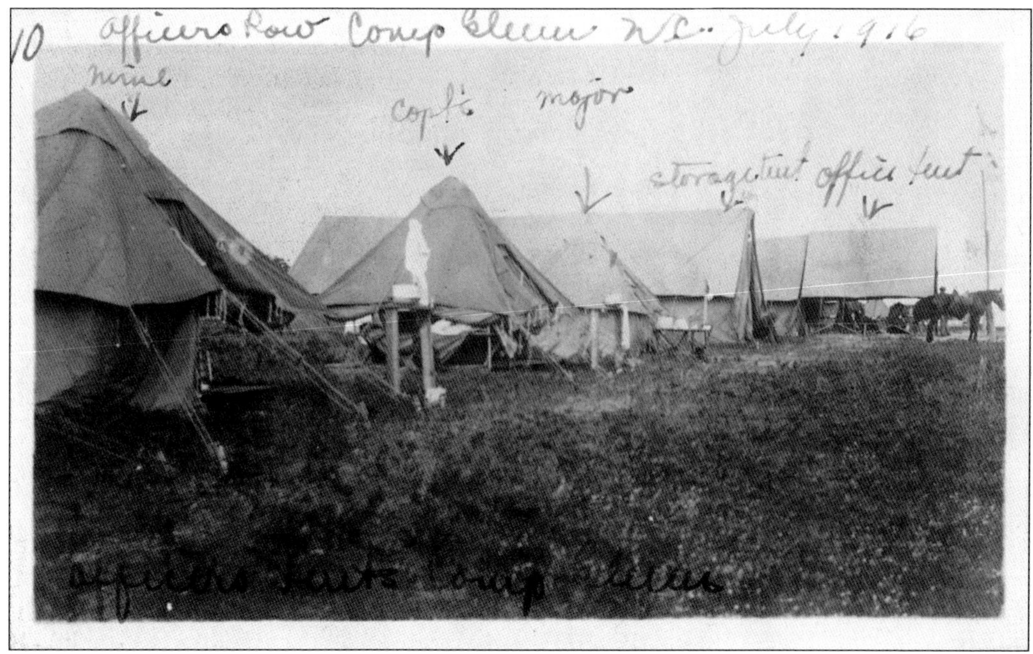


In this photograph, taken in July 1916, Lt. H.B. Hiatt identifies five tents that make up "Officers Row." From left to right, the tents were assigned to Hiatt, other officers in the Sanitary Corps, and Maj. F.J. Clemenger, commander, Field Hospital Company No. 1. A storage tent, an officers' tent, and a saddled horse are shown (right). (Courtesy of ECU.)

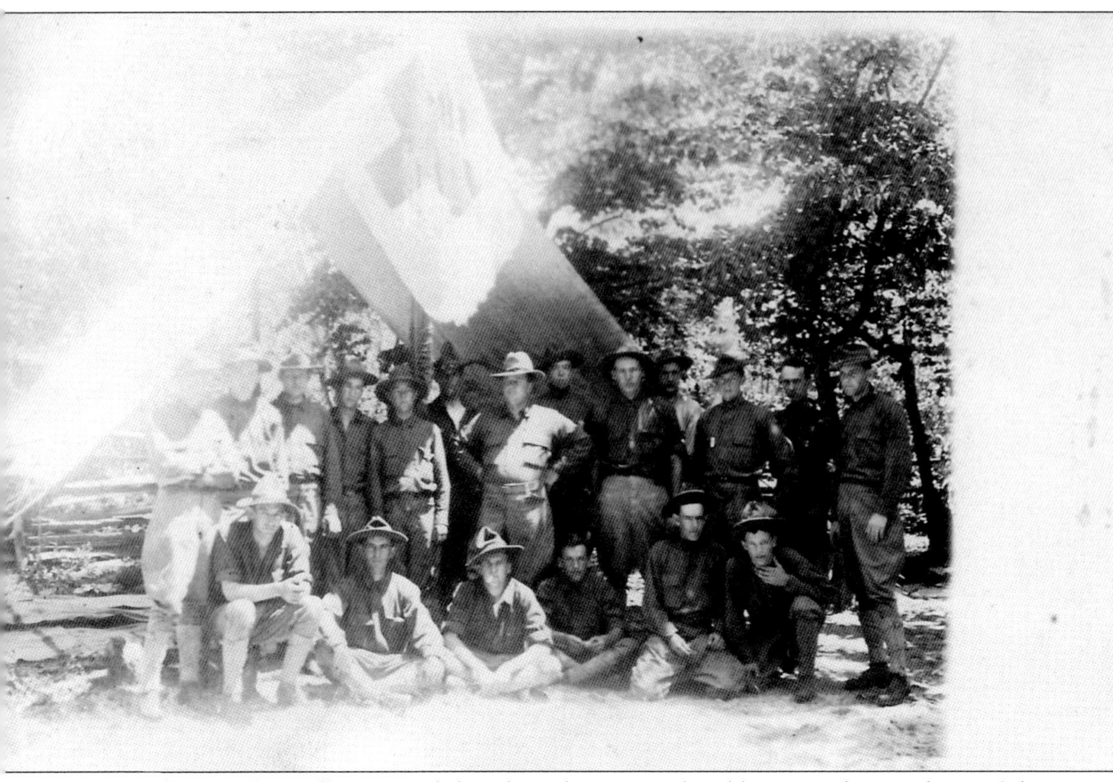

Lt. John MacConnell, seen with hands on hips, is with soldiers standing in front of the camp's hospital tent. MacConnell delivered a short lecture during the 1916 summer encampment to the state and post officers on subjects relating to personal and camp hygiene. As a civilian, MacConnell was a professor at Davidson College, and though he claimed he was not a lecturer, he believed "much good can come of lectures on sanitation and military tactics." Soldiers were mostly free from sickness; though, some men were temporarily on the sick list because of typhoid and smallpox vaccinations. Other complaints treated were digestive tract disorders, sunburn, mosquito bites, and injured feet from stepping on oystershells in Bogue Sound. MacConnell suggested in his report that there should be more time for recreation and pleasure, "as we had absolutely none, as none of us left the camp once."

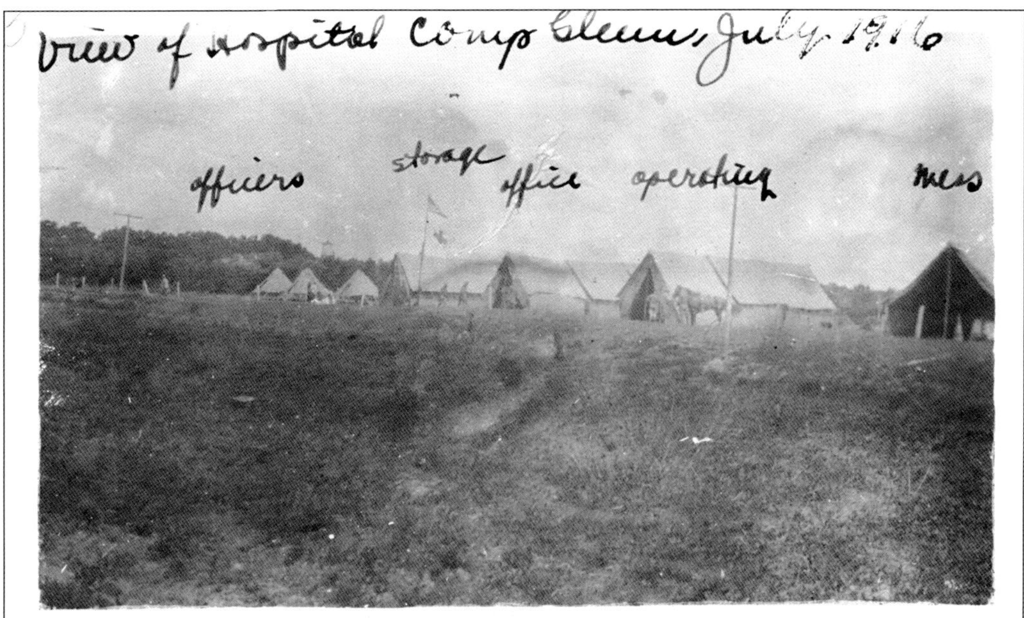


Field Hospital Company No. 1, Asheville, and Ambulance Corps No. 1, Canton, mobilized in July 1916 to prepare for war with Mexico. The hospital had a fully equipped operating room, dispensary, and ward with 25 cots. When first set up, medical supplies were insufficient, and medical staff bought medicines from Morehead Drug Company. Two mess shacks were built for the medical company in 1916. (Courtesy of ECU.)

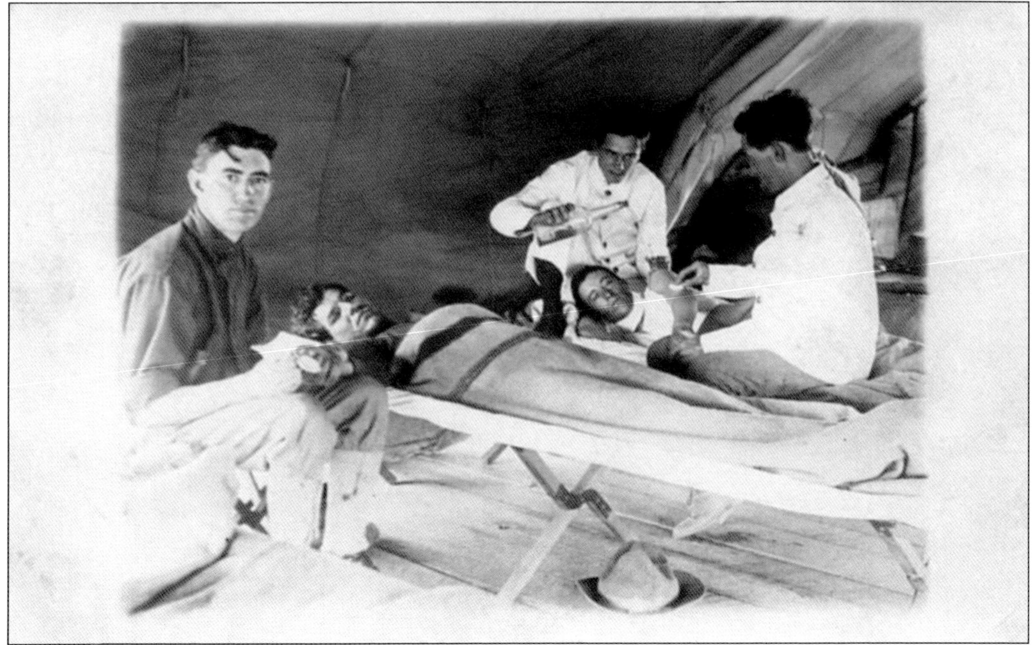

A postcard by Bayard Wootten shows two unidentified soldiers, Company F, 1st Regiment, Asheville, lying on Army cots in Camp Glenn's hospital receiving medical attention from military medical staff. The photograph was taken while Sgt. Elmer Griggs was serving with these soldiers at the time of their hospital stay. (Courtesy of North Carolina State Archives.)

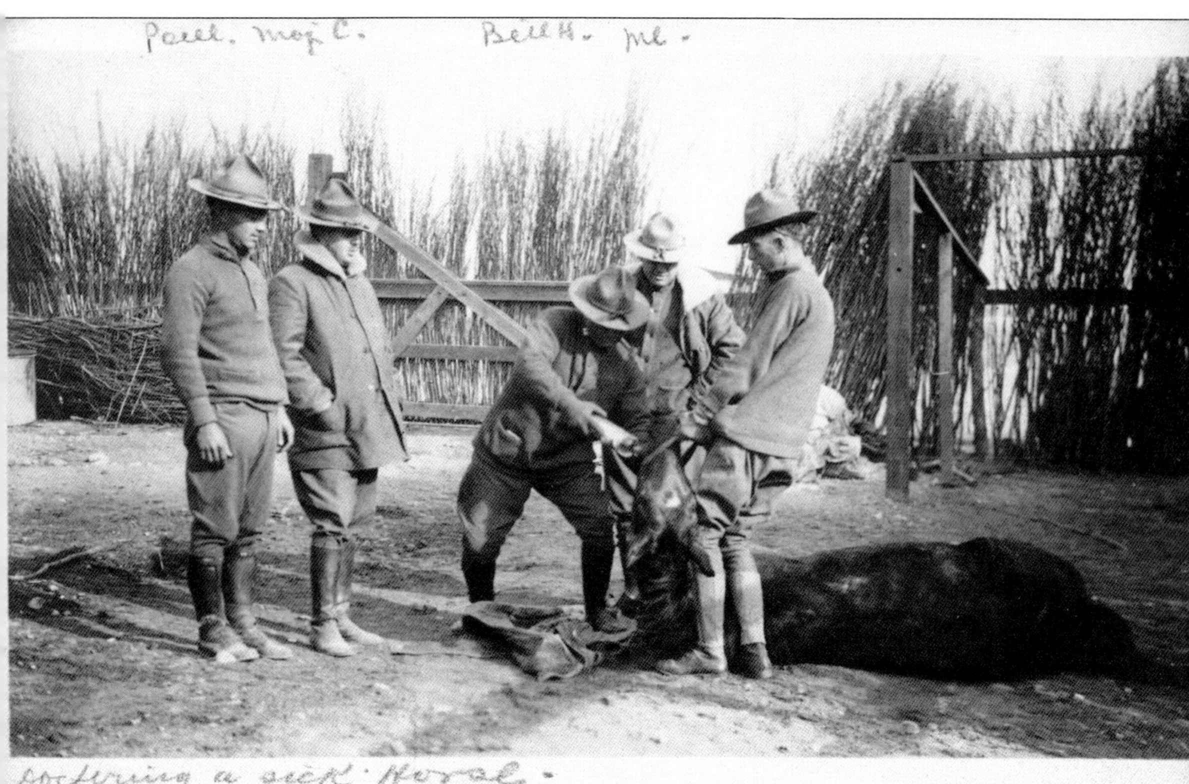


Officers from the medical detachment are shown at the corral assisting the troops' veterinarian in "doctoring a sick horse." The Veterinary Corps was established in June 1916 with the National Defense Act, and at the beginning of World War I, there were 72 veterinary officers and no enlisted men. In 1916, the Veterinary Corps, New Bern, had only one soldier, an officer, who was assigned to the Sanitary Detachment. Since there was only one member in this detachment, it is likely he called on fellow medical officers to assist in pouring medicine down its throat. It is not known if the horse recovered. From left to right are Sgt. 1st Class Paul Mauney (1897–1987) from Kings Mountain; Maj. F.J. Clemenger; Capt. Billl Horton; Lt. H.B. Hiatt; and another unidentified soldier. (Courtesy of ECU.)

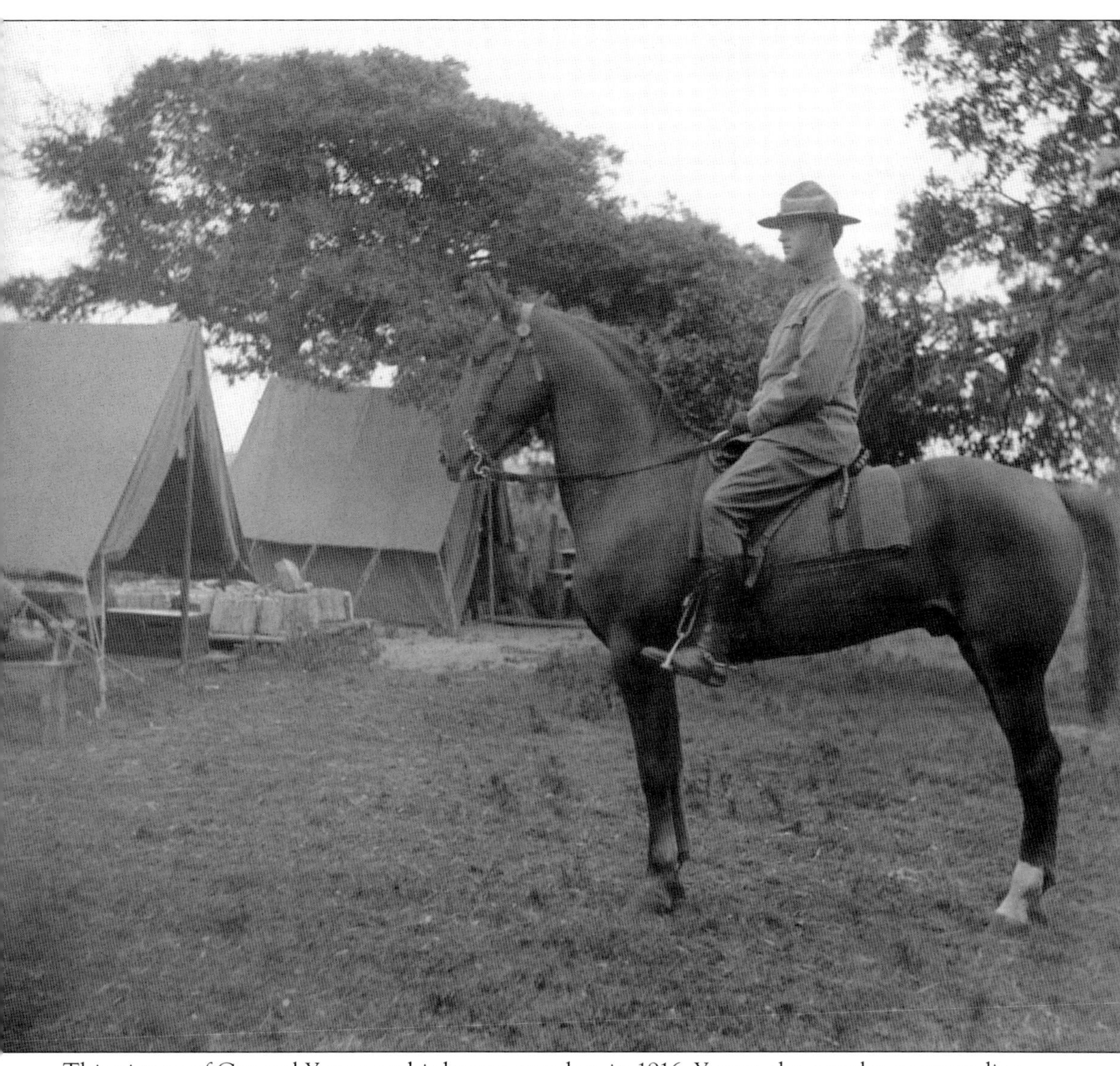

This picture of General Young on his horse was taken in 1916. Young, the popular commanding officer of Camp Glenn, was given this horse in honor of his birthday by his officers of the first North Carolina brigade. Col. S.W. Minor, of the 3rd Infantry, introduced Col. W.C. Rodman, 2nd Infantry, who presented the general with the handsome riding horse named "Sport" that was under the charge of Orderly Yount. General Young accepted the fine animal, declaring that first in his affections was his family, next his brigade, and then a good horse. Afterwards, Young gave a grateful and complimentary speech, declaring, "I know there are men in the brigade who have more ability to command troops than I have but I know there is not one more enthusiastic for the service than I." Then, the band struck up "Dixie," playing while the officers marched back to headquarters. (Courtesy of North Carolina State Archives.)

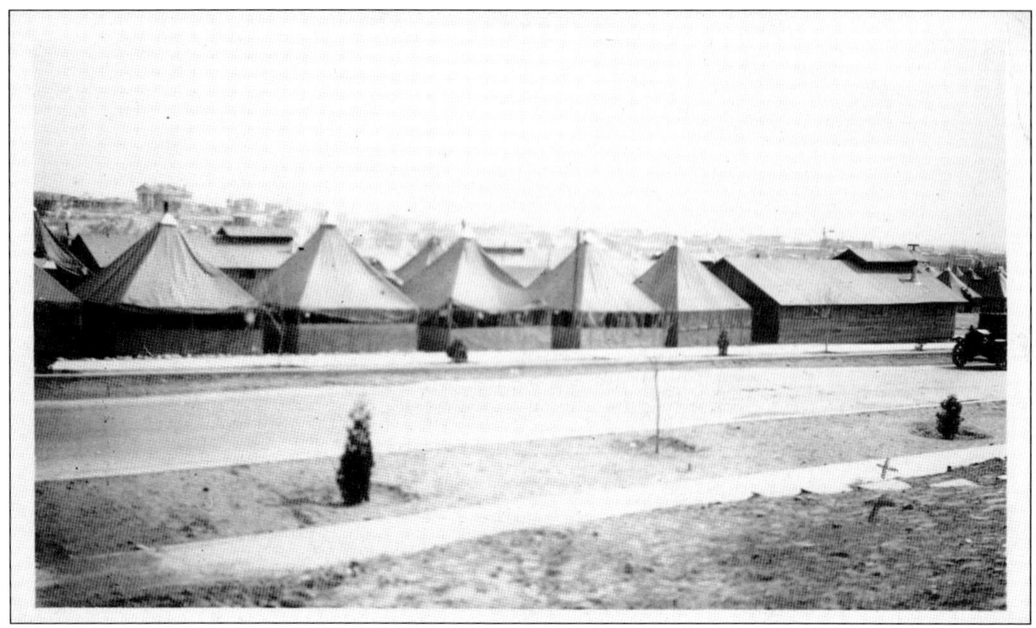

Major camp improvements in 1911 included a new sanitary troops mess pavilion and granolithic driveways and walkways that made more suitable and necessary pathways for walking and wagon service because the sand was deep and heavy. Built for the hospital and ambulance corps, two new mess shacks are depicted here. (Courtesy of ECU.)

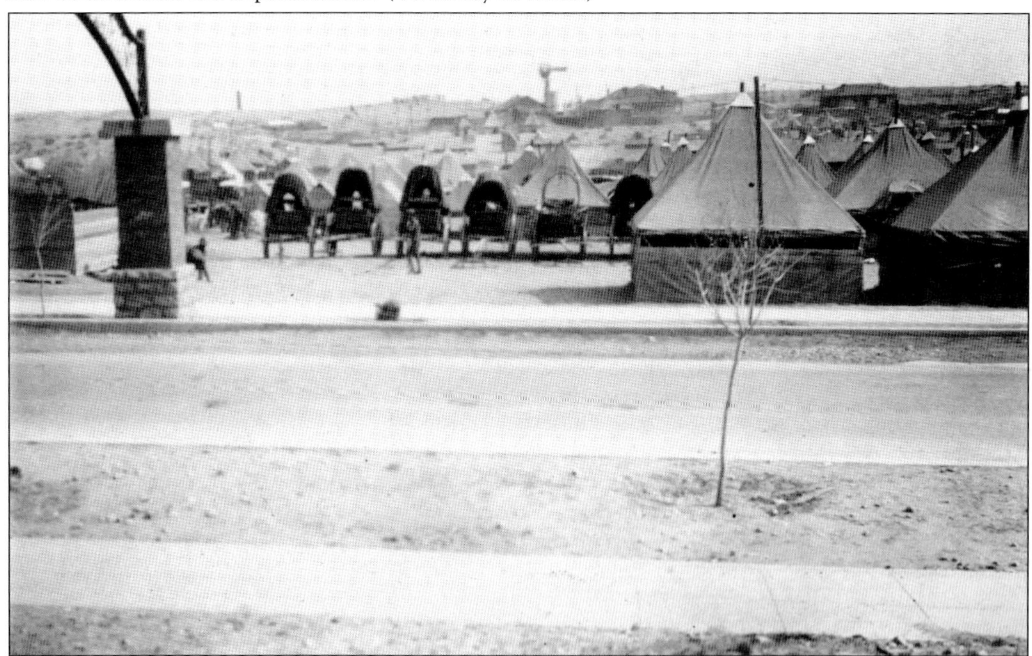

Wagons and tents are shown along with the newly constructed granolithic sidewalks. In 1916, Col. Thomas B. Whitted (1875–1935), chief of engineers, hired two wagonmakers from Charlotte to assemble an entire stock of wagons stored at Camp Glenn. Carpenters, placed in charge of civilians crews and enlisted men, worked diligently constructing wagons and buildings—not stopping even when a terrific storm blew up, soaking them to the skin. (Courtesy of ECU.)

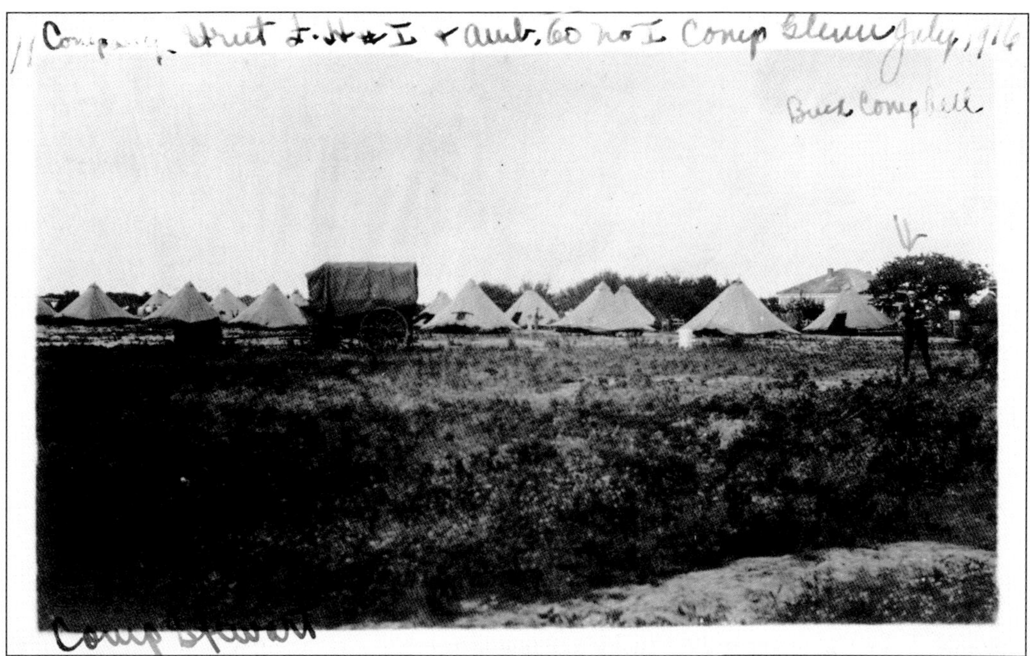


Companies F, Asheville; H, Waynesville; and I, Mount Airy, 1st Regiment occupied the company street in this photograph, taken by Lieutenant Hiatt. Though Camp Stewart is noted in the bottom left corner, this scene is located at Camp Glenn. The arrow pointing to Buck Campbell was Capt. Reuben A. Campbell, Statesville, a surgeon with the Hospital Corps. (Courtesy of ECU.)

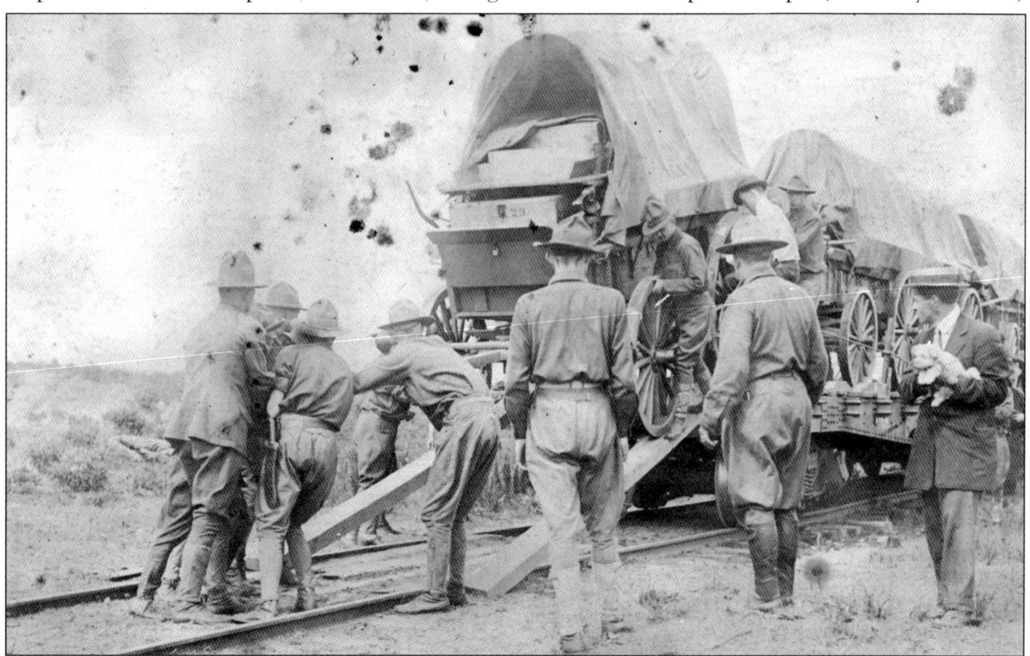

Soldiers are unloading hospital wagons filled with medical supplies from a flat train car at Camp Glenn on June 26, 1916. Ambulance Corps arrived at Camp Glenn to three telegrams from the War Department asking that "the preparations be hurried and rushed to completion as quick as possible." (Courtesy of ECU.)

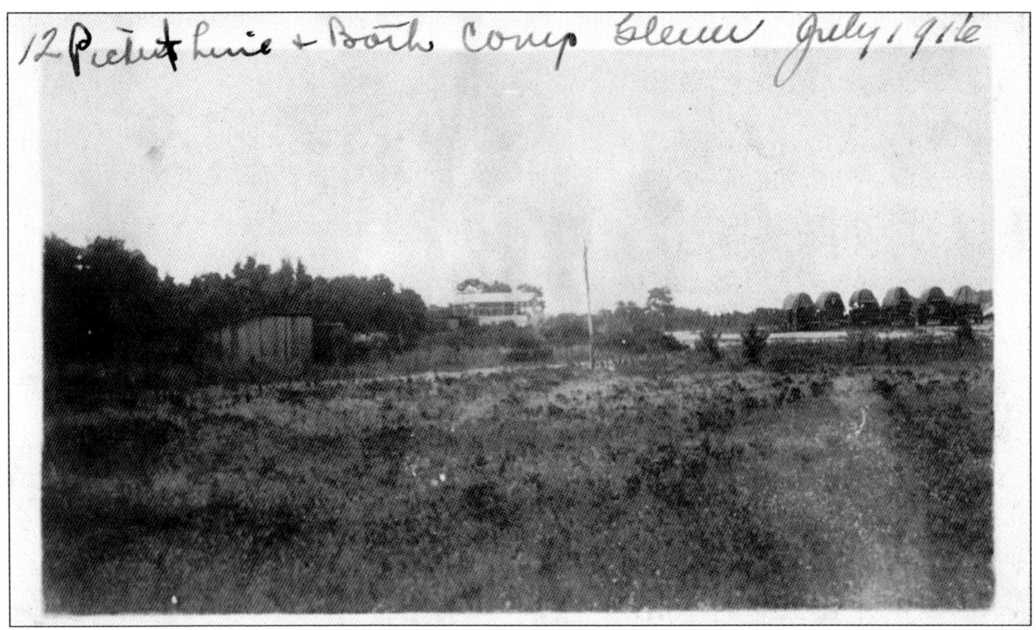


The open bathhouse, constructed in 1916, accommodated the Hospital and Ambulance Corps and other companies. The picket line shown was used by the Hospital and Ambulance Corps to tether horses and mules. Picket line care required broom sweeping daily and disposal of all manure and straw hauled to city dumps and burned weekly to prevent flies and mosquitoes from breeding. (Courtesy of ECU.)

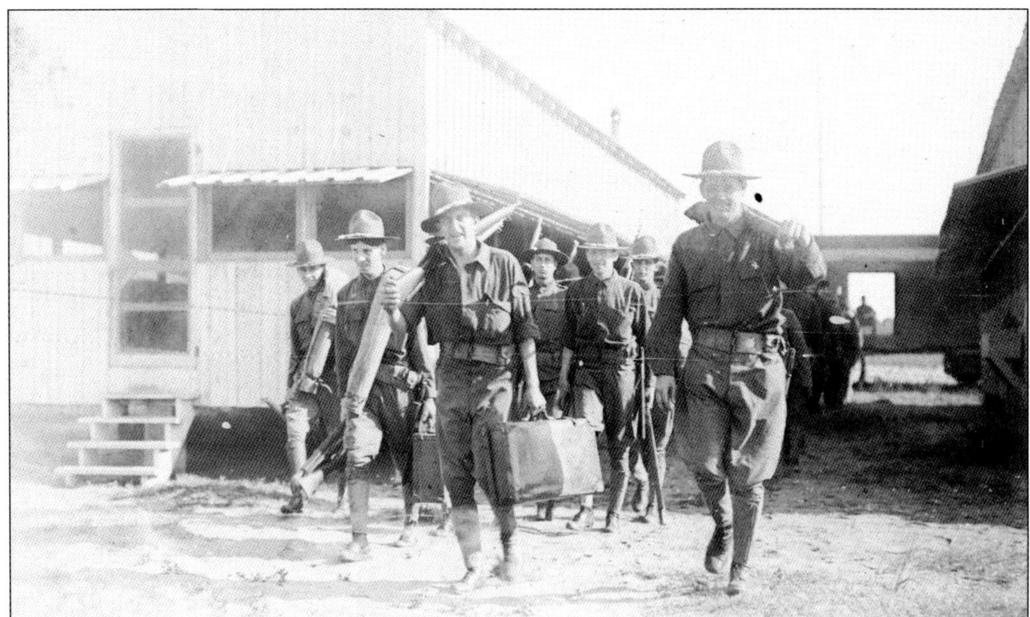

Company A, 1st Infantry, Hickory, soldiers are heading toward their barracks with baggage, bedrolls, and rifles in hand. This postcard, stamped July 30, 1914, was sent to Freddie Hoover, Route 1, Hickory, from Garland Miller. The message reads, "This is a picture of our company going to [illegible] street just after you get off the train." (Courtesy of the University of North Carolina at Chapel Hill.)

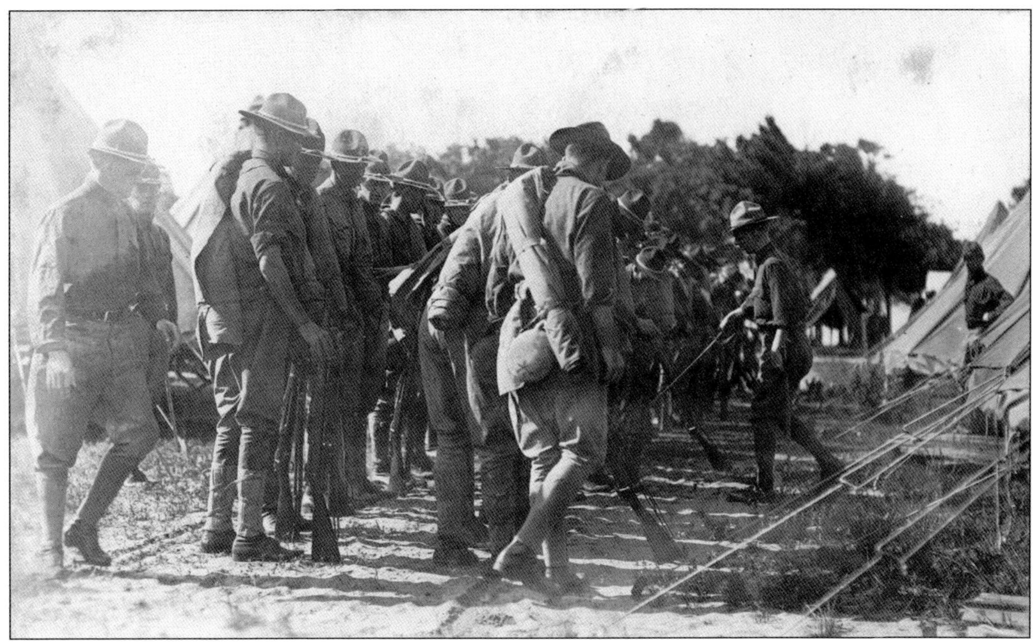

Company A Hickory soldiers, carrying bedrolls and rifles, are preparing for inspection in a company street between tents after their arrival in 1914. This inspection took place after the tents were erected and the cots were arranged in orderly rows. All of this took place under the supervision of the officers. (Courtesy of the University of North Carolina at Chapel Hill.)

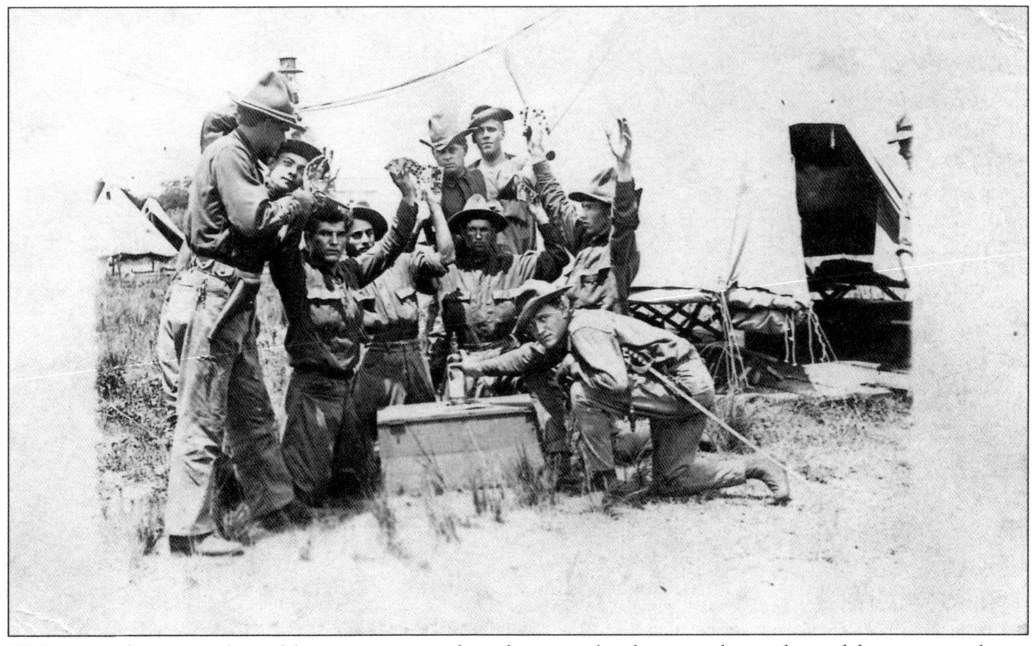

This staged scene of a soldier pointing a handgun and others with cards and liquor may have prompted Col. J.T. Gardner, 1st Regiment, to give the following notice at officer's call: "Hereafter, anyone in the regiment receiving liquor of any kind from the express office, or otherwise, and introducing it into camp will have his name posted on the bulletin board."

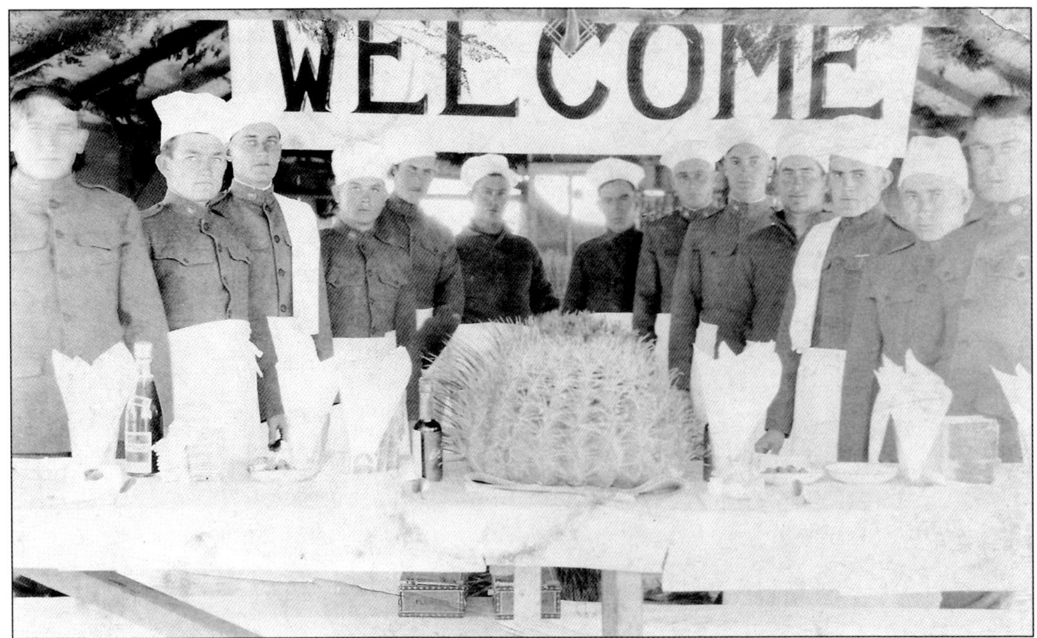


Each regiment had its own mess hall accommodating 12 troops and a band. It appears that the mess crew is serving up a meal of barrel cactus that may have been brought back by Camp Glenn troops who fought in the Mexican Border War. Bottles of ketchup are also supplied. The card's back reads, "Clarence Howell, 3rd Reg, North Carolina State Guard."

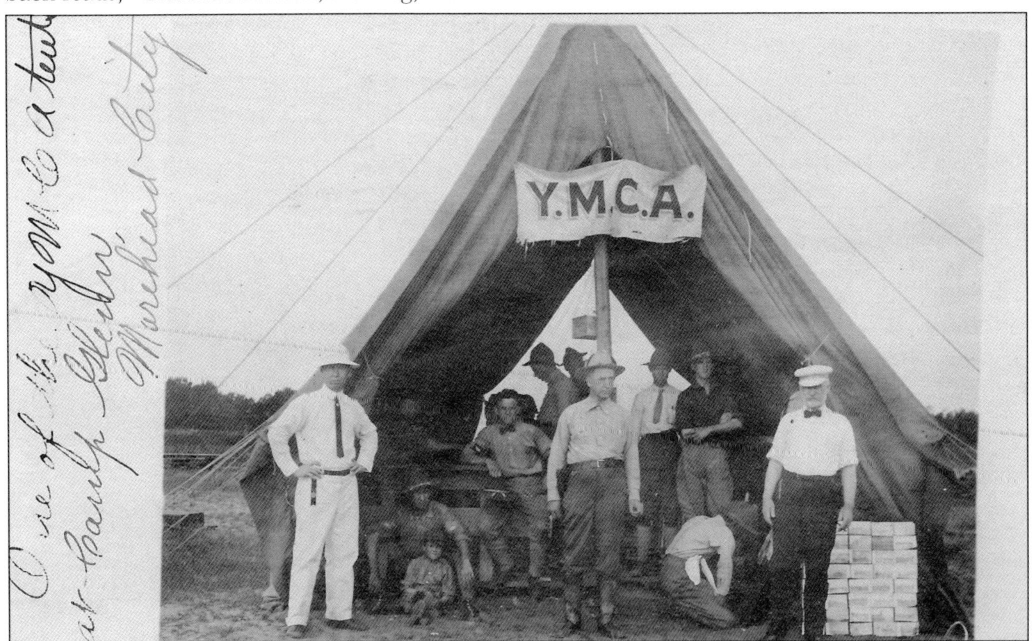


The message on this postcard reads, "One of the Y.M.C.A. tents at Camp Glenn, Morehead City" and shows soldiers and civilians. The YMCA provided writing materials, magazines, newspapers, and games for soldiers' leisure time. Stamps and postal cards, such as the ones shown attached to a board, were sold. Sunday church services held here using a fold-in organ. Motion pictures shown instructed young recruits in warfare. (Courtesy of Linda Willis Sadler.)

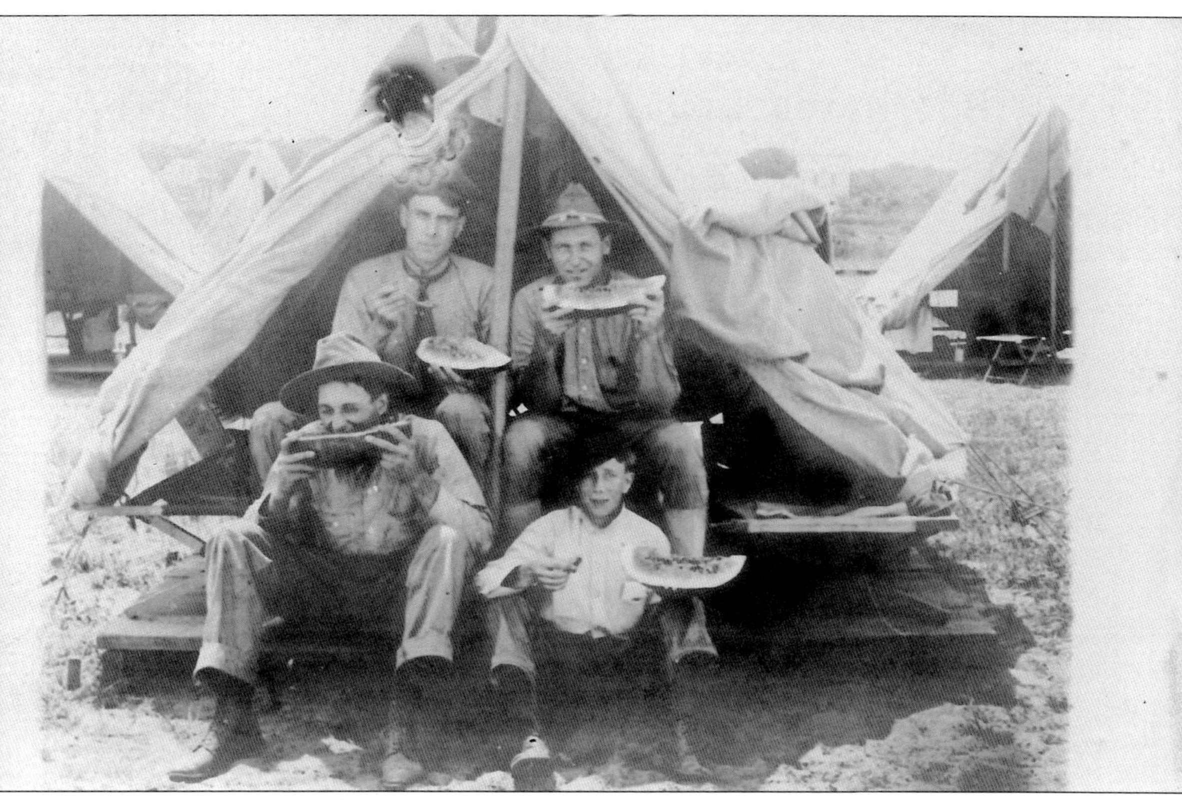

Soldiers and a young friend enjoy a watermelon on a hot summer day during camp. Grown locally and known as the Bogue Sound watermelon, it was a favorite of locals and visiting soldiers. The watermelon was also described as "a luscious treat" on sailing parties. When Camp Glenn held competitive races, the winner's prize was often a Bogue Sound watermelon. After local farmers complained of missing watermelons and blamed soldiers for the theft, camp commanders posted armed guards to prevent marauders from plundering the patch. Though there were times when soldiers were the guilty ones, some of the culprits were local thieves. Once, when General Young and another officer were out inspecting the posting of the guards, both officers were arrested by a guard who thought they were a little too close to the melon patch. After a short argument, the guard was persuaded that neither officer came near the patch with malicious intent. (Courtesy of Linda Willis Sadler.)

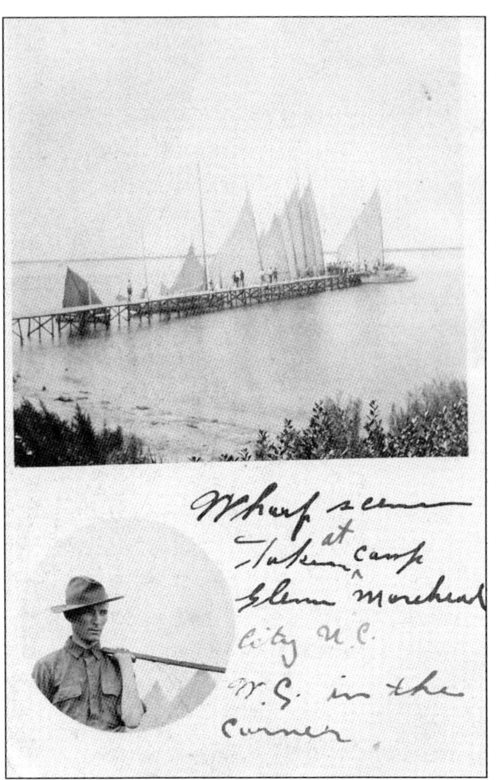


Sailboats lined up along the pier on Bogue Sound are seen along with a message on the postcard's front, "Wharf scene Taken at Camp Glenn Morehead City N.C., W. S. in the corner." Sailing parties for soldiers, their families, and friends were some of the recreational activities that were enjoyed during summer encampments. (Courtesy of Linda Willis Sadler.)

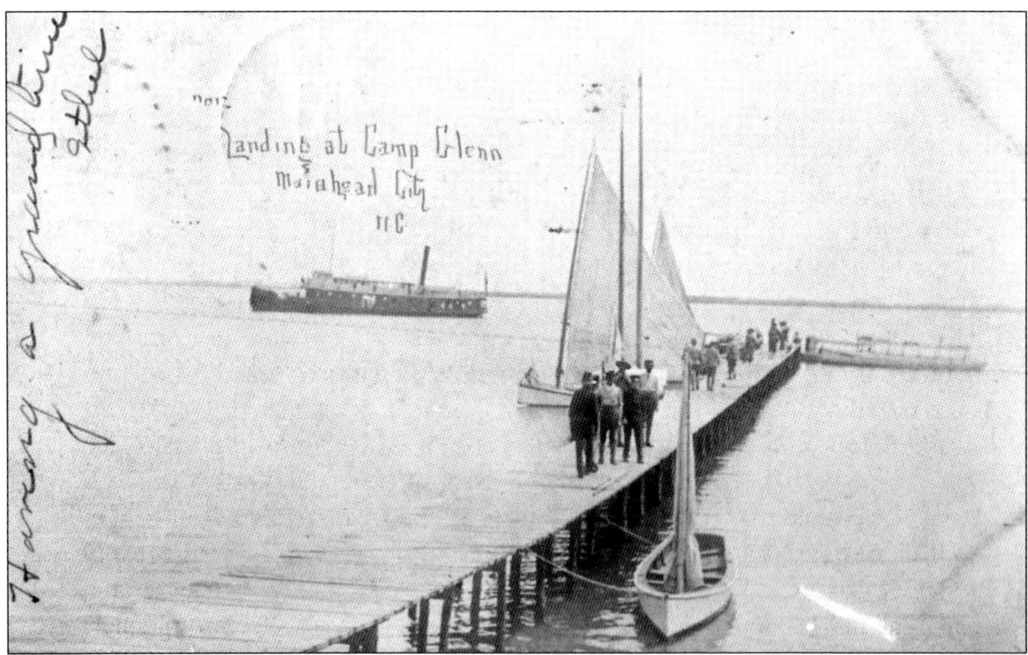


This postcard from Ethel to an unknown person reads, "Having a grand time." It appears that Ethel, a visitor, may have taken part in one of the sailing cruises along Bogue Sound during her stay at Camp Glenn. The scene shows the camp's dock and soldiers with sailboats and a tugboat. (Courtesy of North Carolina State Archives.)

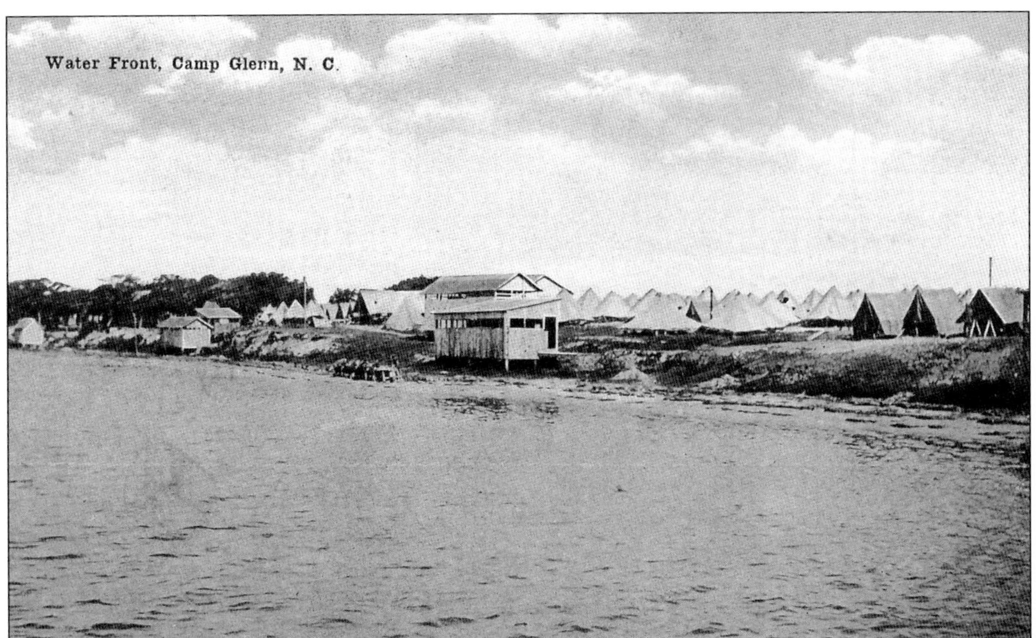


This picturesque view of Camp Glenn along Bogue Sound's narrow shoreline shows tents and buildings—one of which could be a mess hall or kitchen. A group of soldiers can be seen at the water's edge working on an unknown project. Though soldiers enjoyed swimming in the sound, they risked cuts from oystershells found along the shore. (Courtesy of Linda Willis Sadler.)

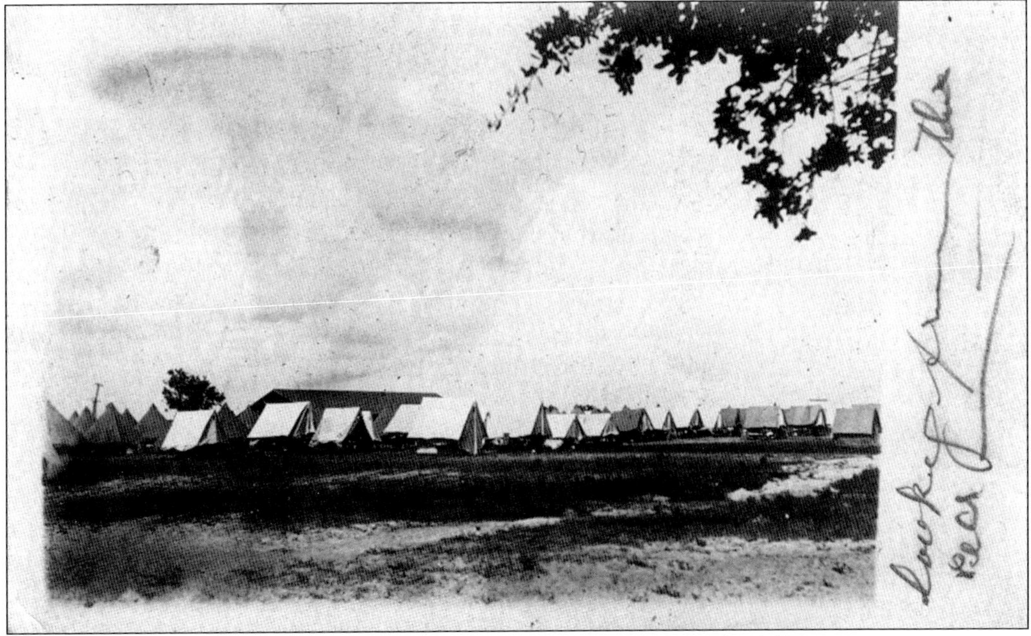

This postcard shows tents lined up along a company street and has the following message written on front: "Lookey from the . . . [illegible]." Two officers slept in wall tents, like the ones shown here, and as many as eight enlisted men slept in the conical tents, shown behind the wall tents. A wagon path runs along the front of the tents. (Courtesy of the University of North Carolina at Chapel Hill.)

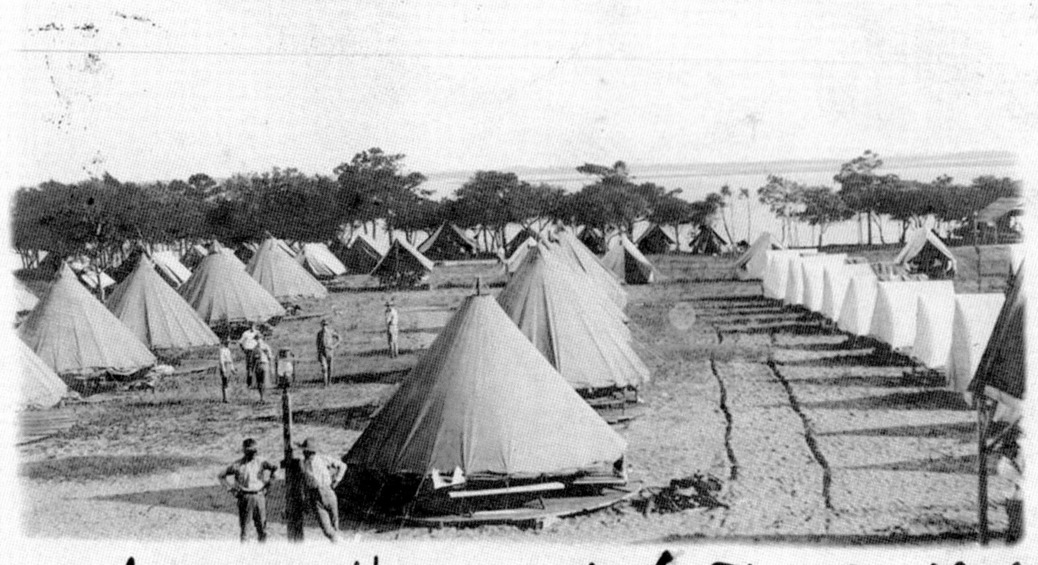


A 1909 postcard shows conical and wall tents lined on Bogue Sound with soldiers in the streets. Two men are leaning against a lamppost. Strong coastal storms kept the men busy pegging down and resetting tents. In 1916, a summer storm blew in after midnight, and a stiff gale wind blew all day. Though a few tents were blown down, not much damage was done due to the men's close attention to ropes and pegs. Later that summer, when another storm hit, soldiers in one tent did not get off so lightly. Henry K. Ennis, Samuel Miller, and Sherrill Wilson Company E, 1st Infantry, Statesville, were lounging on their cots when lightning struck the tent's center pole, breaking it in half and destroying the tent. Miller and Wilson made it out of the tent; they immediately turned around and went back to rescue their friend, Ennis, who was stunned by the bolt but not seriously hurt. That was the first time a tent was struck by lightning at camp. (Courtesy of the University of North Carolina at Chapel Hill.)

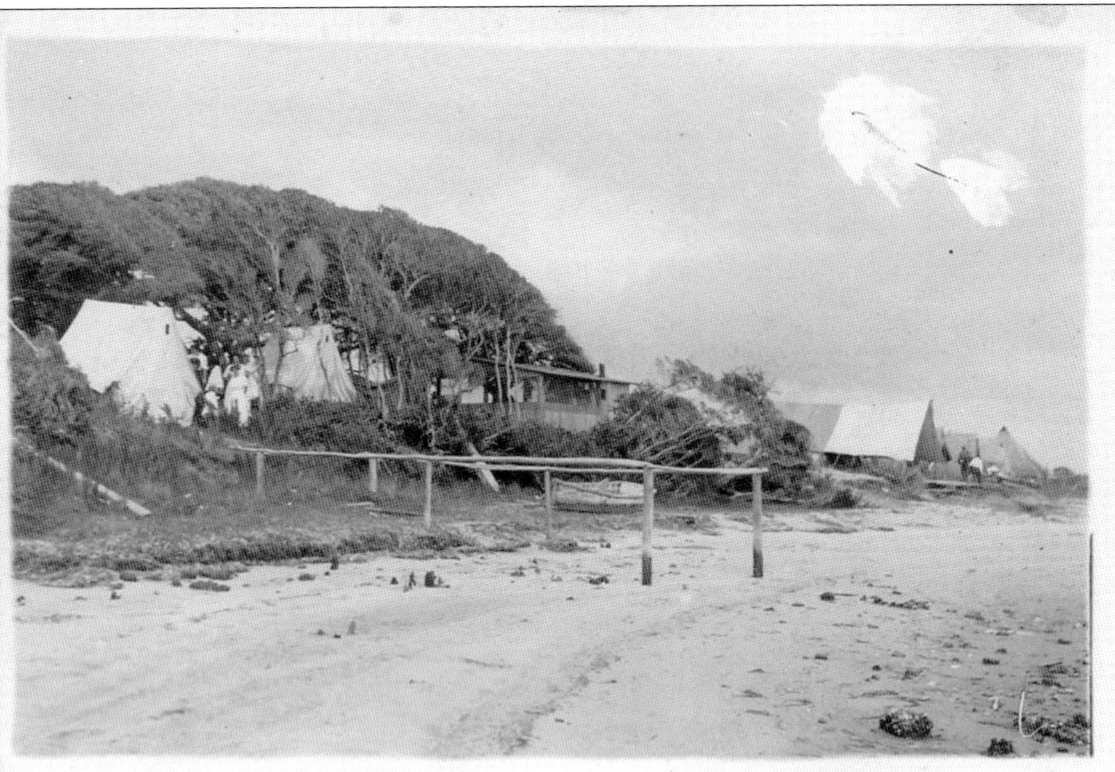

In 1909, the wooded bluff with its live oak trees along Bogue Sound's waterfront was a hotly debated subject among Camp Glenn troops. Critics claimed the bluff blocked refreshing sea breezes, which was one of the important factors for choosing Morehead City as the National Guard's permanent encampment. Bluff defenders countered that it was one of the camp's most attractive and redeeming features; however, they acknowledged that the men and their well-being should be the first consideration. It was also claimed that the mosquitoes were worse in camp than at general headquarters because the camp was sheltered from the breezes by the trees. Furthermore, defenders claimed the headquarters' tents shared in any southeasterly breeze obstruction because of the tents' southward site. One suggestion to solve this problem included stretching out the location for the tents along the shore to allow the breeze to freely circulate through to headquarters and the entire camp. (Courtesy of North Carolina State Archives.)

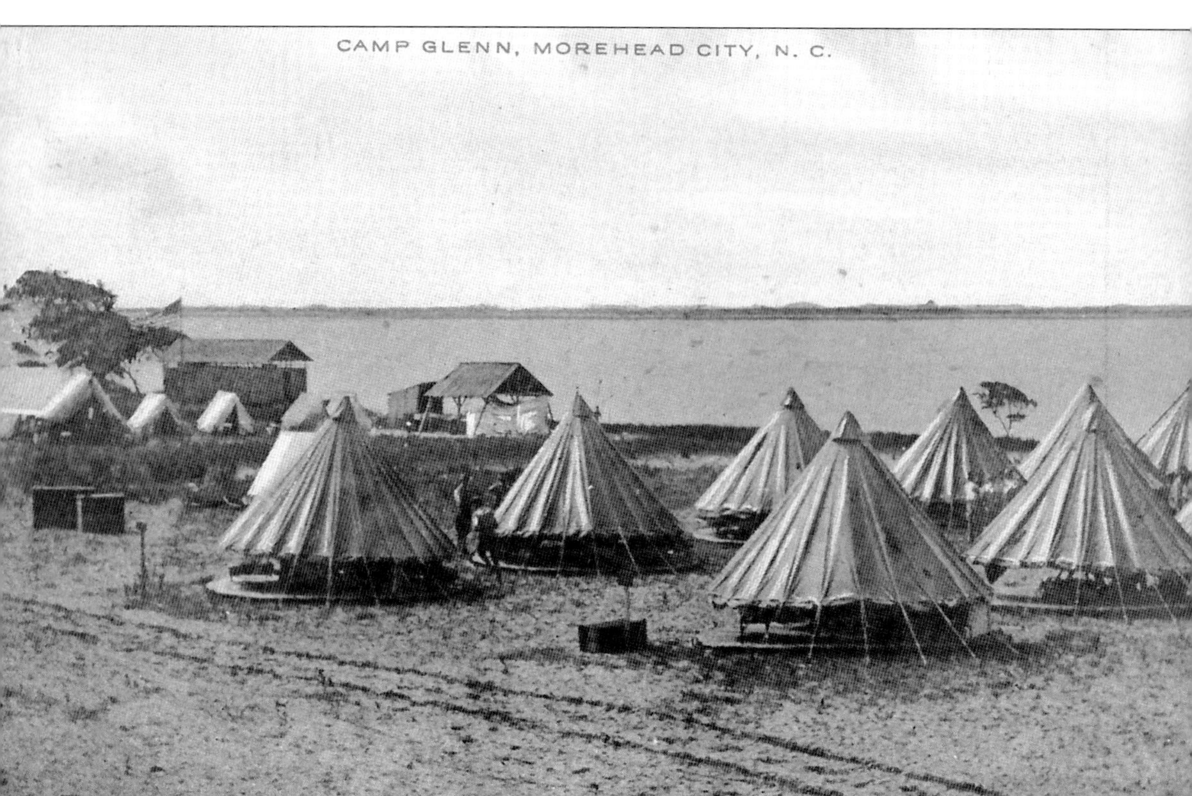


A wagon pathway runs in front of tents pitched along Bogue Sound's shore where the location had the advantage of catching sea breezes helping to keep clouds of mosquitoes at bay. In the *1913 Adjutant General's Report*, Surgeon General Maj. Samuel Westray Battle (1854–1927) noted, "As a whole, I would say it was the most sanitary Encampment I have ever attended, with less sickness and accidents, having only one case of malaria, contracted before leaving Home Station. It is gratifying to note that something is being done each year, looking to a more finished and a more sanitary camp. Something done each year will ultimately bring about the desired result. The breeding place of the mosquito has been ferreted out and all low places have been drained by the efficient authorities in charge of the campgrounds. It is a pity that the campgrounds cannot be enclosed, to prevent the ingress of hogs and cattle, as it is most difficult to keep anything sanitary where the hog has his habitat." (Courtesy of Linda Willis Sadler.)

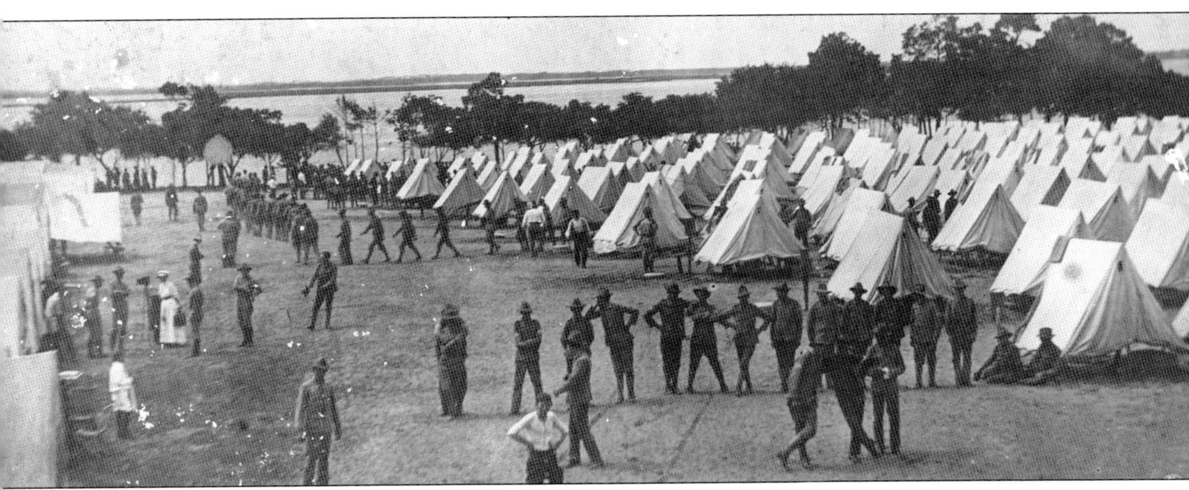

A wide view of Camp Glenn shows shelter tents, soldiers, and Bayard Wootten (left) with her camera setup and ready to take pictures. Bogue Sound is seen in the background. Wootten's half brother and partner, George Moulton, was probably the photographer of this early scene that shows Wootten in a white dress. After Wootten began wearing her khaki uniform in 1908, she was not known to wear any other type of dress during her work sessions at camp. Chief of publicity for the NCNG, she was noted in newspapers, and former commanders recognized her work as "high quality" and necessary for enlistment campaigns and publicity posters. Wootten often said how much she liked her work and her interest in the tar heel soldiers was genuine. She only took photographs, and through this medium, folks back home learned what soldiers' work during summer encampment was about. (Courtesy of the University of North Carolina at Chapel Hill.)

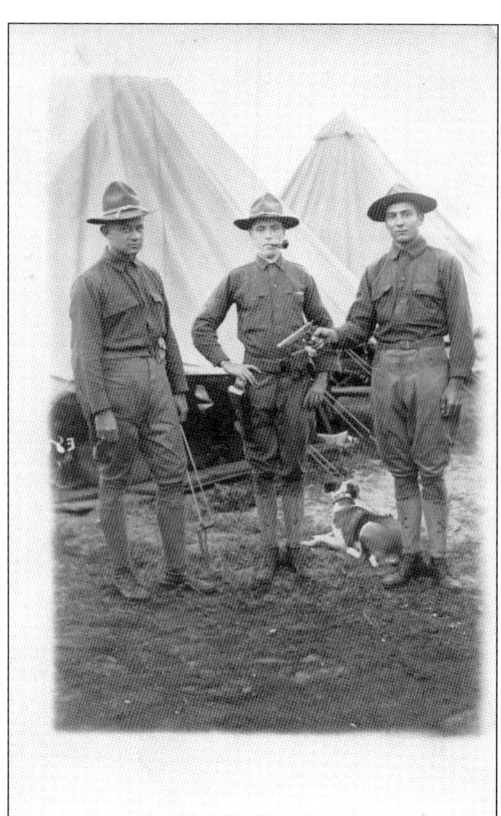

Horseplay often took place in camp and here a soldier is aiming his pistol or maybe just showing it—hopefully, unloaded—at another soldier standing nearby. Meanwhile, a soldier (center) is calmly smoking a pipe while a dog lying on the ground ignores them all. (Courtesy of North Carolina State Archives.)

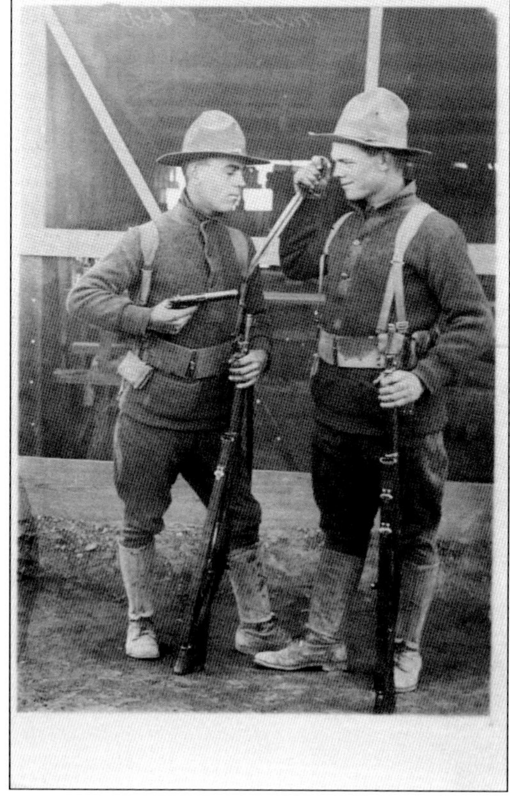

Two soldiers are posing with their rifles outside of Camp Glenn's mess hall. A soldier is aiming his pistol at his companion who in turn is pointing his bayonet at his gun-toting friend while the rifles remain at their sides. A food fight in the mess hall may follow. (Courtesy of North Carolina State Archives.)

This postcard, made from a photograph taken by Bayard Wootten, shows a soldier, Company D, 3rd Infantry, Louisburg, and a dog with a collar and a leash attached to it. It looks like the soldier is holding a medal attached to the dog's collar. (Courtesy of North Carolina State Archives.)

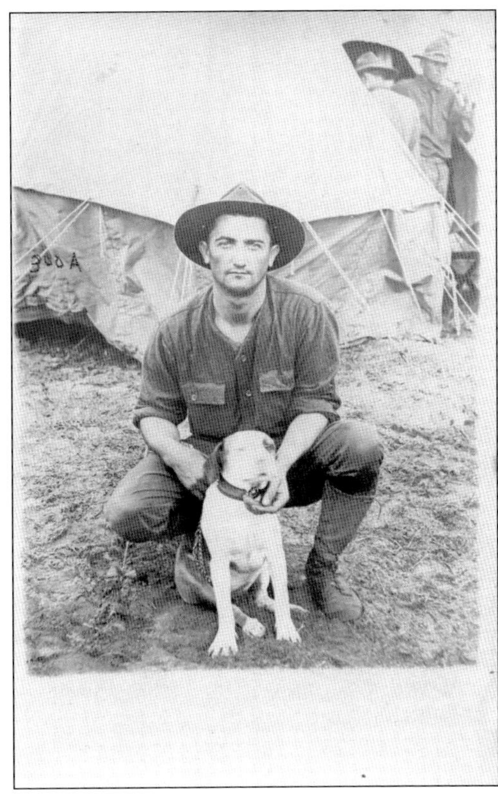

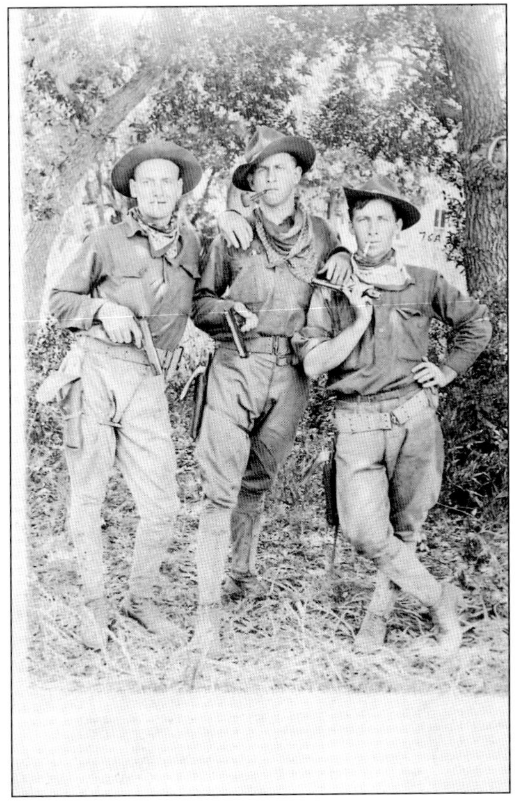

Three soldiers are nonchalantly posing with their sidearms and smoking cigarettes and pipe in the shade of live oak trees. A building, mostly hidden, is shown in the background. Postcards were popular souvenirs with soldiers who sent them back home to friends and family to show what life was about during summer encampment.

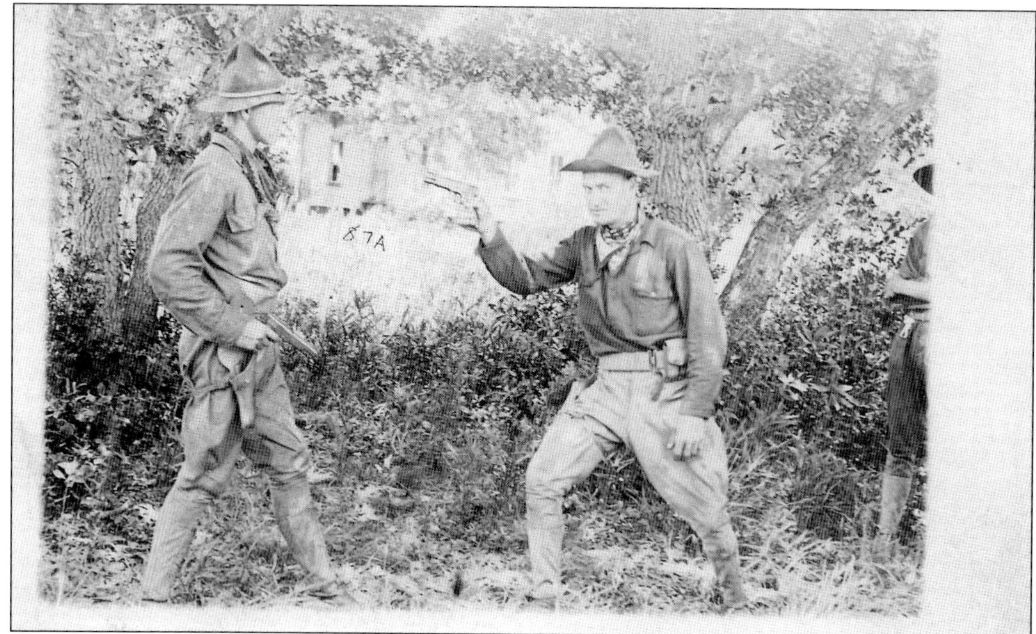


Soldiers draw their guns on one another in what might be a demonstration of what they learned during a mock battle drill. Ambushes were part of mock battles; however, this scene may be more playful and not battle practice. A partially seen soldier (right) is looking on.

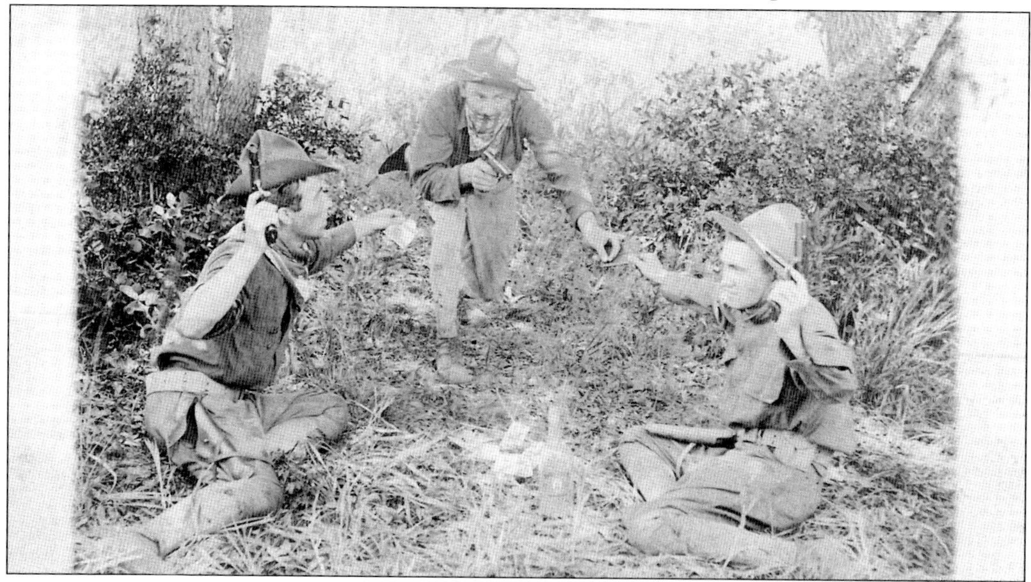

The same three soldiers show up again in a staged hold-up scene. Two soldiers gambling and drinking are robbed by a third who takes their money and a wallet. Note the open bottle of liquor lying on the ground. Soldiers worked hard training during summer encampments, but frequently, Wootten staged scenes like this to show the good times soldiers had during their time at camp. These pictures, as well as the ones of soldiers training on the drill field or on the target practice range, were used as educational propaganda photographs in National Guard recruitment posters. Towns and cities all over North Carolina nailed the posters of Camp Glenn to billboards, which were effective in recruitment efforts.

An enlisted soldier shows off his agility, balance, and coordination by performing a handstand or a backflip as he takes a break from drills and camp duties. This gymnastic maneuver is different from soldiers' typical marching maneuvers practiced on the drill field, and a soldier, or his coach, looking on appears impressed.

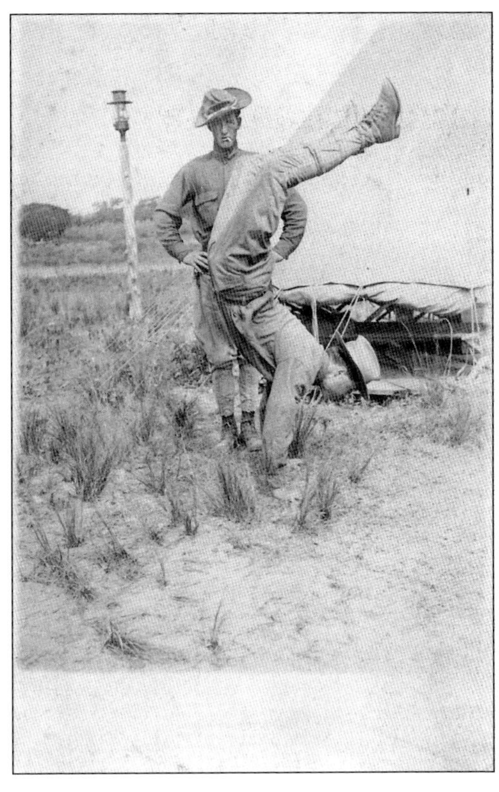

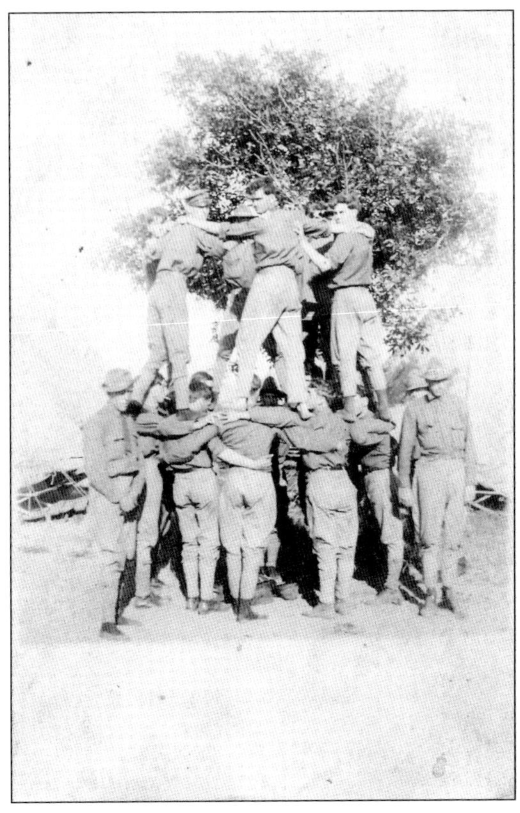

A group of soldiers is displaying an impressive feat of gymnastics in this real-photo postcard. Building a human pyramid took strength, determination, and steadiness, and this is demonstrated as men pose for the camera. During the 1923 encampment, organized games and athletics were part of soldiers' recreational routine during summer training.

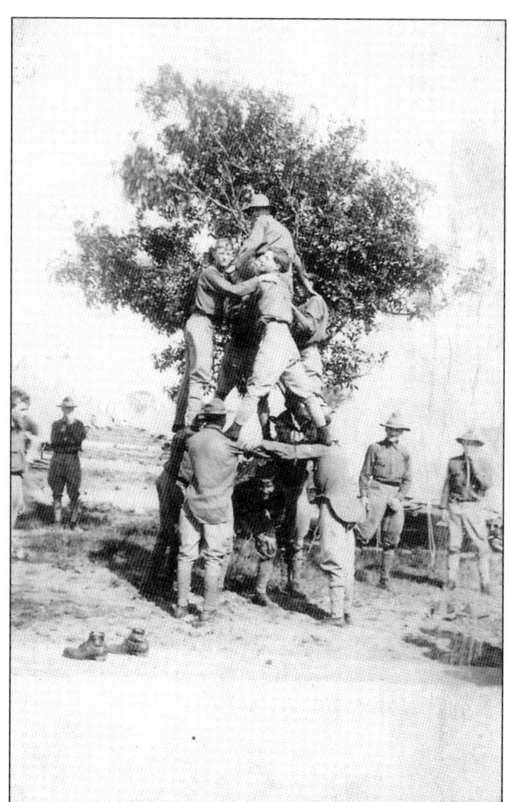

During the 1916 mobilization soldiers already in camp held initiations for the arriving new recruits and troops. Human pyramids were sometimes a part of the initiations, but so were blanket tosses, which placed new recruits in blankets were then flung up into the air several feet. Soldiers' schedules included giving the morning hours to work and the afternoons for recreation, athletics, and as shown here, initiations.

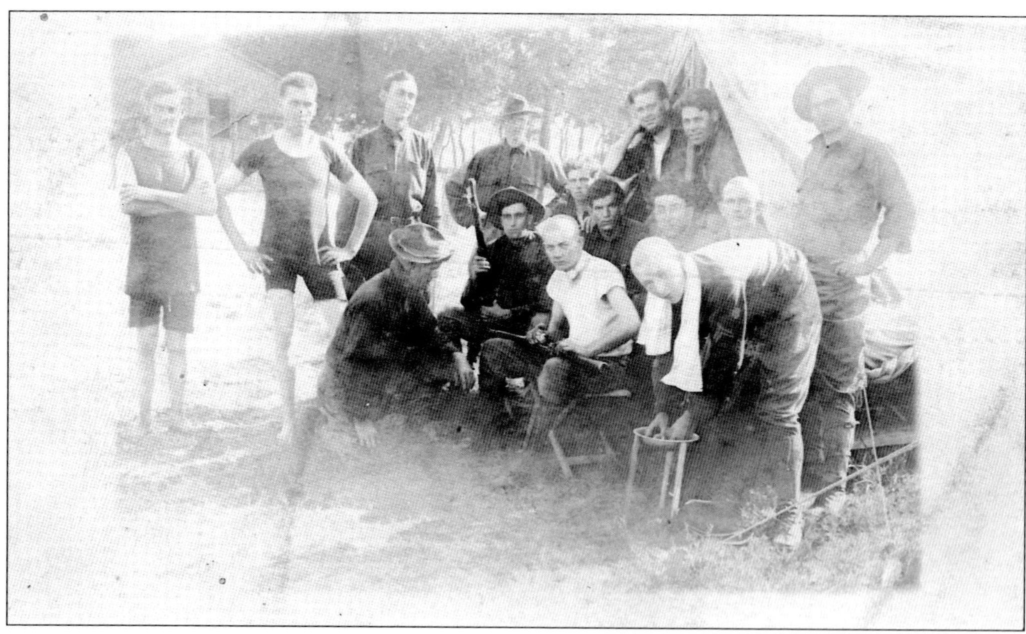

In the early days of camp life, soldiers' bathing routines consisted of using pans of water or washing up in Bogue Sound and risking their feet to oystershell cuts. In 1909, shower facilities and bathrooms were built, and reports that year noted, "The new bathhouses with shower baths added much to the comfort of the regiment."

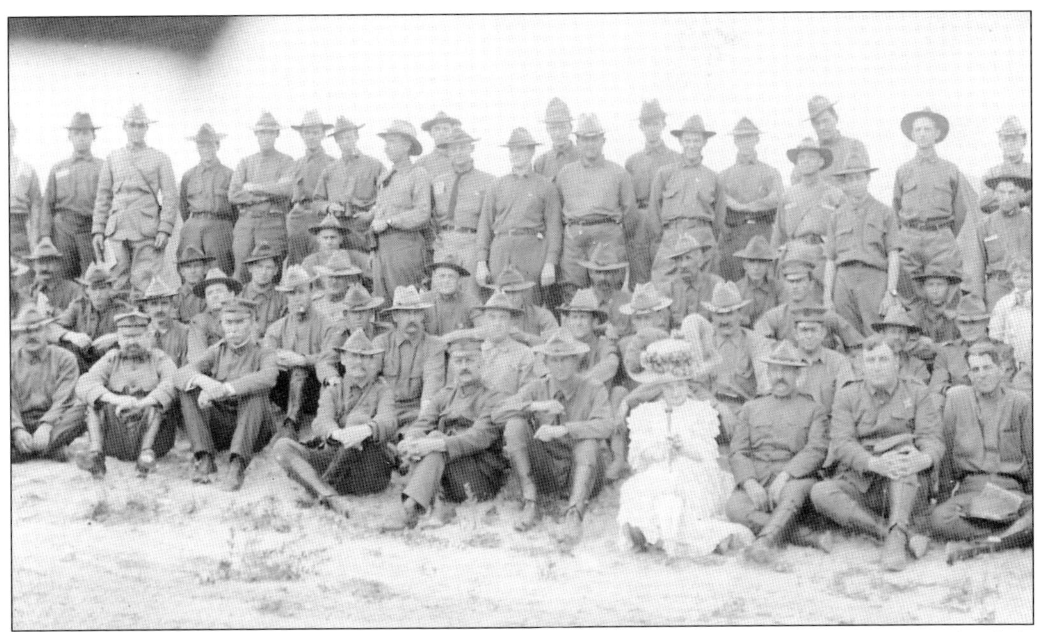

A woman is sitting on the ground dressed in her finery, complete with hat and parasol, while a young boy stands in the row (right) behind her. Soldiers' families and friends were frequent visitors during encampments where they watched dress parades, went surf bathing at the beach, enjoyed sailing parties, and attended military dances and balls at the Atlantic Hotel. (Courtesy of Linda Willis Sadler.)

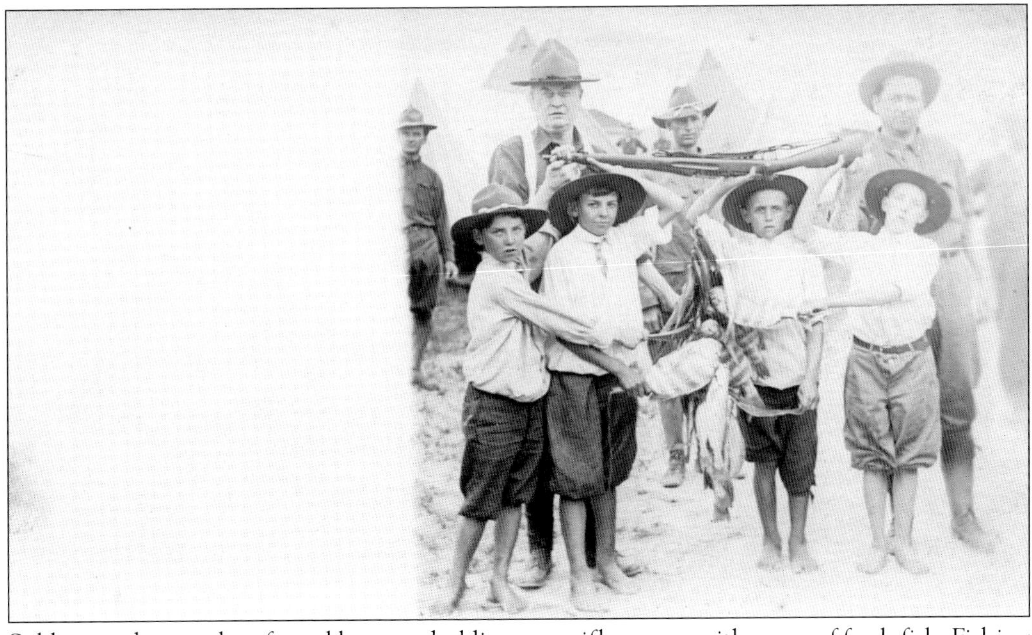

Soldiers and young barefooted boys are holding up a rifle strung with a row of fresh fish. Fishing was a popular summertime activity for both soldiers and their families, and fish were plentiful in nearby Bogue Sound and Atlantic Ocean. In 1906, one soldier reported the following to his hometown newspaper: "A party of our boys were out yesterday and caught enough fish for our whole company." (Courtesy of North Carolina State Archives.)

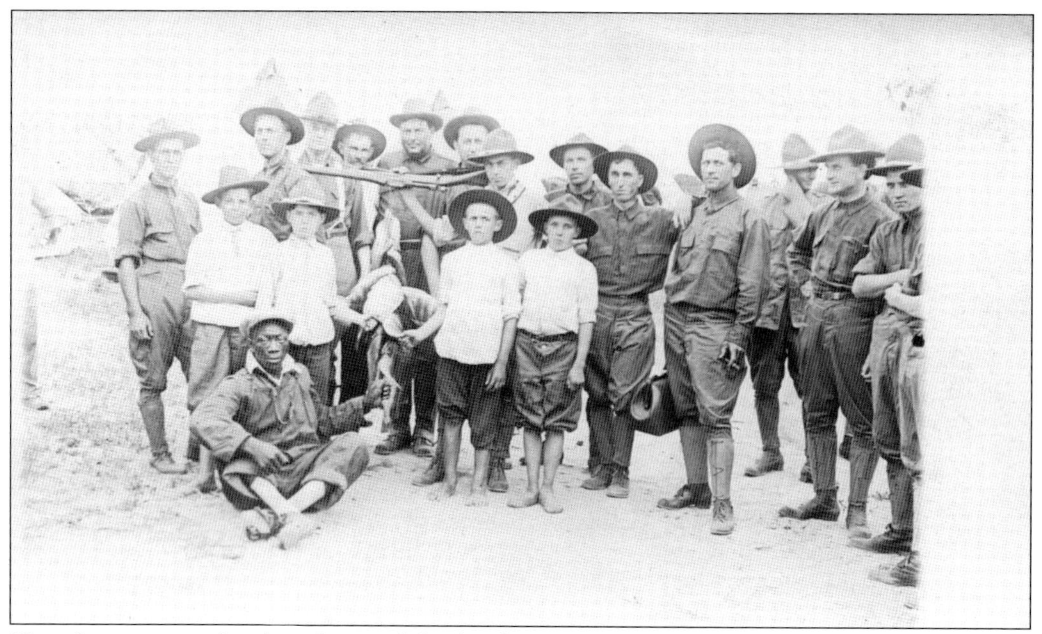

The admiring crowd gathered around the four barefooted boys and their catch of fish is growing, and they all might be looking forward to a fish fry for their next meal. The man sitting on the ground may be a civilian cook employed by the camp. There will be no chance of accusations of "fisherman lies" with this photograph recording the lads' fine catch. (Courtesy of North Carolina State Archives.)

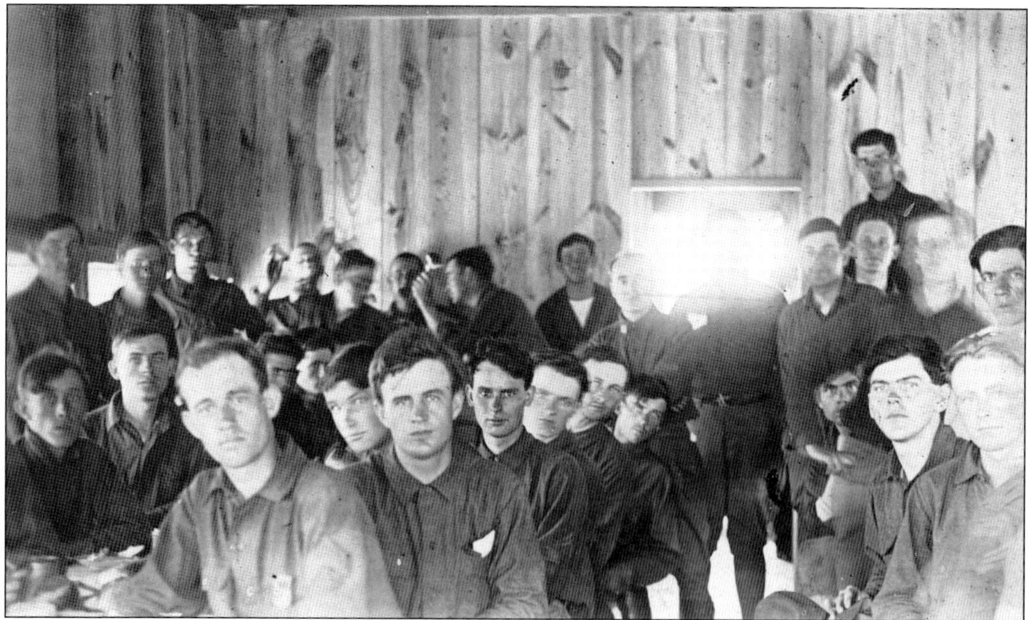

Fifteen modern mess halls were built in 1914, and the old mess hall was moved 300 feet east down the railroad track and converted into a storehouse. Each mess hall had a sanitary water can for drinking water, and eight spigots were placed in each company street so the men could wash up. Wastewater collected in a trough was piped to the sewer. (Courtesy of the University of North Carolina at Chapel Hill.)

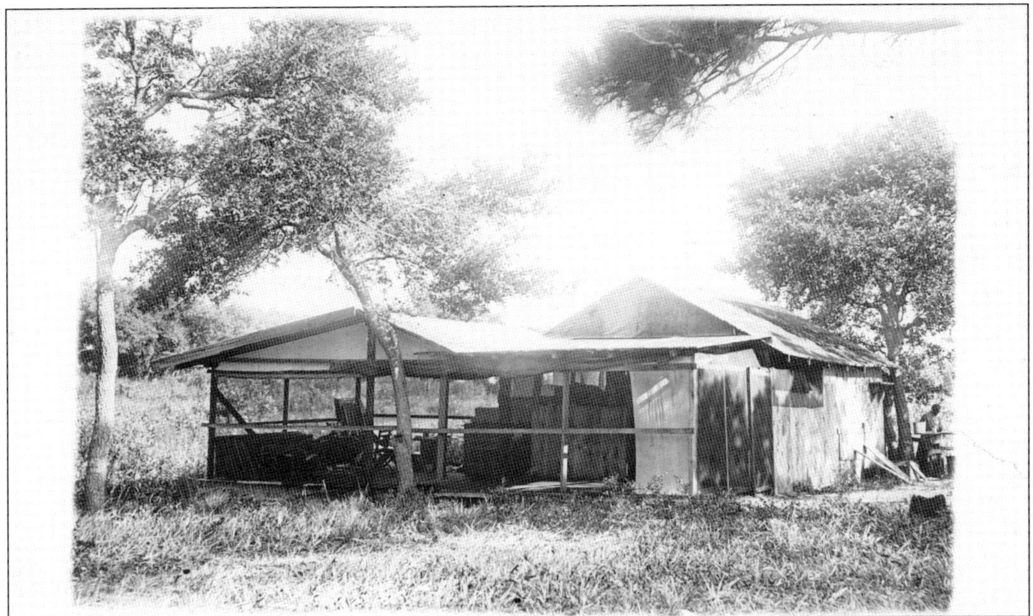

Fifteen modern camp kitchens and screened mess halls were built in 1914 to accommodate one infantry company at war strength. A fully screened kitchen building had water and sewer connections to the sinks and was equipped with a stove, cook table, pan racks, storage facilities, water, and a sink for washing mess outfit and cooking utensils. The cabana chair is folded up inside the screened area. (Courtesy of the University of North Carolina at Chapel Hill.)

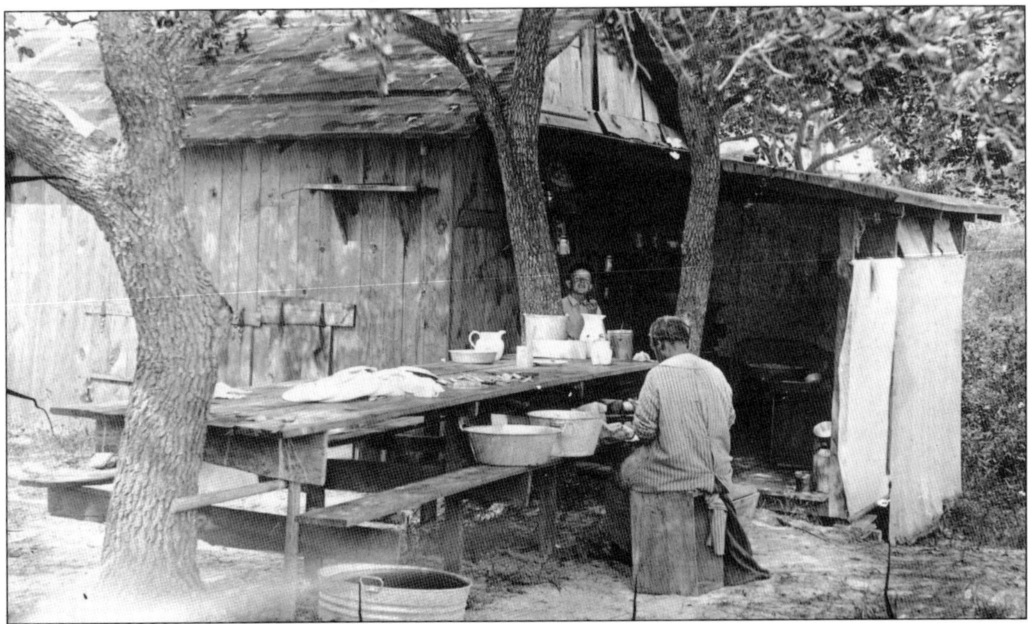

Dishes, mess ware, and pails are shown on an outside table where a woman sits preparing food and a smiling young boy stands with an apple in his hand. The woman may be one of the civilian kitchen help employed by the camp. In 1917, there were two or three enlisted soldiers serving as cooks for each company, with one company employing four civilian and two enlisted cooks. (Courtesy of the University of North Carolina at Chapel Hill.)

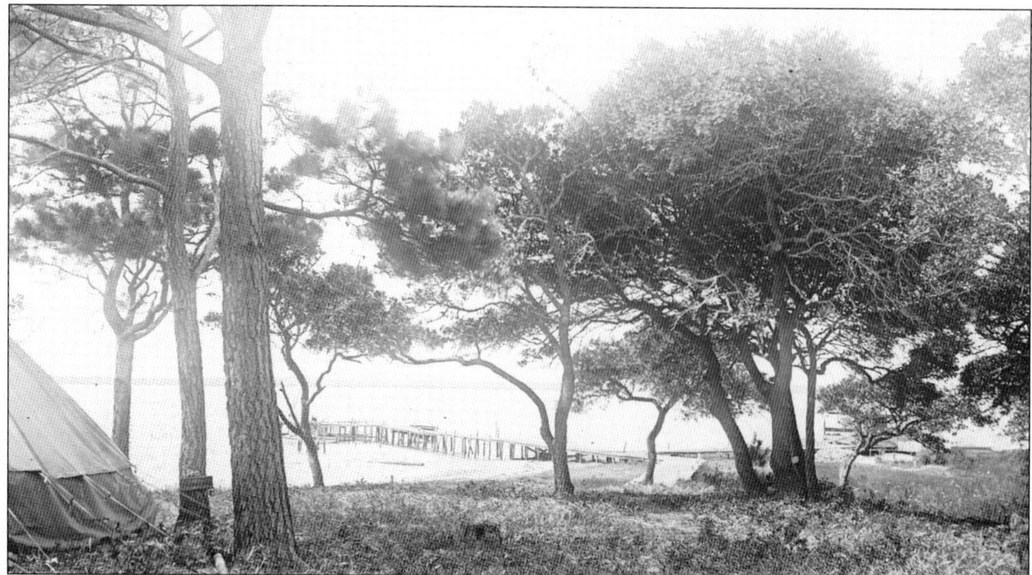

The sun's shines through in a beautiful scene along Bogue Sound's bank. Bayard Wootten used natural light in her photographs whenever possible and would wait patiently until the light was exactly where she needed it. A tent's corner, live oak trees, and a pier in Bogue Sound are part of the picture. (Courtesy of the University of North Carolina at Chapel Hill.)

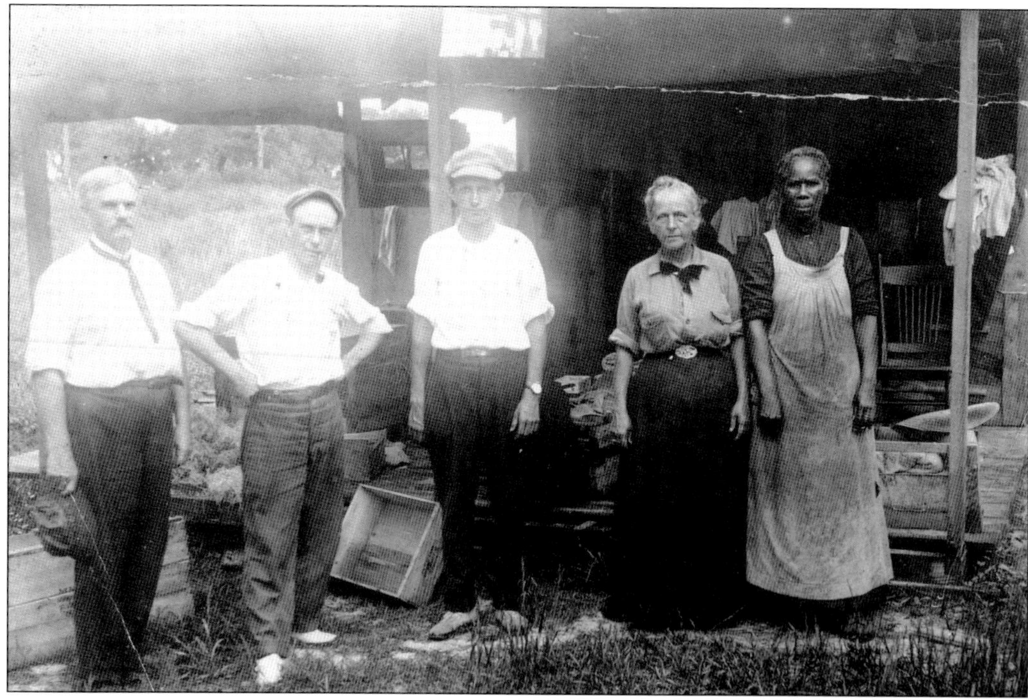

Civilians are posing for a photograph taken by Bayard Wootten. Civilian employees, including an assistant caretaker, were paid $75 monthly. They were responsible for establishing, caring for, and breaking camp. In 1923, local resident Walter Willis was employed as the caretaker's assistant, and camp officers hoped that there was sufficient work to keep him on as he was "was a very conscientious and capable worker." (Courtesy of the University of North Carolina at Chapel Hill.)

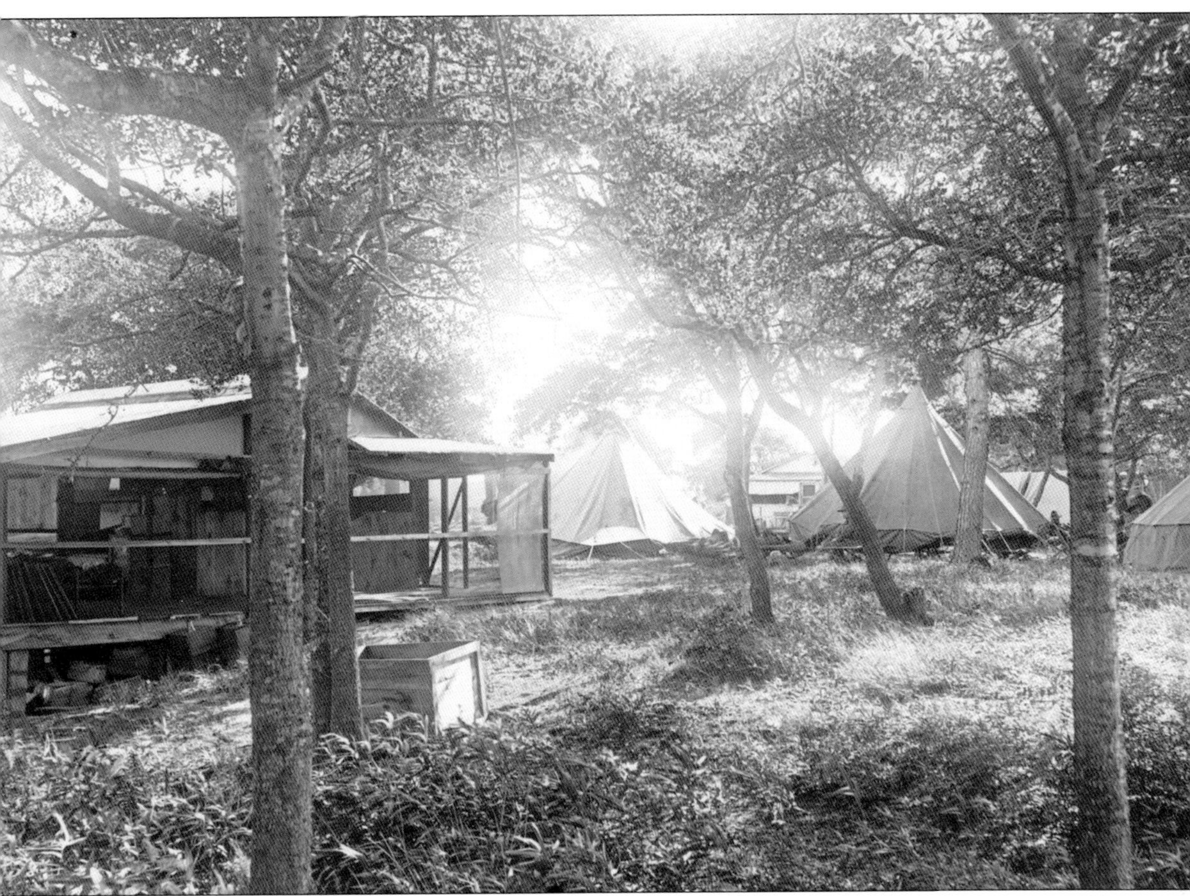

With their tents surrounding a camp kitchen, soldiers are seen lying on cots and standing around. A typical menu for special events held for visiting dignitaries and families at Camp Glenn included Carteret County fried chicken, premium boiled sliced ham, potato salad a la Beaufort Inn, Potter Brothers' sliced tomatoes, Carteret County corn on the cob, old Virginia mashed cream potatoes, North Carolina green peas, New Hanover County "beat" biscuit, New Bern royal peach ice cream, pickles, olives, cake, and ice tea. Coffee, cigars, and cigarettes were served after the meal. The men were mostly satisfied with the food; however, there was a lot of grumbling and complaining once when a spoiled ham was served. Soldiers, looking for a little fun, decided to hold a funeral for the ruined ham, and the event was a grand, hilarious affair showing the lighter side of a sad and serious culinary disaster. (Courtesy of the University of North Carolina at Chapel Hill.)

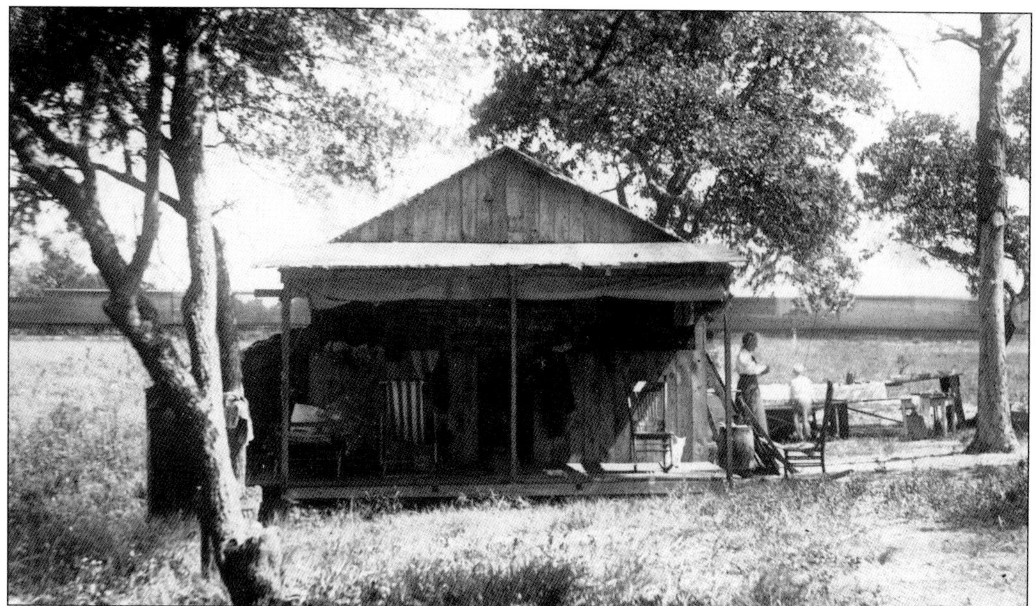

The camp's caretaker looked after the grounds and buildings and lived in a small cottage like this on the grounds. He was paid $125 a month, and the repair work and maintenance kept him busy throughout the year. The woman and young boy, seen previously in the book, are shown alongside a table set for a meal. The traveling cabana chair can be seen on the porch. (Courtesy of the University of North Carolina at Chapel Hill.)

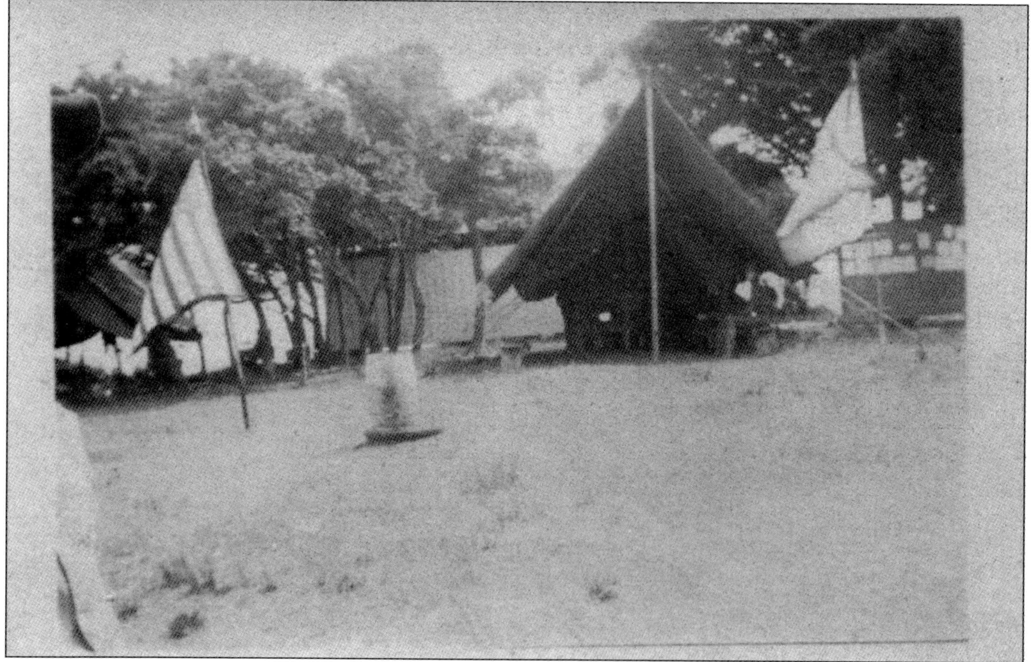

A headquarters tent is seen among live oaks and yaupon holly trees. The tent may belong to Company D, 3rd Infantry, Louisburg, commanders. Buildings and soldiers are seen in the background. The American flag is posted in the foreground along with a regimental flag. A soldier can partially be seen. (Courtesy of North Carolina State Archives.)

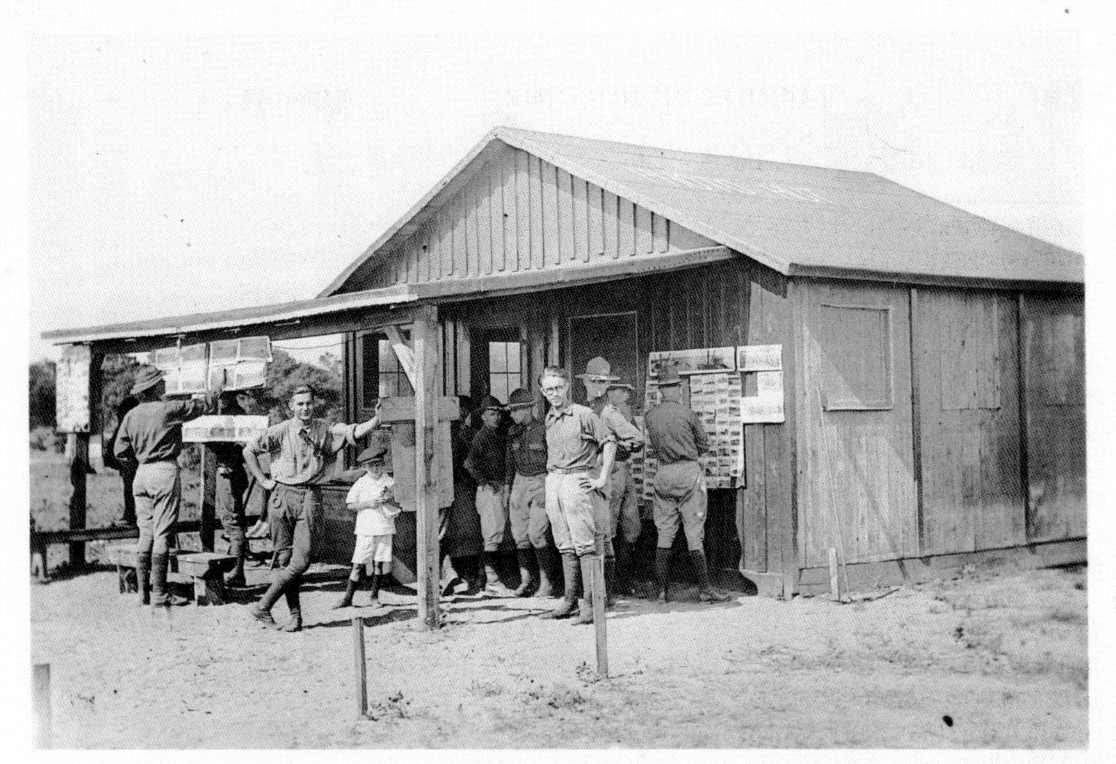

Soldiers and a young boy are looking at postcards trying find themselves in the pictures posted on the Photo Hut's billboards. A panoramic view posted at the top of the board shows boats along Bogue Sound, and the photograph appears to have been taken from an airplane. Wootten was thought to be the first woman in the country to fly in an airplane, and she was the first woman ever to take aerial photographs. The Photo Hut was built in 1923 by a local resident, Mr. Smith, and replaced a much older and smaller studio. Soldiers lined up at the Wootten's studio, eager to have their pictures taken as souvenirs. A newspaper recounted a story about a photograph session that did not go well when a soldier, "stewed to the gills," insisted his picture be made and, later, regretted it. He begged Wootten to destroy them, and she did, however, one slipped through and was posted to the board. The furious soldier threatened the photographer saying, "If you were a man . . . !" Wootten told him that she was glad, for once, she was not. (Courtesy of the University of North Carolina at Chapel Hill.)

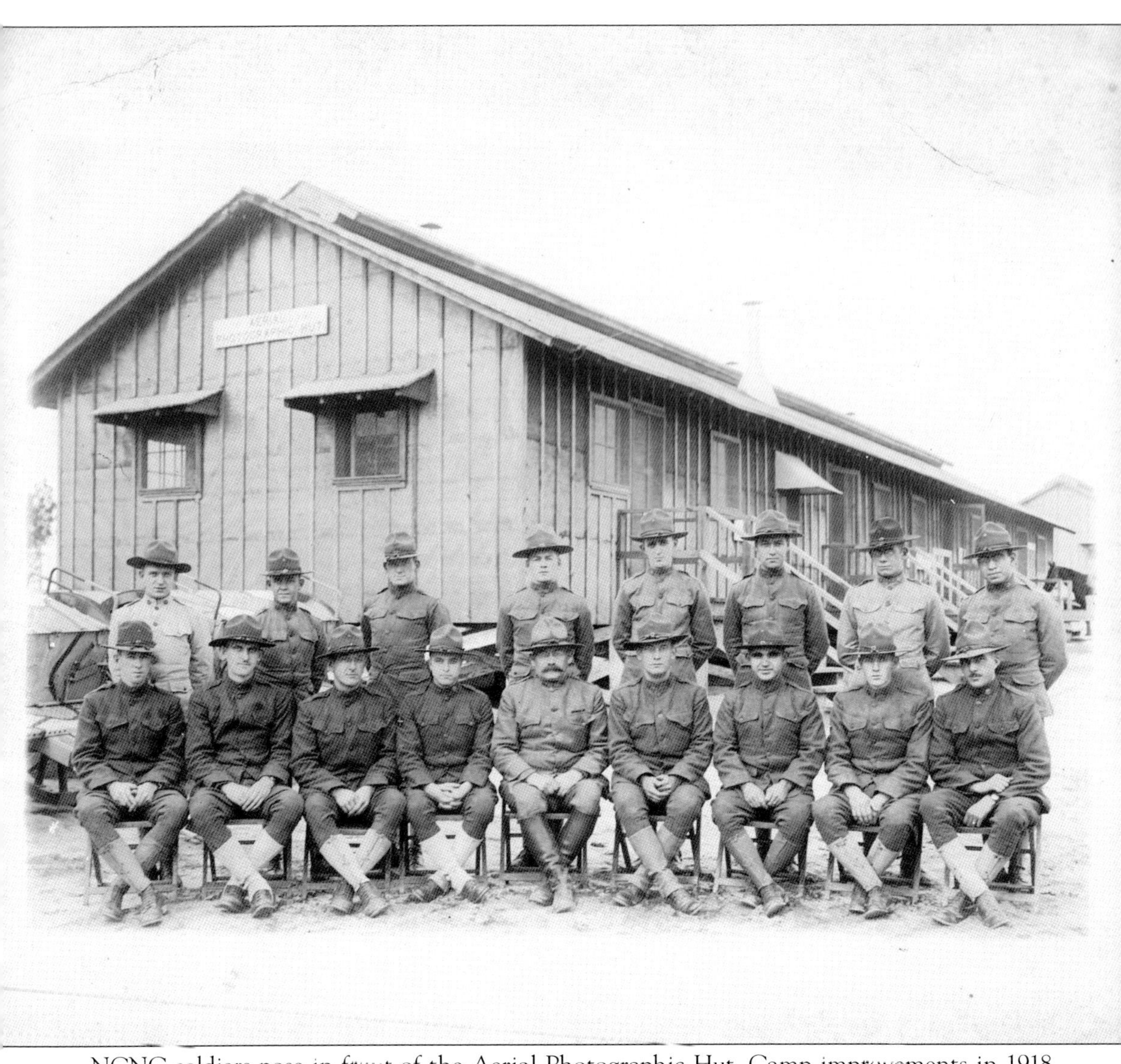

NCNG soldiers pose in front of the Aerial Photographic Hut. Camp improvements in 1918 included building three large hangars and the Aerial Photographic Hut as state leaders prepared to turn Camp Glenn over that year to the US Navy in order to establish a federal seaplane patrol station and training camp. The state made plans to spend approximately $2,000,000 in equipping the naval air station as part of the naval militia for patrolling the coast as far south as Charleston in protection against submarines. The North Carolina Naval Militia, commanded by Lt. Cmdr. J. Kenyon Wilson, was made up of national naval volunteers, both sea and land, and was called into federal service in April 1917. The naval militia was one of three organizations of the militia of the state; the others were the National Guard and the unorganized militia. (Courtesy of the University of North Carolina at Chapel Hill.)

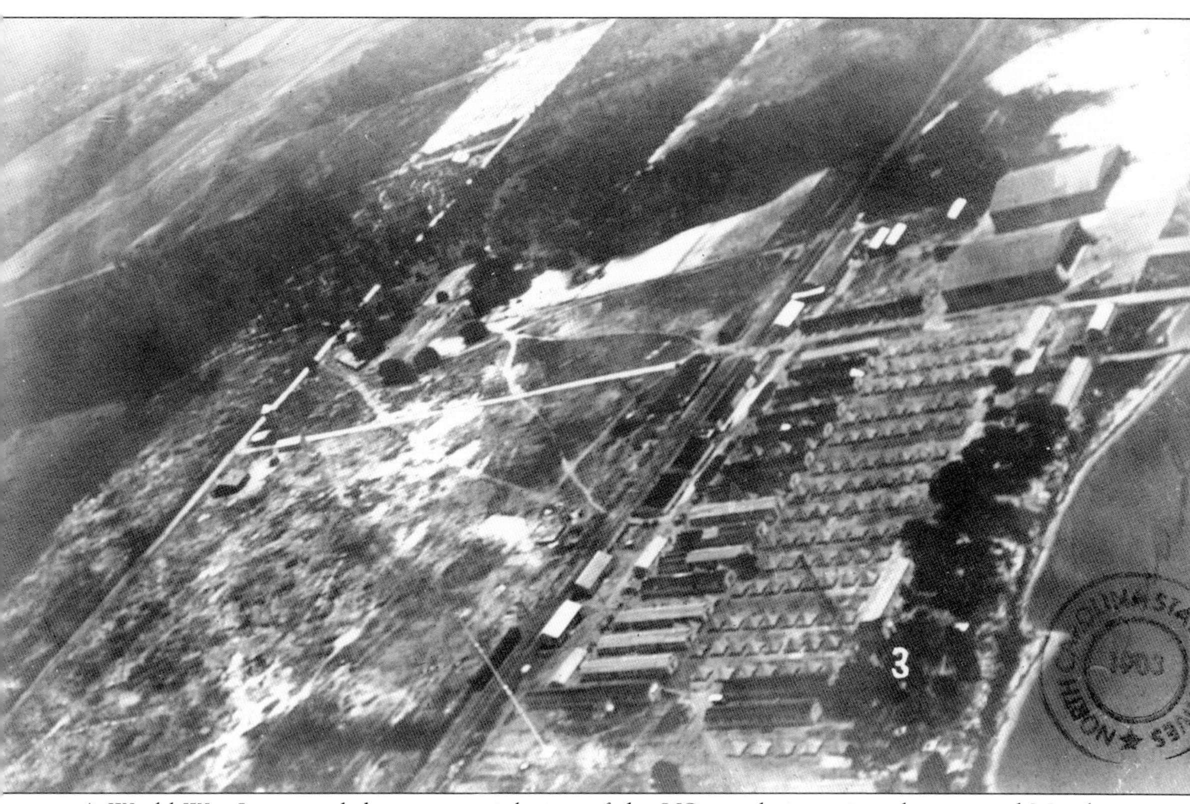


A World War I postcard shows an aerial view of the US naval air station that opened March 24, 1920, on the Camp Glenn site. The air layout and buildings are shown; however, noticeably absent are the tents used as soldiers' quarters that were replaced by wooden barracks. The piers that were badly in need of repair were rebuilt. Numerous storage buildings were constructed as well as permanent medical facilities and radio, telephone, and telegraph facilities. With Camp Glenn's transition to a naval air station, hangars were built to house the airplanes. Initially in 1916, Congress authorized funds to establish the air station at Camp Glenn, but with the event of World War I, those plans were delayed. The Coast Guard station did not last long, and it was discontinued. Other air stations were established at Cape May, New Jersey; Charleston, South Carolina; and Miami, Florida. (Courtesy of North Carolina State Archives.)

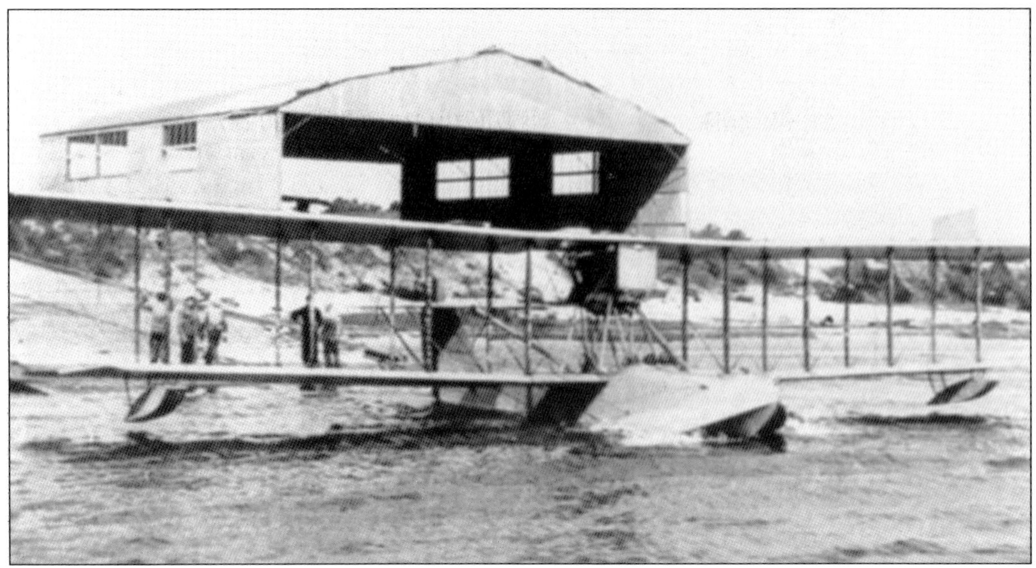

These flying boats on Bogue Sound were used by the first US Coast Guard air station in operation at Camp Glenn. Six Curtiss HS-21 hydroplanes were loaned by the Navy to the Coast Guard for the experimental base. The National Guard was still allowed to hold summer training camps, sharing some of the new facilities built in 1918–1919 for use by the Coast Guard. Lt. Robert Donohue commanded the air station when it opened in 1920. During that time, hydroplanes were used for rescuing and locating vessels in distress, finding schools of fish for fishermen, and conducting surveillance, including searching for liquor smugglers along the coast. During the war, the US Navy maintained an air base with 500 men stationed there. A refueling base for the Navy also operated on the site. The Coast Guard base project ended on July 1, 1921. (Courtesy of the National Archives, Washington, DC.)

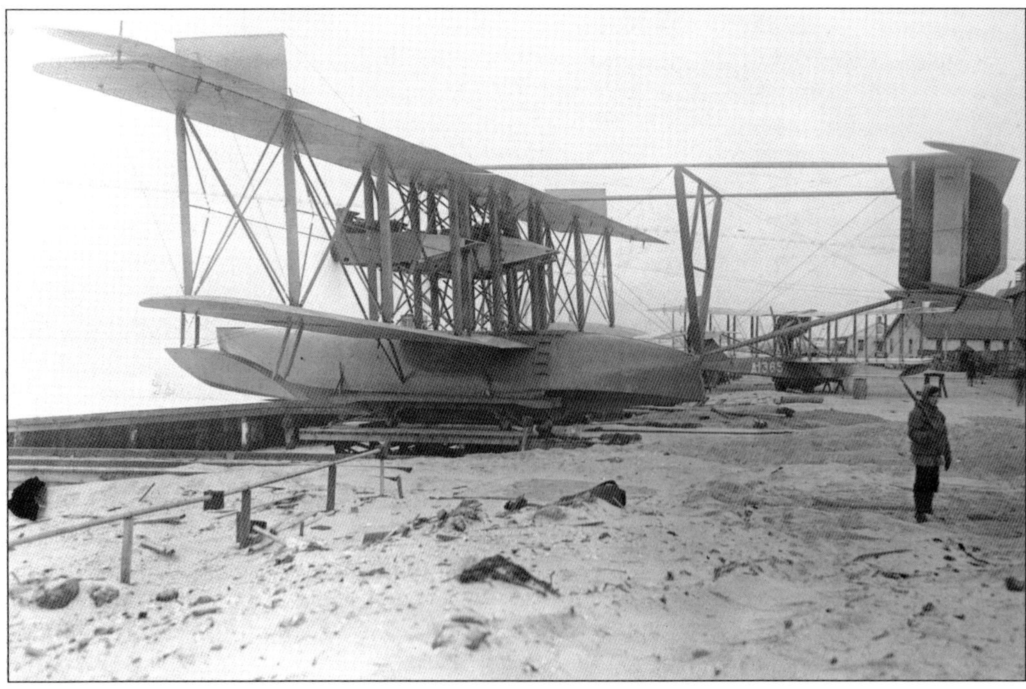

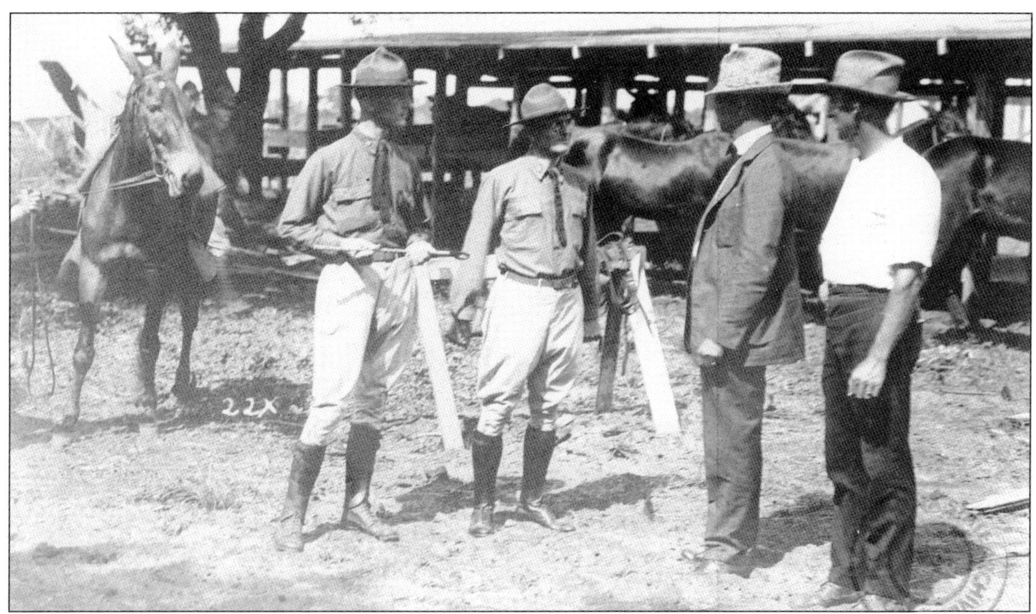

A covered corral and a stable with stalls for 50 horses were built at one end of the camp. During encampment, the state supplied mounts, and soldiers furnishing their own mounts were given yearly allowances of $150 for one and $200 for two horses. Drills in care of the horses in camp or on the march were conducted as part of military training exercises. Drill instructions for pistol firing while mounted were to lean slightly forward and bear on the stirrups, and when firing to the front, lean well to the right and slightly forward, to avoid burning or frightening the horse. The men shown in these photographs may have been purchasing horses from local sellers where it was reported that "good horses cost in the vicinity of the station of this troop $250 or $300. Sixty or seventy horses could be secured at once at this price." (Courtesy of North Carolina State Archives.)

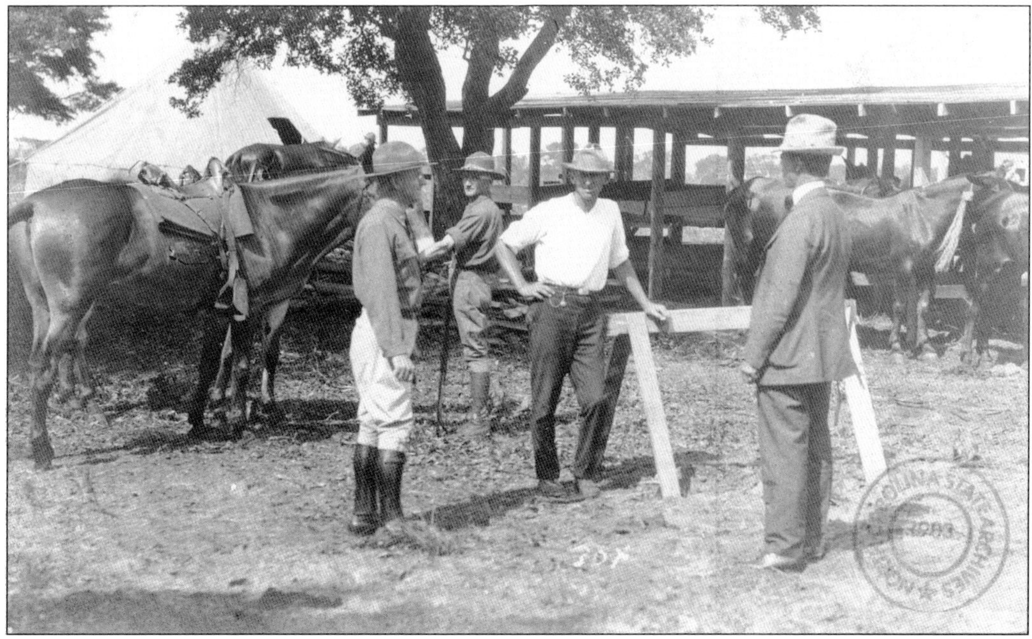

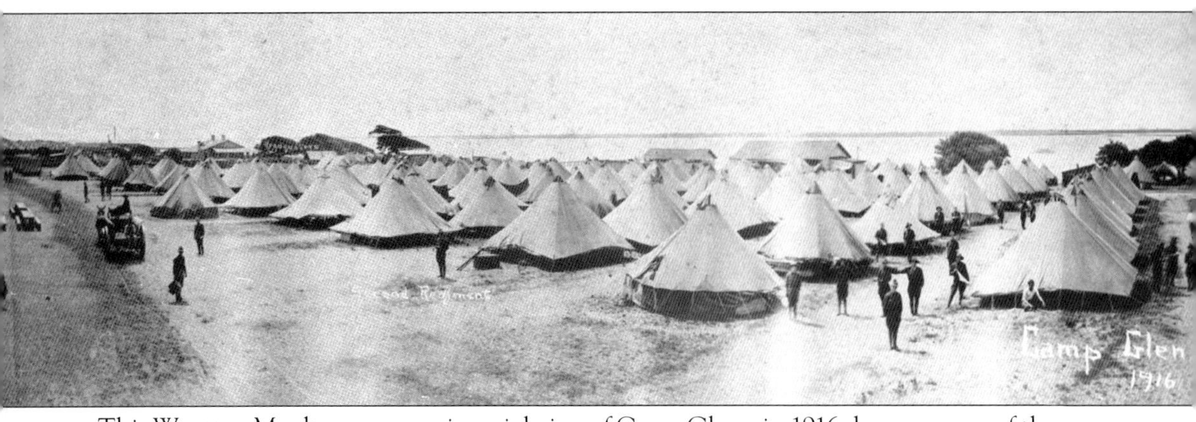


This Wootten-Moulton panoramic aerial view of Camp Glenn in 1916 shows a scene of the camp that is neat, orderly, and active during the mobilization training period. Over 5,000 soldiers were preparing to go to the border and fight in the Mexican Border War against Pancho Villa. The three regiments' locations labeled in the photograph and company mess halls and buildings can be seen (right). Soldiers, wagons, and horses (left) are seen in company streets. In the lower right

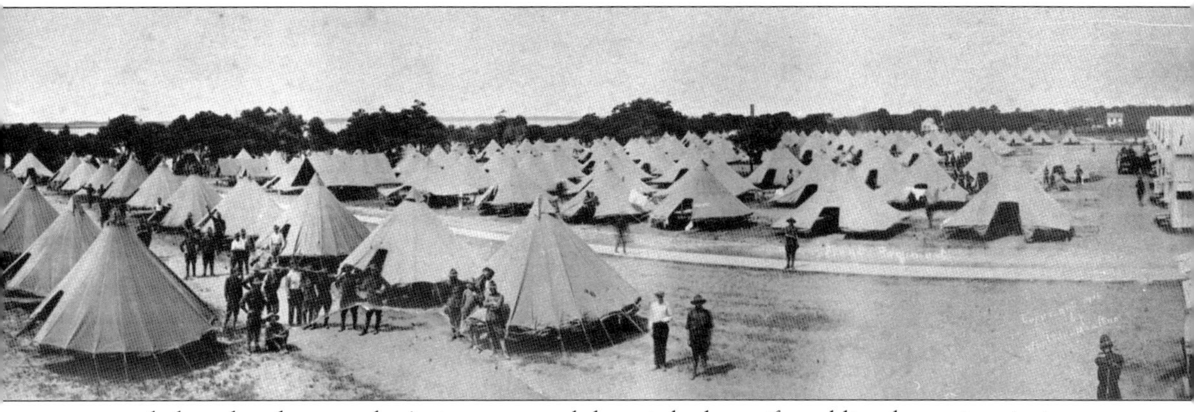

corner below the photographer's signature and date, it looks as if a soldier shown is pointing a weapon toward the photographer (or perhaps just leaning on a rake). When Bayard Wootten took this photograph, she had been a fixture at Camp Glenn for 10 years, thus establishing her reputation as one of earliest and leading female photographers in the country. (Courtesy of North Carolina State Archives.)

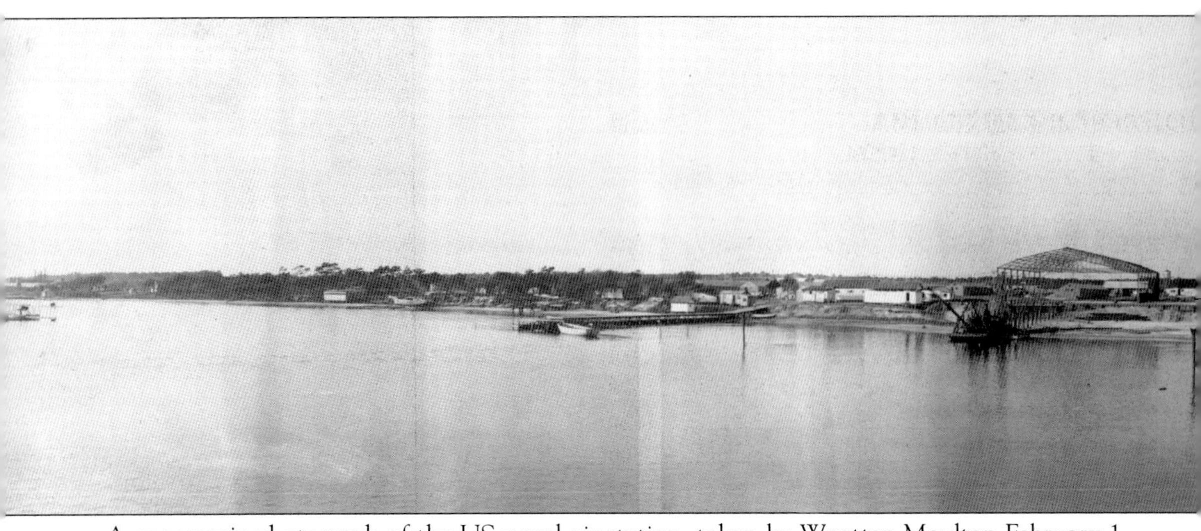

A panoramic photograph of the US naval air station, taken by Wootten-Moulton February 1, 1919, shows the hangars built in 1918 on Bogue Sound. Almost 40 buildings were constructed for the air station, including the barracks for housing naval military personnel. One of the two flying boats (left) stationed here can be seen anchored in the sound, and daily training trips were made by pilots and students. Gov. Thomas Walter Bickett (1869–1921) authorized almost $2,000,000 to be spent on established a naval seaplane patrol station and training camp in 1918.

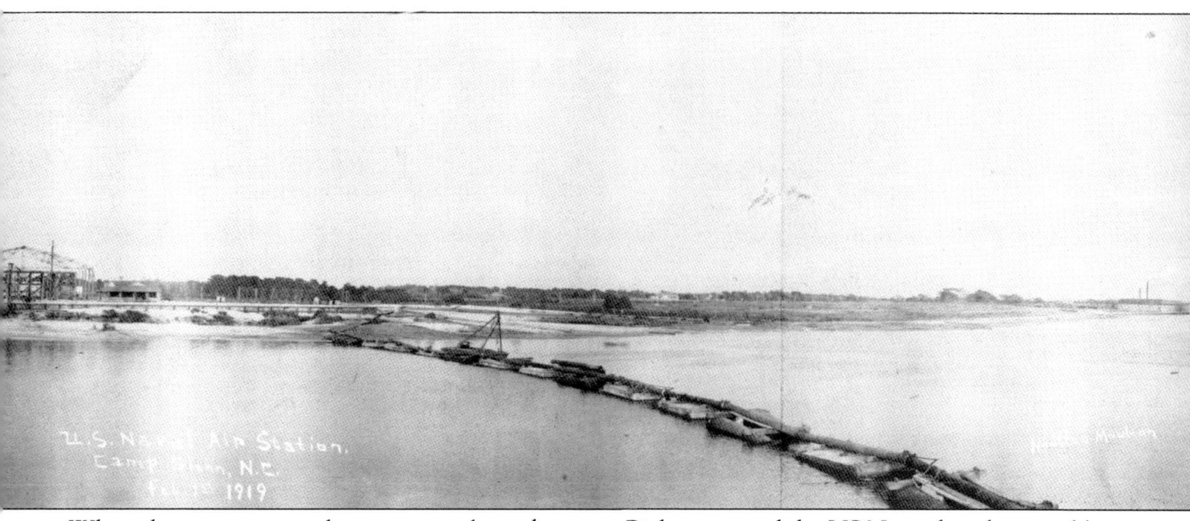


When the camp was made permanent later that year, Bickett assured the US Navy that they would have full use of the state's camp. More than 200 men were stationed at Camp Glenn under the command of Lt. Cmdr. Robert Livingston "Liv" Ireland Jr. (1895–1981), who moved here with his family. While here, Ireland rented John Motley Morehead's summer cottage for his family's stay. Seaplanes flew as far south as Charleston, patrolling for submarines along the coast. (Courtesy of North Carolina State Archives.)

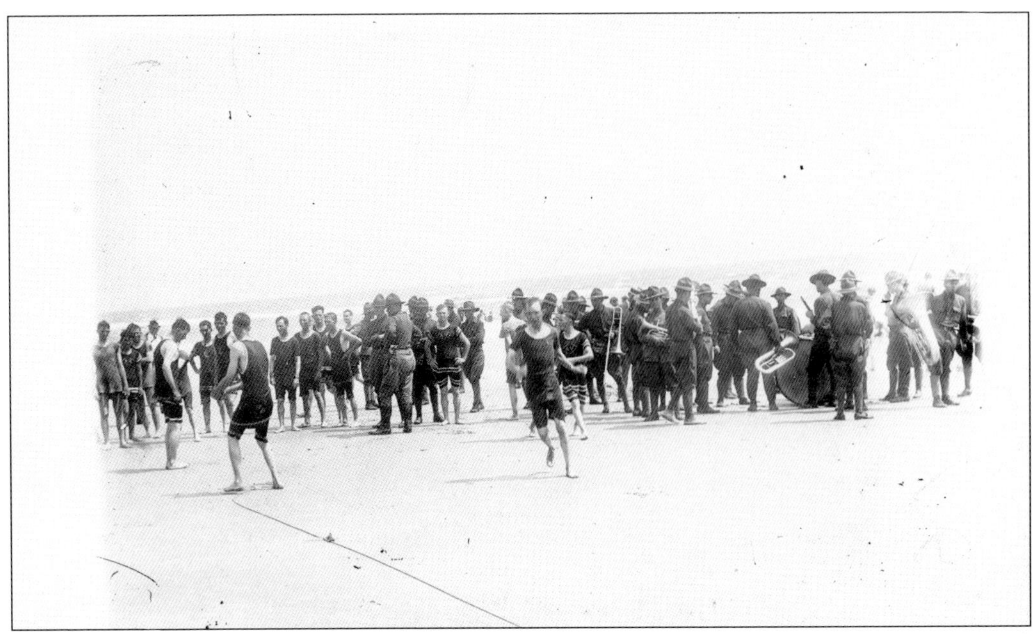

Soldiers in uniform, a band, and men in bathing costumes are enjoying a day at the beach and, perhaps, a concert. Soldiers along with visiting families and friends enjoyed fishing and sailing parties in sharpie sailboats, and occasionally, visiting dignitaries, like Governor Bickett and his wife, Fannie, were among the guests enjoying the ocean waters on their trips to the coast. (Courtesy of the University of North Carolina at Chapel Hill.)

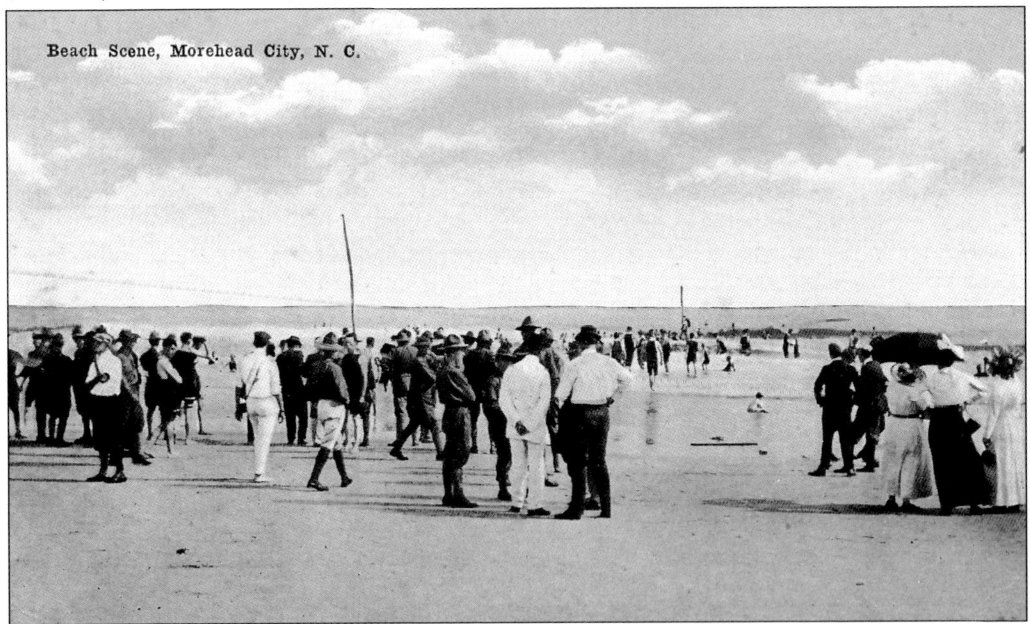


"Beach Scene, Morehead City, N. C." shows uniformed soldiers, men in suits, and women in long dresses with parasols strolling on the beach. Children are playing in tidal pools between the shore and sandbars. This scene illustrates why the site of Morehead City was chosen over Wrightsville Beach as the permanent site for Camp Glenn. The prevailing southwesterly winds off the ocean make for a comfortable setting for all to enjoy.

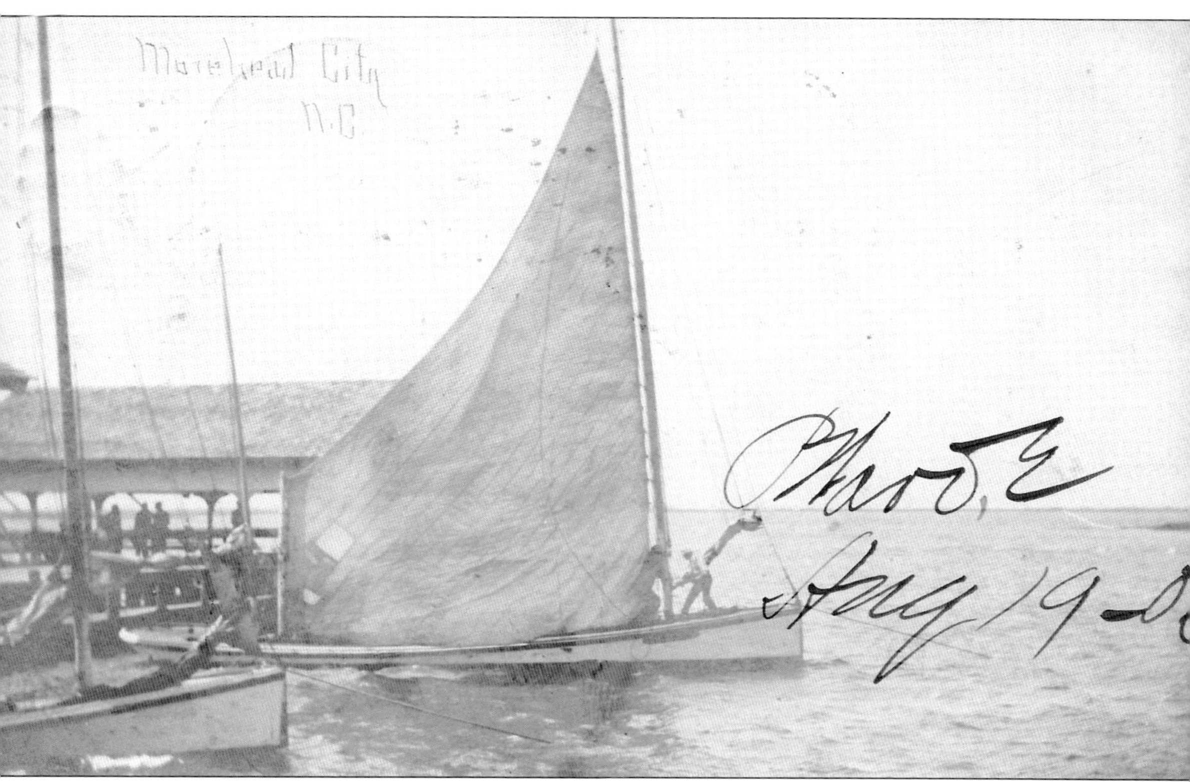


Sailing parties often took place on small sailboats like this one, which is known as a sharpie. These sailboats were flat-bottomed with an extremely small draft perfect for sailing along North Carolina's shallow coastal waters. Also used for oystering, the boat's design was believed to have originated in New Haven, Connecticut. The Thomasville newspaper, *The Davidson*, reported in the summer of 1911 that Charles R. Thomas and his wife, Susie, a local businessperson, gave a complimentary sail to Company L, the Thomasville Blues. The guests embarked at the Atlantic Hotel, sailed up to Camp Glenn where they spent a delightful three hours along the sound visiting Beaufort, Old Fort Macon, and other points of interest. After stopping awhile at the Atlantic Hotel to enjoy music and dancing for an hour the party resumed their sail back to camp where the company's quartet "rendered several splendid selections." Along with sailing parties, there were fishing parties and clam roasts held on the beach. Moonlight sails on the beach and Bogue Sound were often held with guests sometimes numbering 50 or more.

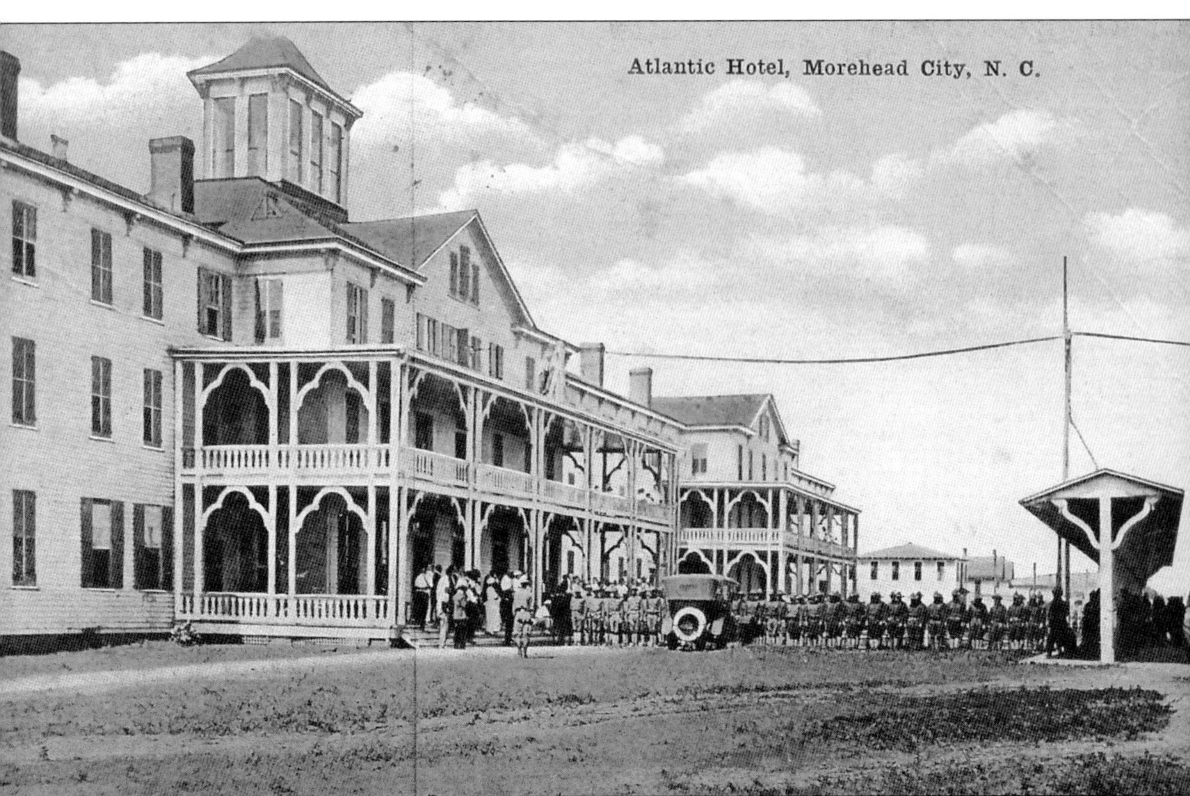


Built in 1880, the Atlantic Hotel opened that year on June 21 and quickly became known as the "Summer Capital by the Sea." With 233 rooms, the Atlantic offered its guests surf bathing, sailing parties, lawn tennis, bowling, billiards, and card parties arranged by the ladies. Open for the season from June to October, the Atlantic Hotel was located on Bogue Sound and the Newport River that mingled with it. Sailing parties' guests were promised outings that were as "sheltered from storm and shipwreck as a lake in Central Park" (according to *The Atlantic Hotel,* published in 1885). The hotel was also the summer home for many of Camp Glenn's officers and their families. Soldiers seen in this postcard are in formation drill in front of the Atlantic Hotel, located near the train depot. They often rode the train's special line from the camp to the hotel, but since the camp was located just a few miles west, they sometimes just walked or rod a horse to the hotel.

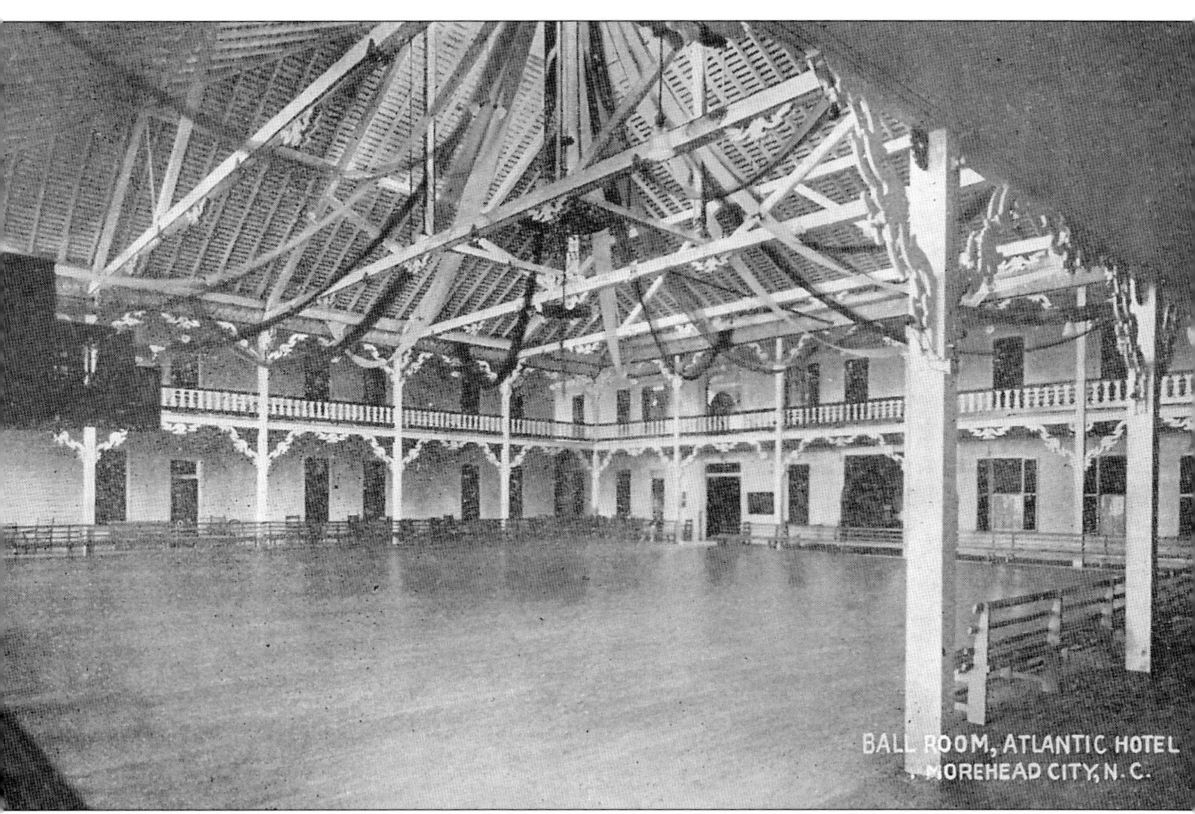


A grand regimental ball was held at the elegant Atlantic Hotel to mark the end of each two-week summer encampment. The night began with a reception held in the100-feet-square ballroom, or the Pagoda room as it was sometimes called, that was topped by a ceiling with an eight-foot-wide reflector fueled by 83 burners. Ribbons, festooning the rafters, greeted guests as they entered. The men were in dress uniform, and women were fashionably dressed in the latest-style gowns. The brigadier general and his wife led the grand march signaling the beginning of the ball. From 9:30 p.m. to the wee hours of the morning, guests danced to music provided by the National Guard's infantry band and enjoyed the refreshments that were served. The menu included stone crabs, clams, fish, shrimp, scallops, and the freshest fruit and vegetables from nearby truck markets. Occasionally, a midnight sail followed the military ball where guests were entertained by a string orchestra on board.

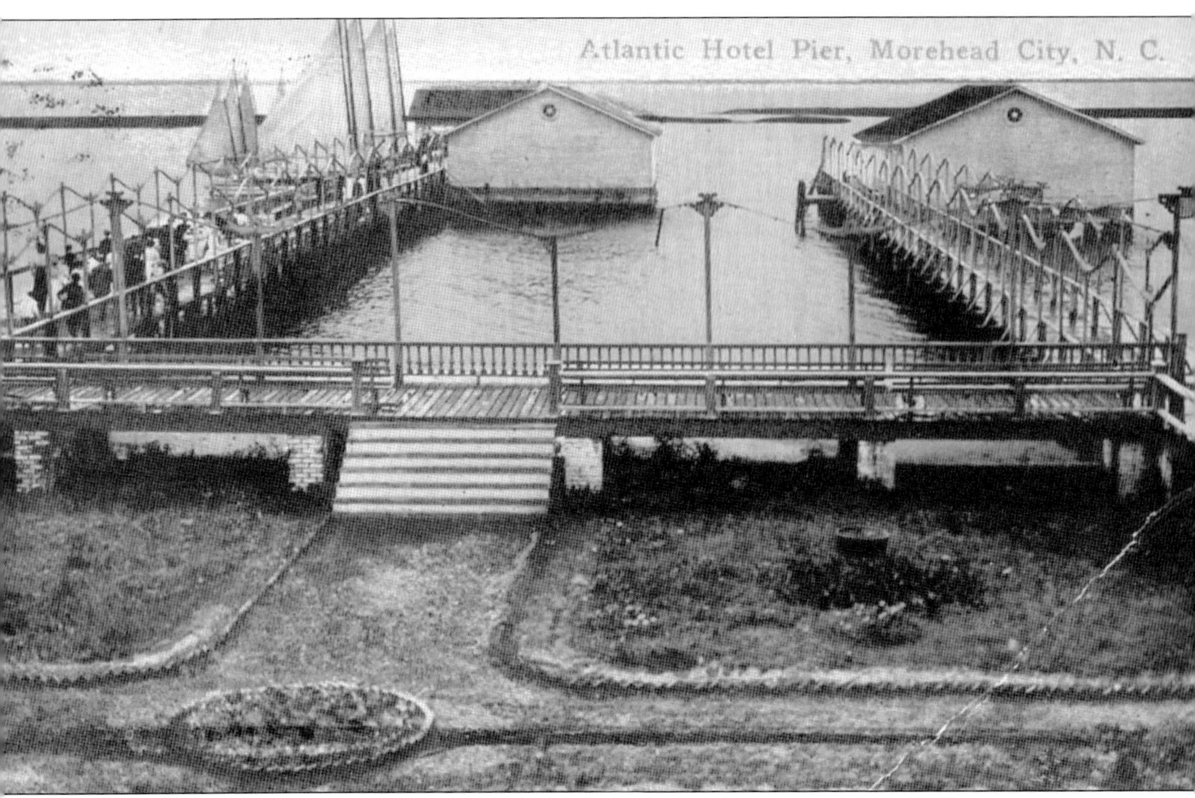


Guests lined the Atlantic Hotel's extensive piers to embark on sailing parties in boats for hire or privately owned boats. A boardwalk lined Bogue Sound, and boathouses jut out into the water. For fishermen, there were fishing parties sailing and trolling along the sound or into the ocean for bluefish or Spanish mackerel, as well as perch, striped bass, black bass, or sheephead that were waiting to be hooked and then cooked by the Atlantic Hotel's chefs. In 1913, motorboats began to make their appearance along the Atlantic Hotel's waterways. Local fishermen, tied up at the docks waiting for passengers, bitterly resented this newfangled trend. They did, however, enjoy the sight of the noisy and smelly vessels getting stuck on sandbars, and when the landlubbers tried to pole off the shoal with straw hats flying in the breeze, old-timers did not bother to hide their grins. (Courtesy of North Carolina State Archives.)

# BIBLIOGRAPHY

Cotten, Jerry W. *Light and Air: the Photography of Bayard Wootten.* Chapel Hill: University of North Carolina Press, 1998.
*Annual Report of the Adjutant General of the State of North Carolina.*
*Carteret News-Times*, Morehead City.
*Charlotte Daily Observer.*
*Coaster*, Morehead City.
*Durham Recorder.*
*Franklin Times*, Louisburg.
*Goldsboro Weekly Argus.*
*Hickory Democrat.*
*High Point Enterprise.*
*Independent*, Elizabeth City.
*Monroe Journal.*
*New Berne Weekly Journal.*
*New York Times.*
*Raleigh Times.*
*Semi-Weekly Messenger*, Goldsboro.